KU-522-098

Baudelaire's Tragic Hero

A Study of the Architecture of
Les Fleurs du Mal

Baudelaire's Tragic Hero

A Study of the Architecture of
Les Fleurs du Mal

by

D. J. MOSSOP

OXFORD UNIVERSITY PRESS
1961

Oxford University Press, Amen House, London E.C.4

GLASGOW   NEW YORK   TORONTO   MELBOURNE   WELLINGTON
BOMBAY   CALCUTTA   MADRAS   KARACHI   KUALA LUMPUR
CAPE TOWN   IBADAN   NAIROBI   ACCRA

© Oxford University Press, 1961

B61 11923

HERTFORDSHIRE
COUNTY LIBRARY
841 / BAU
1993798

PRINTED AND BOUND IN ENGLAND BY
HAZELL WATSON AND VINEY LTD
AYLESBURY AND SLOUGH

CONTENTS

ABBREVIATIONS

The edition of Baudelaire's works to which references are made is that published by Louis Conard and edited by Jacques Crépet. The following abbreviations have been used:

FM: *Les Fleurs du Mal* (1922).

CE: *Curiosités esthétiques* (1923).

AR: *L'Art romantique* (1925).

PPP: *Petits Poèmes en Prose* (1926).

PA: *Paradis artificiels. La Fanfarlo* (1928).

JOP: *Juvenilia, Oeuvres posthumes, Reliquae* (t.I, 1939; II et III, 1952).

CORR: *Correspondance générale* (t.I et II, 1947; III et IV, 1948; V, 1949; VI, 1953).

NHE: *Nouvelles Histoires extraordinaires* (1933).

Occasional references are made to the following works:

OC: *Oeuvres complètes*, Bibliothèque de la Pléiade, Gallimard, 1954.

FM (Crépet): *Les Fleurs du Mal*, édition critique par Jacques Crépet et Georges Blin, José Corti, 1942.

'One of the chief problems with regard to Baudelaire is to explain the duality of the *Fleurs du Mal*, the opposition between his idealism . . . and his "satanism".'

A. R. CHISHOLM *(Towards Hérodiade)*

INTRODUCTION

THE first statement made on the subject of the architecture of *Les Fleurs du Mal* has often been echoed but never bettered. Within a month of the publication of the first edition, Barbey d'Aurevilly wrote in his article for *Le Pays:*

> ... il ne faut pas s'y méprendre, dans le livre de M. Baudelaire, chaque poésie a, de plus que la réussite des détails ou de la fortune de la pensée, *une valeur très importante d'ensemble et de situation,* qu'il ne faut pas lui faire perdre, en la détachant. Les artistes qui voient les lignes sous le luxe et l'efflorescence de la couleur percevront très bien qu'il y a ici une *architecture secrète,* un plan calculé par le poète méditatif et volontaire. Les *Fleurs du Mal* ne sont pas à la suite les unes des autres comme autant de morceaux lyriques, dispersés par l'inspiration et ramassés dans un recueil, sans d'autre raison que de les réunir. Elles sont moins des poésies qu'une oeuvre poétique *de la plus forte unité.* Au point de vue de l'art et de la sensation esthétique, elles perdraient beaucoup à n'être pas lues *dans l'ordre* où le poète, qui sait bien ce qu'il fait, les a rangées.[1]

Both indirectly and directly the author of *Les Fleurs du Mal* encouraged this manner of approaching his work. He did so indirectly by his evident concern, from 1846 onwards, when *Les Lesbiennes* was first announced, to produce a volume of poems grouped in a unity about some central theme. He did so directly by his repeated statements to that effect. The most striking is the one contained in the letter that he sent to

[1] The article was published in the Appendix to the third edition of *Les Fleurs du Mal* (Paris, Michel Lévy, 1868).

Vigny together with a copy of the second edition of *Les Fleurs du Mal:* 'Le seul éloge que je sollicite pour ce livre est qu'on reconnaisse qu'il n'est pas un pur album et qu'il a un commencement et une fin'.[1] The words have not perhaps excited the wonder that they deserve. If Baudelaire meant what he said, he had come to set so high a value on the architectural element in the work which he denoted by the unpretentious terms 'commencement' and 'fin', that he was prepared to forgo all praise arising from other considerations, not excluding the purely poetic value of the individual poems. If his statement was not a gross exaggeration of his feelings, either his judgement was sadly at fault or there is a greater secret in the architecture than his readers have found.

The obstacles that stand in the way of appreciation of this aspect of the work may seem many and great. Even though far more poems than we realize may have been written with a plan in view, this plan itself seems to have been subjected to major alterations which not only called for new poems to fit the new versions, but inevitably altered the meaning which the poet himself attached to poems and groups of poems written for the older versions.[2] In some cases the poet's view of the meaning may actually have evolved further than is warranted by the form of the poem or poems. A poem may therefore have several meanings: that which was attached to it when first composed, with or without the plan of the volume in mind, and all the more or less different meanings which it has had in subsequent versions of the

[1] CORR, IV, p. 9.

[2] The traditional assumption that the meaning of every poem was irrevocably fixed at the time of writing, allows neither for the flexibility of meaning in art nor for that of an artist's plan.

plan and sometimes in more than one position in the volume. It is possible that *Le Reniement de Saint Pierre* originally expressed a mood of personal religious revolt on the part of the poet; it may later have become a more or less sympathetic reflection of 'les agitations spirituelles de la jeunesse moderne';[1] in the first edition of *Les Fleurs du Mal* we have Baudelaire's assurance that it is 'le pastiche des raisonnements de l'ignorance et de la fureur'[2] and it therefore stands for a mood of ironical condemnation of the very attitude it seems to express; but almost certainly, also, it is designed to produce the grim pathos which may attach to the situation of a 'hero' who has been so far seduced by Satan as to attempt what for him is the impossible task of renouncing all allegiance to God. What then is the meaning of the poem? The historian's answer must be: 'all the meanings considered separately'. He could therefore render valuable aid to the student of poetry who justifiably felt that the true meaning of the poem was the last that the poet attached to it. But neither the literary historian nor the student of poetry could be content with a mere confusion of the meanings. It would be tantamount to making an arbitrary amalgam of a poem with its earlier versions and textual variants and calling that the true poem.

Unfortunately the historian is seriously handicapped in this case by the lack of evidence. Prior to 1857, nothing is known of Baudelaire's plans save what can be tentatively deduced from the various titles assigned to the work and the brief indication given in 1850 and 1851 as to its content. The

[1] Cf. the notes announcing *Les Limbes* in *Le Magasin des Familles* of June 1850, and in *Le Messager de l'Assemblée* of April 1851.

[2] FM, p. 473.

circumstances surrounding the composition of all but a few of the poems are equally vague. Nothing of importance can be deduced, either, from the publication of isolated poems or of groups of poems. Even the group of eighteen published under the title of *Les Fleurs du Mal* in the *Revue des Deux Mondes* of June 1, 1855, reveals no more than Baudelaire's desire (as explained later to Calonne in the letter of November 1858) to pitch the tone of his poems 'tantôt très-haut et puis très-bas'.[1] The 1857 edition must be approached without any real knowledge of the stages through which it has evolved and which, for better or for worse, may still be reflected in its final form. It must be read with the knowledge that the meaning of every poem not only contributes to the meaning of the architecture, but is simultaneously dependent on its place and meaning within the architecture as Baudelaire understood it at the time. And the very uncertain result of that reading must serve as the basis for the equally uncertain study of the architecture of the second edition. In reality, of course, complete understanding of the first edition implies a careful utilization of knowledge of the second.

Great as such difficulties may appear when envisaged in detail, they are inseparable from the study of every play, every novel, every epic and even every lyric poem. The second edition of *Les Fleurs du Mal* corresponds to the final form of any work of art. In fact we are more fortunate in this case than in most others inasmuch as we possess an earlier version of the work in the form of the first edition. The only difficulty which is peculiar to *Les Fleurs du Mal* is the discontinuity inherent in the medium itself, together with the

[1] CORR, VI, p. 233.

instinctive feeling of readers that only the barest minimum of continuity and architectural meaning can be expected from a collection of lyric poems. And this is aggravated by the omnipresent problem of the relation of the man to the work which he produces.

The critics who show the greatest readiness to treat the poems as autobiography are not those who study the architecture, but those who consider the poems as separate entities, whether for literary or for biographical purposes. However outmoded the idea may be as poetic theory, it has not proved easy to avoid the dangers of the Romantic assumption that a lyric poem is a sincere personal confession. The 'Je' or 'Poëte' of the poems is thought to be necessarily Baudelaire, Baudelaire as he was at a moment or a period of his life which is not always specified. Nor has it always been thought necessary to adduce more evidence than the poems themselves, which are credited with the dual power to explain the man in terms of the work and the work in terms of the man.

Critics who have concerned themselves with the architecture have reacted against this tendency in varying degrees. Albert Feuillerat, whose essay of 1941 remains the most detailed study in this field,[1] is extremely careful to distinguish the plan that he finds in *Les Fleurs du Mal* from the chronology of Baudelaire's own biography. In no sense, he insists, is *Les Fleurs du Mal* the story or drama of Baudelaire's own life. He does not however consider the possibility that the

---

[1] *L'Architecture des 'Fleurs du Mal'* in *Studies by members of the French Department of Yale University*, New Haven, Yale University Press, 1941, pp. 221–330. (It has not been possible to consider here the study by Alison Fairlie: *Baudelaire: Les Fleurs du Mal*, London, Edward Arnold, 1960, which appeared when this work was in the hands of the publisher.)

work could relate to anyone other than Baudelaire, and to that extent he remains exposed to another form of the same danger that he denounces in its dramatic form, when he goes on to explain the architecture as 'une analyse psychologique' which Baudelaire makes of his own heart and mind, 'avec le souci de découvrir, autant pour lui-même que pour le lecteur, le rapport existant entre les mouvements ou expériences de son coeur et leur expérience par cet esprit'.[1] Although he qualifies his use of the term, Albert Feuillerat does indeed regard the work as a 'confession' of a straightforward kind, and he makes little allowance for irony on the part of the poet. Marcel Ruff is more cautious. Like Feuillerat he discards the idea of chronological autobiography and, with it, the idea of drama, but although he accepts Baudelaire as the 'sujet' of *Spleen et Idéal*, he thereafter reduces the poet's role to that of a 'témoin', writing in a general way of the follies of mankind.[2] He is thus enabled to distinguish his picture of Baudelaire from such biographical implications as might conflict with it in the latter books of *Les Fleurs du Mal*. L. J. Austin represents a third school of thought inasmuch as he has suggested that there is no real incompatibility between the psychological analysis which Feuillerat finds in the work, and 'un certain mouvement dialectique, qui reflète jusqu'à un certain point l'itinéraire spirituel du poète'.[3] And this writer so far favours the idea that the work is dramatized autobiography, as to advance a theory which ascribes to Baudelaire himself the adventure that is thought to be outlined in *Spleen et Idéa*

[1] *Ibid.*, p. 287.
[2] *Baudelaire, l'homme et l'oeuvre*, Paris, Hatier-Boivin, 1955, p. 113.
[3] *L'Univers poétique de Baudelaire*, Paris, Mercure de France, 1956, p. 99.

and involves a disastrous attempt to use Satan and evil as instruments for good, with the help of art.[1] L. J. Austin is certainly justified in querying the absolute validity of Feuillerat's distinction between psychological analysis or confession, and dramatic autobiography. When Feuillerat explains how, in the first edition, Baudelaire confesses to ever greater sins which culminate in Satanism, before envisaging two ways of escape from the Devil in *Le Vin* and *La Mort*,[2] one may begin to feel that this confession is closer to drama, if not to autobiography, than Feuillerat allows. To sum up, the architecture has been explained in terms of autobiographical confession or self-analysis, autobiographical drama, and non-dramatic critical reflections on humanity at large. What does not seem to have been fully explored, is the possibility that the architecture is intended to represent a drama which is that of an anonymous 'Poëte' who cannot properly be called Baudelaire however much he may resemble his creator, and who is designed to have a universal, as well as an individual, significance.

Baudelaire's own comments on this aspect of his work are typical. His very breadth of view, his feeling for the relation which unites extremes, combines with his despair of making others see more than one extreme at a time and forces him both to encourage and to discourage all parties to the dispute. Nowhere does Baudelaire give the slightest support for

[1] *Ibid.*, pp. 54–56, p. 112, p. 131. The theory is related to the ideas of L. F. Benedetto (*L'Architecture des Fleurs du Mal* in *Zeitschrift für franzözische Sprache und literatur*, vol. 39, 1912), and of A. R. Chisholm (*Towards Hérodiade. A literary genealogy*, Melbourne University Press, 1934, pp. 68–86).

[2] *Op. cit.*, p. 288.

Albert Feuillerat's contention that no dramatic element can be found in the architecture. But those who insist that the work is impersonal can quote the letter to Calonne of November 1858 which contains the sentence: 'Il n'y aura plus que les gens d'une mauvaise foi absolue qui ne comprendront pas l'impersonnalité volontaire de mes poésies'.[1] To it may be added the celebrated passage from the *Projets de Préface* of 1859–1860 which ends with the words: 'Ce livre, essentiellement inutile et absolument innocent, n'a pas été fait dans un autre but que de me divertir et d'exercer mon goût passionné de l'obstacle'.[2] In reply, the partisans of autobiography can quote Baudelaire's letter of February 1866 to Ancelle: 'Faut-il vous dire ... que dans ce livre *atroce*, j'ai mis tout *mon coeur*, toute *ma tendresse*, toute *ma religion* (travestie), toute *ma haine*? Il est vrai qui j'écrirai tout le contraire, que je jurerai mes grands dieux que c'est un livre d'*art pur*, de *singerie*, de *jonglerie*; et je mentirai comme un arracheur de dents'.[3]

The statements must certainly be understood in relation to the situations in which they are made. One of the main purposes of the *Projets de Préface* was to counter the charge of immorality that was directed at Baudelaire and his work. By his words to Ancelle, Baudelaire had little or nothing to gain. What is more, they concur both with Baudelaire's theory of the 'naïveté' of the great artist and with the commonsense view that the thoughts and feelings which a poet is most likely to express, and to express best, are those which affect him most as a man and inevitably form part of his personal biography. This does not however mean that the

[1] CORR, VI, p. 233.   [2] FM, p. 373.   [3] CORR, V, p. 279.

statement in the letter to Ancelle should be taken to cancel and supersede the earlier ones. There is truth in both just as there is exaggeration in both. They are complementary half-truths. The portrait of a writer that appears in his work can never be more than a special form in which the writer has chosen to appear. The form will be at best a selection and arrangement of some of the thoughts, feelings and possibly actions which helped or help to constitute the ever-changing insubstantial creature called 'the man'. And the more artistic the writer's purpose, the less will be the semblance of bio-graphical truth—though a deeper, less obvious form of psychological truth will almost certainly be reached on the artistic plane. What appears in the work will be a form of the man which only he could assume and which is uniquely he. But it will not be the same person that the biographer studies however much it may resemble him. When Baudelaire speaks of putting 'all his thought, emotions and religion' in his work, one must mentally add: 'selected and arranged and indeed disguised not only by the most ironic and subtly perverse of confessants, but also, and above all, by the most conscious, conscientious, and therefore "innocent" of artists, over a span of some twenty hectic years'.

Like the difficulty which is raised by changes or develop-ments in the plan of *Les Fleurs du Mal*, there is nothing in the least unusual about the problem of the man and the work. It presents itself in the humblest poem no less than in the longest epic. There is only one answer to it: the work both is and is not the man. That being so, it seems only reasonable to avoid making either of the two assumptions unless it can be proved beyond reasonable literary doubt. This can hardly

be done if the 'Je' in the work is called Baudelaire and confused from the start with the historical figure—whose legend
it has helped to create. At least to begin with, the work must
be treated as what it manifestly is—something apart from its
creator. The principle is so obvious that it would be as
absurd as it would be ungrateful to imply that none of the
distinguished critics who have passed beyond it, to lend their
authority to one or other of the aforementioned schools of
thought, was aware of what he was doing. Important though
it is for critical theory in general, if the principle has been
established here at such length, it is chiefly in the hope that a
positive contribution to the particular problem can still be
made by applying it to the study of the architecture of *Les
Fleurs du Mal* as strictly as it would be applied in the case of
a tragedy or epic poem presented in a more conventional
form. The hope was the offshoot of a growing conviction
that the architecture itself demanded this approach in order
that the full richness of its detail and structural patterns
might be seen. And this conviction sprang originally from
examination of the group of poems on Beauty which have
hitherto yielded surprisingly little of value to attempts at
exegesis, but which are in fact a central feature of the architecture and serve to make the problems arising from an
aesthetic the starting-point of a human tragedy.

For the reasons already set forth, Baudelaire is treated here
as the author of this tragedy and the creator of the 'Je' or
'Poëte' who takes part in it and is accordingly referred to as
the 'poet-hero'. In a sense, the term is a provisional admission
of ignorance—ignorance of the precise extent of the creature's
likeness to, and difference from, the creator whom he both is

and is not. In many respects, no doubt, good estimates may be made, but they do not have to be made in order to follow the architecture and it may be a positive danger to make them before the poet-hero has been allowed to emerge as a figure in his own right. For understanding of him and his adventure may then be limited to the real—or fancied—points of similarity between him and his creator: he may be denied altogether, as he is by Feuillerat; or he may find his splendid tragic role cut off in the middle to save the author's good name, as it is by Marcel Ruff. He is certainly a 'témoin' as well as a 'sujet', but why not both at once, as are all the other heroes of literature and drama?

In this case, as in others, admission of ignorance may possibly further knowledge. To free the poet-hero from assumptions of likeness to, or difference from, his creator, is not to let the imagination run riot. It certainly tends to confirm L. J. Austin's contention that the architecture does not consist merely of the suggested connecting-links between the different books, but exists within the books themselves to a hitherto unremarked degree.[1] And perception of this detail leads to the perception of new major structural patterns which affect the balance and meaning of the whole. But although the architecture may come to seem more complex and coherent as a result of this distinction between the man and the work, the drama which it represents and which is treated in this study as if it were fiction, is actually no more strange and improbable than many interpretations of the architecture, or portions thereof, which have been presented as biographical fact. Nor does it differ greatly in its broad

[1] *Op. cit.*, p. 99.

outline from such conservative general surveys as that given by Crépet and Blin in their excellent critical edition of *Les Fleurs du Mal*.[1]

The reserves which have been expressed above with regard to the use of biography imply no disrespect for that science. In the more general form of literary history its aid has been enlisted here in connection with every poem. Intellectual autobiography, in the shape of Baudelaire's other writings, has however been regarded as a more reliable and valuable aid than other kinds in the present instance. What have been consciously omitted are attempts to support exegesis with reference to Baudelaire's biography in cases where he himself has not provided strong documentary evidence apart from the poems themselves, and discussion—but not consideration —of Baudelaire's love-affairs in cases where understanding of the relevant cycle of poems offers no special architectural problem. Lastly, no attempt has been made, before the concluding chapter, to 'explain' Baudelaire in terms of his poet-hero and the latter's tragedy. As the conclusion may show, this is not to say that no biographical inference can be drawn nor that a work treated as fiction cannot reveal the personality and convictions of the author in a truer light than the same work considered purely as the expression of the drama of the author's life—about which we may know far less than we think. It is simply that the first aim of this study is to add what it can to understanding of the drama of *Les Fleurs du Mal*.

To speak of the drama of *Les Fleurs du Mal* is to assume

[1] FM (Crépet), p. 247. The survey is preceded by a brief history of early studies of the architecture.

that there is no *essential* difference between the plans of the
first and second editions. It is therefore to disagree with the
findings of Albert Feuillerat who distinguishes sharply
between the two. For Feuillerat, the true basis for any study
of the work must be the first edition. This of course is true,
but only in a chronological sense. Where two or more versions of a work exist, we do not normally regard the first
as the most reliable guide to the author's intentions: we assume, on the contrary, that the last version published by the
author is the definitive form. Feuillerat, however, takes the
view that the second edition of *Les Fleurs du Mal* was, on
the whole, an artistic error: the new poems introduced a tone
of lassitude and discouragement which conflicted with the
enthusiastic virility of the first edition and so spoilt the unity
of the work.[1]

This view of the two editions may result in part from a lack
of logic in the manner of Feuillerat's approach to the problem.
Having dismissed the studies of Prince Ourousoff, Benedetto
and Ruff, on the grounds that they are based on preconceived
ideas (one might wonder what studies are not, and reflect
how easy it is to condemn as a preconceived idea, what is
actually a conclusion), he proposes to undertake a systematic
study of the poems of the first edition in order to put himself
'à la place de Baudelaire' and to 'revivre les intentions qui le
dirigèrent dans l'organisation de son plan'.[2] To the extent
that he does so, he rejects the valuable assistance that knowledge of the second edition can give us in understanding the
first, and it may be that too dogmatic a stand on conclusions
based on part only of the available facts, has led him to exag-

[1] *Op. cit.*, p. 320. [2] *Ibid.*, p. 223.

gerate the difference between the two. The critic cannot ride
one horse only when several are available: he must ride them
all at once—which means that their respective positions do
not really matter. One should, theoretically speaking, be able
to arrive at the same conclusions about both editions of
Les Fleurs du Mal, whether one chooses to study the second
edition in the light of the first, or the first in the light of the
second. These considerations, together with the preconceived
idea (or conclusion) that Baudelaire may indeed have improved his work at the second attempt, explain why the second
edition has been given pride of place in this study.

A summary of the architecture of the second edition is
contained in Chapter I. It thus serves as an introduction to
the detailed study on which its findings are based. It designedly
postpones discussion of the attendant problems, including
those which arise from the chronological growth of the work.
In the following chapters, the architecture is related to the
individual poems and groups of poems to be found in the
first and second editions. The later poems have not been
considered: admirably adapted as many of them are to the
architecture, they add nothing of importance to our knowledge
of the editions of 1857 and 1861. In general, comment on the
poems has been limited to discussion of their relation to the
architecture, but in the case of *Correspondances* and the group
of poems on Beauty, this relation itself has necessitated ex-
tensive reference to the vexed problems of Baudelaire's
aesthetic theory. So rich is the architecture of *Les Fleurs du
Mal* that all the problems which it raises, human as well as
literary, cannot adequately be treated by a single writer, much
less in a single book. This survey will have fulfilled its pur-

pose if it helps to make that view more general than it is at present. What should be looked for in *Les Fleurs du Mal* over and above the purely poetic value of the poems considered individually, is not limited to an abject confession combined with a didactic 'message', to be judged according to one's taste in such messages. It is, in the first place, a tragedy or poetic drama, to be judged in terms of the artistic value proper to the genre.

I

AN OUTLINE OF THE TRAGEDY

1. THE STRUCTURE

THE second edition of *Les Fleurs du Mal* may be considered as a tragedy in six parts corresponding to the six books into which it is divided. The tragedy is primarily the personal one of the anonymous poet-hero but he is clearly intended to represent also the 'jeunesse moderne' referred to in the note in *Le Magasin des Familles* of June 1850 which announced Baudelaire's forthcoming work. The sweeping nature of the indictment contained in the introductory poem, *Au Lecteur*, indicates moreover that the poet-hero is ultimately representative of Everyman, and that impression is confirmed by the tragedy itself. For in the action from which it springs, religious, moral and aesthetic issues which are particularly, but not exclusively, the concern of a nineteenth-century French poet and Catholic, have been superimposed on a problem which is the universal one of appetence—the quest for happiness envisaged in its basic, instinctive form.

The terms in which the problem is stated provide the title of the first book: *Spleen et Idéal. Idéal*, like Spleen itself, should be understood primarily as an emotional state, and together they constitute the emotional poles between which all experience, both instinctive and rational, is contained.

Whatever its source, the Ideal is a state of pleasurable excitement towards which man is constantly striving but which, owing to the limitations of his own nature and the imperfections of his environment, he can enjoy for brief moments only. Spleen is a state of emotional depression which may range from the boredom that is merely consciousness of the absence of excitement, to any degree of suffering that is felt as undesirable and not as an ingredient in masochistic pleasure—for as such it may enter into certain forms of the Ideal.

Envisaged in its simplest form, the conflict which opposes the poet-hero to himself and to his environment is a struggle to escape from Spleen towards the Ideal. This struggle determines the primary motif revealed by the architecture of the work: it may be thought of figuratively as a movement upward or outward followed by a return to rest. From Spleen comes an aspiration towards the ideal state of pleasurable excitement, some degree of satisfaction is achieved, the energy needed to maintain this state is temporarily exhausted, and the aspiration collapses with a consequent return to Spleen. Each of the six books of *Les Fleurs du Mal* represents at least one such cycle. The movement is as simple as that of breathing, the simplest and most regular of all rhythmic patterns and an archetype of every kind of physical or moral movement (the *voyage* in the flesh or in the imagination and the *transport* of the emotions) which returns to its point of departure. Few works of literature can show such a rigid adherence to so simple a basic plan: few can show such remarkable structural coherence and unity.

The value of coherence in art is, however, relative to the

degree of complexity that enters into it. And the basic pattern in *Les Fleurs du Mal* is not repeated without constant variations. These affect, not the type of movement involved, but its direction—that is to say, the precise form of the Ideal at which it is aimed, and, less obviously, the precise form of the Spleen in which it begins and ends. Although the Ideal remains constant in the sense that it is always an emotional excitement which is felt as pleasurable, it may be derived from very different kinds of experience and assume correspondingly different forms: religious, artistic, sexual and so on. Not only has Baudelaire introduced such variations, but he has presented them in an order which is itself necessary, logical and coherent. It imposes on successive examples of the primary movement, a secondary movement which determines the progress of the action of the tragedy. This can be summarized by means of the following simple diagram:

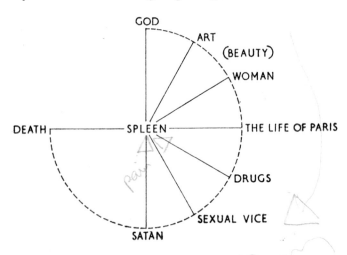

The successive forms of the poet-hero's ideal are here arranged in the order in which they appear in *Les Fleurs du Mal*: those of God, art and woman (with the transitional ideal of beauty) are treated in *Spleen et Idéal*, the life of Paris (or of the world in general) in *Tableaux parisiens*, drugs in *Le Vin*, sexual vice in *Fleurs du Mal* (anticipated, of course, by the cycles dealing with woman in *Spleen et Idéal*), Satan in *Révolte*, death in *La Mort*. In respect of his struggle to escape from Spleen, the poet-hero's situation is the same at the end as it was at the beginning; the primary pattern of the architecture remains unchanged. But in respect of the form taken by his ideal, his situation changes constantly, and even if one limits one's view of the matter to the primary level of purely appetitive, non-rational experience, one can see something of the logic of the order in which the successive ideals are explored. The logic lies in the degree of unpleasantness or pain which enters into the later forms of the Ideal as compared with the earlier ones. The poet-hero becomes a man whose instinctive tastes in pleasurable excitement (the Ideal) become more and more degraded in so far as they make excitement and pleasure itself conditional upon an ever-increasing admixture of pain. In the language of psychology, he develops the marked sado-masochistic complex which Georges Blin has so thoroughly studied with reference to Baudelaire himself.[1]

This vice is of the greatest importance in the architecture since it constitutes the poet-hero's tragic 'flaw'. It is the perversion of his aspiration towards the Ideal, which is, or should be, his noblest attribute. To avoid a gross misunder-

[1] *Le Sadisme de Baudelaire*, Paris, José Corti, 1948.

standing, it must indeed be insisted from the start that although the poet-hero may share with the brute this attraction towards what pains and repels, it is not in him a sign of brutality. It is, on the contrary, a sign of the very intensity of his revulsion from brutality, ugliness, immorality and sin in all its forms. Therein lies the full irony of his tragedy. Remembering that the poet-hero's nature is more masochistic than sadistic, and that his sins are mostly confined to his own mind and imagination, one could say of him what Proust has so excellently said of his own Mlle Vinteuil:

Une sadique comme elle est l'artiste du mal, ce qu'une créature entièrement mauvaise ne pourrait être, car le mal ne lui serait pas extérieur, il lui semblerait tout naturel, ne se distinguerait même pas d'elle; et la vertu . . ., comme elle n'en aurait pas le culte, elle ne trouverait pas un plaisir sacrilège à (la) profaner. Les sadiques de l'espèce de Mlle Vinteuil sont des êtres si purement sentimentaux, si naturellement vertueux que même le plaisir sensuel leur paraît quelque chose de mauvais, le privilège des méchants. Et quand ils se concèdent à eux-mêmes de s'y livrer un moment, c'est dans la peau des méchants qu'ils tâchent d'entrer et de faire entrer leur complice, de façon à avoir eu un moment l'illusion de s'être évadé de leur âme scrupuleuse et tendre, dans le monde inhumain du plaisir.[1]

In so far as such people are 'naturellement vertueux', the 'plaisir sacrilège' which they find in profaning virtue is a pleasure in which the essential ingredient is pain, not necessarily the sadistic pain that may be inflicted on others, but first and foremost the pain which comes from awareness that they are degrading themselves by acting against the instincts of their better nature, and which may therefore be termed

[1] *Du côté de chez Swann*, t. I, Paris, Gallimard, 1929, p. 236.

Considered in terms of aesthetic values, the poet-hero's struggle to escape from Spleen towards the Ideal is synonymous with his struggle to convert his experience of life into great poetry. The Ideal, in its aesthetic form, therefore remains constant throughout, in the sense that it is aimed at in every poem and enjoyed as the 'principe de la poésie', the specific kind of pleasurable emotional excitement which characterizes successful poetic activity for poet and reader alike. What varies is not the pure aesthetic ideal but the kinds of ideal that serve the poet as *subject-matter* for his art at different stages of his poetic career. These are so varied and so arranged as to allow him to treat the whole range of human passions from the most beautiful to the most ugly. All are transformed with equal success into the specifically artistic beauty of the pure aesthetic ideal and the poet-hero achieves an artistic triumph. He nevertheless lives the tragedy which is unfolded in the subject-matter of his poems and his very aspiration towards the aesthetic form of the Ideal helps to bring about his moral and spiritual ruin and indeed the ruin of his basic mental health. For although the aesthetic ideal is itself a perfectly pure and healthy one, closely connected, moreover, with the highest form of the religious ideal, pursuit of it encourages him to give expression to morally dangerous tendencies in the appetent or instinctive level of his personality which underlies (and, to a large extent, assimilates) the rational levels formed by aesthetic and religious culture. He thereby fosters the development of tastes which cause him to be gradually seduced from his original allegiance to the ideal of God and led down through what he hopes is a neutral position (the ideal represented by the contemplation of the life of

Paris in *Tableaux parisiens*) to the extreme of moral and spiritual evil (allegiance to the ideal of Satan) before seeking a final, morally neutral ideal in and beyond death.

The religious and moral aspect of the poet-hero's tragedy must be considered in the light of a generalization made by Baudelaire in *Mon Coeur mis à nu*:

> Dans tout homme, à toute heure, il y a deux postulations simultanées, l'une vers Dieu, l'autre vers Satan. L'invocation à Dieu, ou spiritualité, est un désir de monter en grade; celle de Satan, ou animalité, est une joie de descendre.[1]

The psychological justification of this alarming statement lies in the probability that a relatively mild form of the sado-masochist complex is part and parcel of normal human nature, a consequence, perhaps, of physiological laws which have decreed that pleasure and pain, like heat and cold, should be overlapping and highly subjective measurements of the intensity with which a set of nerves is stimulated. Even normal pleasures range between an 'upper' extreme of pleasure which is relatively far removed from pain, and a 'lower' extreme of impure, but not necessarily less intense pleasure which obviously overlaps into the zone of pain. Interpreting the matter in terms of religious morality, Baudelaire associates with God the 'upper' extreme in so far as it is consistent with moral law, and the 'lower' extreme in so far as it may involve a morally justifiable form of masochist pleasure or suffering (in repentance or self-denial, for example, though in *Le Voyage* these pleasures are condemned as: 'la Sainteté . . . dans les clous et le crin cherchant la volupté'). All other

[1] JOP, II, p. 93.

forms of undiluted pleasure and masochistic pleasure, together with sadism in all its manifestations from malice to murder, are classified as satanic.

The poet-hero of *Les Fleurs du Mal* is indeed a being whose destiny it is to be pulled in two seemingly opposed directions by forces which must, in the final analysis, be deemed superhuman. His situation is reminiscent of that depicted by Lord Herbert:

> ... God stoops o'er his head,
> Satan looks up between his feet—both tug—
> He's left, himself, i' the middle; ...

But whereas Lord Herbert optimistically infers an awakening and healthy growth of the human soul, Baudelaire characteristically prefers the tragic view. In the case of his poet-hero, God and Satan tug, it seems, with exactly equal strength—except when his own efforts to cleave to one, confer upon the other an increase in strength just sufficient to restore the balance. It is from the poet-hero's initial aspiration towards God that there develops the movement which carries him through intermediate positions and ideals to the ideal of Satan. But for reasons which are grounded in psychology no less than in theology, and which will be outlined in the second part of this chapter, the further the poet-hero moves away from God in the direction of Satan, the stronger becomes the pull of the force that binds him to God. And when at last the aspiration towards Satan himself weakens, the poet-hero's soul relapses into a state of frustrated inertia in which the two *postulations* cancel each other out completely. This spiritual inertia is the specifically religious and moral form assumed by Spleen—for it must be remembered that Spleen, as the negation of the Ideal, has as many different forms as the Ideal itself. It also has different intensities: the mildest form of religious Spleen, suggested rather than expressed in the final stanza of *Les Phares*, is merely the consciousness of the separation of man from God. In its worst form, in *La Destruction* and Part VI of *Le Voyage* for example, it is a bitter consciousness of the satanic *postulation*; it is a horrified and despairing consciousness of being spiritually torn apart by forces that hold man forever suspended between God and Satan, Heaven and Hell, unable to identify himself with either of the two absolutes whose conflict makes him suffer. And so it is that the poet-hero's last aspiration is to the absolute itself, any absolute—'Enfer ou Ciel, qu'importe?'

It is interesting to compare the theological conception which underlies the tragedy, with Swedenborg's conception of 'the equilibrium' between Heaven and Hell:

> All existence, that is, every effect, is produced in equilibrium, and it is produced by one force acting and another allowing itself to be acted upon ... There is a perpetual equilibrium between heaven and hell, for from hell there continually breathes forth and ascends the endeavour to do evil, and from heaven there continually breathes out and descends the endeavour to do good ... Spiritual equilibrium in both men and spirits is liberty ... In order that man may be in freedom, for the sake of his being reformed, he is conjoined as to his spirit with heaven and with hell. For there are with every man spirits from hell, and angels from heaven.[1]

The human will, which this equilibrium leaves free, is itself defined by Swedenborg in terms of love and desire. That being

[1] *Heaven and Hell*, London, The Swedenborg Society, 1931, pp. 367–73.

so, it is easy to conceive of a state of complete freedom of the will in which the energy of love or desire is in abeyance and which may therefore be characterized by feelings of ennui or Spleen. When, on the other hand, man throws in his will on the side of either the heavenly or the infernal spirits, we have the state of excitement characteristic of the Baudelairean Ideal. It is not suggested that Baudelaire was necessarily influenced by Swedenborg, but it does seem possible that such 'mechanical' conceptions of man's relation to the two opposed forms of the supernatural were not uncommon at the time.

Whether or not it corresponds at all points to Baudelaire's own considered beliefs at any period of his life (there is no reason why it should), this grim view of human destiny is incorporated, through the hero, into the dramatic structure of the volume and does indeed dominate it. The human drama is presented as an episode in a dimly-seen cosmic drama which enriches and completes the work by making it communicate with the mystery of the infinite. Although the poet-hero retains ultimate responsibility for his fate, the hand of God or of Satan must be seen even in the simplest manifestations of appetence within him. It is both a sign of Satan's power and a condition of it, that the values of appetence conflict with religious and moral values. The poet-hero's religious and moral convictions force him to regard God as the Ideal and Satan as the opposite of the Ideal. Thanks to the sado-masochistic complex, however, he discovers in the appetent level of his personality a taste for a pleasure mingled with pain which he interprets as a *postulation* towards Satan, and this obliges him to contradict the religious and moral judgement to the extent of regarding both God and Satan as ideals, having a common opposite or negation in the state of Spleen. What is more, he finds that the conflict between the values of appetence and those of religious morality is contained in another conflict between the latter and aesthetic values. It is in this clash of values that God and Satan join battle for the soul of the poet-hero, and from it Baudelaire develops the tragic action.

2. THE ACTION

Poems I to XXI form an exposition which introduces the reader to a poet who is not precisely at the outset of his career, but who is at a sufficiently early stage of it to be able to contemplate making a fresh and more systematic start. To this end, he is engaged in taking stock of the vocation of poet and artist (Poems I–VI), of his personal poetic talent (Poems VII–XI) and of certain enigmatic characteristics of his moral nature (Poems XII–XVI). His ideal is presented as a very pure and lofty one in which God and art are closely associated, thanks to his conception of the sacrificial, semi-divine role which the artist must play. It seems to him that he is called upon to seek the ideal of God in and through the ideal of art, and on his success depends his freedom from a Spleen which arises partly from his impatient eagerness to attain his ideals, but partly also from certain sombre depths in his own nature which perversely breed and foster Spleen as if the accompanying pain were a good and not an ill.

The opening movement of aspiration culminates in Poem XVII (*La Beauté*) in which the poet personifies as a celestial goddess the austerely Platonic ideal of absolute beauty which must be the goal of the efforts of all artists. But, as the first of the group of five poems devoted to the ideal of beauty, this same sonnet marks the beginning of a critical phase in the poet-hero's development, one which serves to link the end of the exposition with the *coup du hasard* that sets the tragic action in motion. For it is here that the poet-hero becomes fully aware of the conflict of values which divides his own nature, and ultimately the cosmos itself, into two warring camps.

To attain to the absolute beauty of art envisaged in *La Beauté*, the poet-hero must write great poems. To write great poems he requires inspiration in the shape of subject-matter. For not any subject-matter will do: if he is to give of his best, it must be subject-matter of the kind which holds the greatest interest and appeal for him personally, subject-matter which will itself be 'beautiful' in the loose, relative sense that it affords him pleasurable excitement. In the next three poems of the exposition (*L'Idéal*, *La Géante*, *Le Masque*), he therefore proceeds to take stock, more consciously and deliberately than before, of his tastes in this relative kind of beauty. And by a natural association of ideas, he is led to envisage it in the particular form of the physical and moral attractions of types of womanhood. The results are disconcerting and not what one might expect from the poet of *Bénédiction* and *La Beauté* who quite genuinely aspires to very high and pure religious and artistic ideals. They confirm earlier hints as to the sombre depths of this nature, by revealing, alongside the more elevated aspirations and indeed not wholly distinguishable from them, incipient sado-masochistic tendencies which cause the poet to be attracted to what, in some measure, is painful, to find a strangely stirring beauty, distinct from the absolute beauty of art, in what is in some measure ugly or evil.

This is the problem which the poet-hero envisages with remarkable lucidity in the final poem of the group and the exposition, the *Hymne à la Beauté*. He shows complete awareness of the spiritual and moral ambiguity with which his ideal of Beauty has come to be invested, for on the one hand there is the semi-divine beauty of art itself, and on the other, the satanic beauty of the tragic, ugly and evil experiences which can serve the artist as material for his art—and serve the man as a source of pleasurable excitement and an escape from Spleen in everyday life. Quite clearly, the spiritual and moral values which he tacitly recognizes in aspiring to the ideal of God, demand the sacrifice of the ideal of satanic beauty both in his art and his personal life. But his aesthetic ambitions join with appetence to persuade him that the sacrifice is too great. As the concluding stanzas of the poem show clearly, he determines to accept all forms of beauty, including the satanic, into his Ideal, his art and his life. By this acceptance to which the *Hymne* bears witness, he assumes complete moral responsibility for his subsequent tragedy. He takes the right course as a poet, but the wrong course as a man—a piece of irony which Baudelaire, with his tragic view of life, was not in the least concerned to explain away. And like the conventional tragic hero, he is at once innocent and guilty.

Tragic consequences do indeed follow, just as swiftly as the poet himself passes from dreams to action, and, content no longer with imaginary forms of the ideal of beauty, seeks it in the person of the black Venus. This development is so well prepared that one might hesitate to speak of it as the *coup du hasard*. The true *coup du hasard* lies in the fact that, without fully realizing it, the poet selects as his ideal a woman who is the incarnation of the extreme of satanic beauty. Only by degrees is her true nature revealed to poet and reader alike, for in *Parfum exotique* and *La Chevelure*, she does no more than answer the prayer of the *Hymne* by opening the door of a purely artistic infinite. But when the sexual element in their relationship overpowers the artistic, when the ideal of Beauty becomes the ideal of woman, she develops into a monstrous vice the poet's tendency to find pleasurable excitement in what he finds repulsive as well as attractive—in this case, the sinful black Venus herself. She leads him, not merely back to Spleen, but, so to speak, 'below' Spleen and on to the ideal of sexual vice which will never cease to haunt him and to which he will later return. So it is that the black Venus fulfils her double task of leading him to greatness as a poet and to his ruin as a man. It is she who knots the threads of the tragedy and from this time onwards the poet-hero is irrevocably trapped.

Nor, despite appearances, is he blind to the fact. The episode of the white Venus is best understood ironically, as a deliberate but none the less pathetic 'mensonge' or 'songe', for both these words are applied to it by the poet-hero himself in *Semper eadem*, the poem which introduces the cycle. The episode of the green-eyed Venus is less equivocal in this respect and it presents, in the title of Poem LIV, the word 'irréparable' which reverberates throughout the following cycle of increasingly splenetic *divertissements* (Poems LVIII–LXXIII). So, with the collapse of the aspiration towards the ideal of woman, the poet is returned to a worse state of Spleen (Poems LXXIV–LXXX) than any he has yet encountered. Having progressed so much further from the ideal of God in the direction of the ideal of Satan, he must feel the increased 'pull' of God in the form of a horrified and despairing disgust with himself which is projected upon his environment as well. Poems LXXXI to LXXXV conclude *Spleen et Idéal* with an agonized analysis of the irreparable damage that was done in the crucial cycle of the black Venus. What has happened is possibly simpler and more truly irreparable than commentators have allowed. The poet-hero has lost the very ability to be pleasurably stimulated otherwise than by what is in some sense repulsive to him ('Le Printemps adorable a perdu son odeur'), and although he bemoans his fate in moods of genuine suffering, he quite literally wants no other, because the joys of Paradise itself now seem too insipid to satisfy his perversely sophisticated taste. He is in all truth what Joseph de Maistre and Baudelaire believed all sinners to be—'l'Héautontimorouménos', his own tormentor, he whose sin itself brings its own punishment.

At the end of *Spleen et Idéal* the poet-hero has progressed so far from the ideal of God that its attraction can be felt only as pain: it may be the pain that is an essential ingredient in the satanic pleasure of conscious wrongdoing, or the undiluted pain of the periods of remorseful Spleen which follow such orgies of excitement. But although he realizes that he cannot go back, the poet-hero is loath to go forward

and continue with his own perdition. He therefore tries to
stay where he is, and, like an invalid at a window, to seek
forgetfulness of self, or at least some peace of mind, in contemplating the life of the city around him and using it as
material for his poetry. This is the innocent, morally neutral
ideal of pleasure towards which he cautiously aspires at the
opening of the second book, *Tableaux parisiens*. It proves to
be as ambiguous as the ideals of beauty and woman, for
despite his attempt to forget God and Satan, he and the city
are both in their grip, and within the city he can and does find
a reflection of his own vice and his own Spleen. This ideal
also becomes corrupted in so far as he uses it to indulge his
vice by finding pleasurable excitement in the pain, the ugliness
and the evil that he uncovers. But the excitement itself seems
perilously close to Spleen and the end of the book may be
taken to indicate abandonment of this ideal and a reversion
to the state of Spleen itself.

Having failed to achieve peace of mind and forgetfulness of
self by natural methods, the poet-hero seeks the artificial
consolation of drink, as suggested by the third book, *Le Vin*.
As it stands, however, the book is clearly the weakest of all,
and the least finished, in the sense that its poems were designed to fit an earlier plan than the one which Baudelaire
had evolved at the time of the publication of the first edition
of *Les Fleurs du Mal*. When one remembers the effort
expended by Baudelaire on his *Paradis artificiels*, one cannot
but agree with Marcel Ruff that the significance of *Le Vin*
within the architecture of the volume must be understood in
relation to the work in prose. To understand it thus is to see
in this ideal also an ambiguity which the poems of *Le Vin*

do not bring out with sufficient clarity and force. For wine, like drugs, may be classed as a vice which is analogous with the poet's own, and all the more likely to attract him, not merely as a consolation, but as a source of satanic pleasure and excitement. Like the poet's mental vice, drink and drugs also have the power to kill the taste for purer pleasures that are free from sensations normally regarded as unpleasant; as with the poet's mental vice, indulgence in drink and drugs can be followed by moods of intense depression, remorse and Spleen, from which the only escape is a return to the vice itself.

The same analogy can serve to explain the logic of the poet-hero's passage from the ideal of wine or drugs in general to the ideal of sexual vice presented in the book of *Fleurs du Mal*. Drunkards and drug-addicts have often to increase the dose of their drug in order that it shall continue to stimulate them. A similar psycho-physiological law of diminishing returns may operate in the case of mental vice, and it does so in the case of Baudelaire's poet-hero. In order to stimulate his increasingly blasé sensibility, the degree of pain or re-pulsion which enters into his pleasure must constantly be increased. His ideal must become increasingly corrupt and satanic. So it is that he is driven to what for him is a greater vice than drink, and seeks an escape from Spleen in an imagin-ary form of the ideal of sexual vice into which the black Venus first initiated him. It appears here as the excitement which can be derived from a fascinated and horrified con-templation of sexual vice in its more perverse forms. But in so far as the poet is led to sympathize with the 'Femmes damnées' of Lesbos, and even to admire them as 'coeurs ambitieux' and 'chercheuses d'infini', he is prepared for the last step that he will take on the road to his own damnation.

These poems illustrate the operation of another psychological law which is a consequence of the one referred to above. The poet's ideal has become more corrupt in the sense that a higher degree of repulsion and pain has entered into the excitement that is his pleasure. But this means that the ideal, which is the only escape from Spleen, has been brought a step nearer the level of pure repulsion and pure pain which is the state of Spleen itself. The only step which can increase the diminishing efficacity of the Ideal has, in the end, the opposite effect. The same paradox can be expressed in terms of religious morality by saying that the pleasure which the poet finds in vice depends in very large measure upon his inward adherence to the principles of virtue. So the greater his vice, the closer his state of mind to actual remorse and revulsion from vice. All the more quickly and surely therefore does this ideal lead him back to Spleen in the poems of moral and physical destruction which end this book.

The same laws govern the passage to the ideal of Satan in the fifth book, *Révolte*, and the eventual abandonment of this ideal also. The fascination of the supreme sin depends more than ever on consciousness of sinfulness; the fascination of adherence to Satan depends upon tacit adherence to the law of God; such adherence can never be absolute and the excitement that it brings must sooner or later be replaced by remorseful Spleen.

So at last the poet turns his back on Satan, God and life and seeks his last ideal in death. For a time the mere contemplation of death is emotionally exciting and sufficient in itself as an escape from Spleen. In *Le Voyage*, however, the poet turns to the only possible solution of his problem which remains—that offered by the concrete reality of death and whatever may lie beyond.

Such is the tragedy which Baudelaire develops with perfect logic from his exposition and, in particular, from the poems on Beauty. It is of the *Hymne à la Beauté* that the final stanzas of *Le Voyage* should remind us, for in the words of Jean Massin, the only critic who has commented on the fact, the endings of the two poems give out 'un son identique'.[1] Both poems were specially written for the second edition of the work, at a time, that is, when we may be sure that Baudelaire was writing with the architecture clearly in mind. Beauty and death have the same ambiguous character, monstrous, repulsive, yet attractive. So does the unknown 'infini' or 'nouveau' which the poet demands from both. The same plea is made to death as was made to beauty in the same movement of escape from Spleen and with the same indifference to consequences ('Enfer ou Ciel, qu'importe?'). There could be no more effective way of underlining the basic unity of the poet's nature and of the tragedy which springs from it.

[1] *Baudelaire entre Dieu et Satan*, Paris, René Juillard, 1946, p. 34. Jacques Crépet (FM (Crépet) p. 531) has remarked on the repetition of 'Qu'importe'.

II

THE INTRODUCTORY MATTER

I . THE TITLE

As Enid Starkie has remarked in her introduction to the Blackwell edition of *Les Fleurs du Mal*, the meaning of the title has frequently been misunderstood. The same writer is also one of the very few commentators who have made an effort to assist their readers to a better understanding of the title which almost all admit to be obscure. Unfortunately the interpretation that is given leaves some of the mystery unexplained. It is argued from the nature of the frontispiece which Baudelaire wished Bracquemond to produce for the 1861 edition, that he intended the title to be interpreted in its mediaeval and symbolical sense, that is to say that certain plants are the emblems of sins and vices. Leaving aside for the moment the implications of this idea, and granting that the argument holds good for the 1861 edition, it must still be asked whether Baudelaire could seriously have expected the public of 1857 to relate his title to mediaeval symbolism, for at that period, as far as we know, there was no question of providing any frontispiece to guide them. If we feel this to be unlikely, then we must suppose that Baudelaire was willing to accept a more obvious interpretation. But what precisely was it?

The primary meaning of the title is: 'Poems (i.e. works of aesthetic beauty) written on the subject of evil'. A poem, however, is not merely a work of art: it may be confused with the experience which provides its subject-matter and judged in consequence, not as art, but according to one's taste in pleasurable non-artistic experiences. This confusion is so common that the word 'Fleurs' in Baudelaire's title, inevitably invites interpretation in this sense also—in the sense of the representational content of the poems instead of their aesthetic effect. It therefore gives rise to two additional meanings of the title, which may combine to form a third.

The first of these additional meanings is obtained by stressing the pleasant suggestions of 'Fleurs' at the expense of the unpleasant suggestions of 'Mal'. We are then presented with the idea that evil can produce forms and experiences which are beautiful in the sense that they are alluring, evil 'flowers' which the poet has plucked with a pleasurable thrill, before distilling their evil but attractive essence in his poems. This is the *pseudo*-aesthetic, perversely immoral interpretation of the title which a Swinburne and an Oscar Wilde would tend to prefer. It is also, one suspects, the interpretation that many modern critics deprecate. They seem to prefer the moralistic interpretation given by emphasizing the word 'Mal'. We then have the moralistic counterpart of the previous libertine interpretation: life, it is suggested, contains many attractive and superficially beautiful forms of which we should beware because they are rooted in evil and therefore fundamentally ugly and repulsive.

One may unhesitatingly agree with Enid Starkie and those who feel as she does, that of the two secondary interpretations

Baudelaire himself would wish to emphasize the moralistic interpretation, and that the overall tendency of the tragedy narrated in his poems is to do precisely this. The attitude towards life expressed in the content of the volume as a whole, and which we may with some confidence regard as that of Baudelaire himself, is deeply and desperately moral. But this does not mean that we should simply rule out and abandon the immoral meaning distinguished in the title. One's attitude may be no less moral when one is conscious of the evil that is within one, than when one is conscious of one's own virtue and the evil of others. One may be none the less *against* evil, for being aware that part of one is *for* evil, inclined to emphasize the pleasant suggestion of 'Fleurs' in the expression 'Fleurs du Mal'. Similarly, Baudelaire's attitude, as expressed in his work, is not the simple attitude of being 'against evil', nor is it the equally simple attitude of being 'for evil': it is the complex attitude of being '*against* evil including the evil part of himself which is *for* evil'. This attitude may well appear ambiguous, and the title of *Les Fleurs du Mal* does in fact show the same ambiguity that generations of readers have recognized in the volume itself. We should not therefore reject the immoral meaning of the title, any more than we should shut our eyes to what corresponds to it in the poetry. In all probability it is this very ambiguity, or richness of meaning, that explains the appeal which the title held for Baudelaire.

To conclude, misunderstanding of the title can occur only when its ambiguity and the implications of its ambiguity are forgotten, that is, when only one of the two secondary meanings is accepted. This happened in 1857 when the authorities who prosecuted Baudelaire preferred to ignore the moralistic attitude of repulsion implicit in the title and the work alike, and so failed to grasp the complex but still moral attitude which resolves the apparent antithesis. This fact no doubt goes some way towards explaining why Baudelaire came to feel the need of a frontispiece for the second edition. It would serve to emphasize the moralistic attitude of repulsion, by portraying the 'fleurs', not as beautiful, but as grotesque, deformed and horrific, in keeping with the mediaeval philosophy which identified moral evil and aesthetic ugliness. Nor would such a frontispiece exclude the other meanings of the title. The illustration eventually produced by Rops for *Les Épaves* may have little merit as a work of art, and the plants which it depicts are certainly not attractive in a conventional way. But no Romantic writer was more aware than Baudelaire of the unconventional attractiveness and 'beauty' of the grotesque and the horrible. In that sense, the illustration remains as ambiguous as the title of the major work.

Since Baudelaire's death, the title of *Les Fleurs du Mal* and the poetry itself have been partly misinterpreted by French and English Decadents, who emphasized the immoral aspect of the work. In its reaction against this extreme view, modern criticism has, on occasion, swung too far to the opposite extreme, and has ignored the deepest and most sombre tones that enter into the extraordinary symphony of *Les Fleurs du Mal*.

2. THE DEDICATION

The published version of the dedication of *Les Fleurs du Mal* raises no difficulty save for critics who emphasize the differences of outlook which separate Baudelaire and Gautier and minimize the area of agreement and sympathy. On the other hand, the first version of the dedication has proved as enigmatic as the title, and, since it has a direct bearing both upon Baudelaire's intentions in writing *Les Fleurs du Mal* and upon his theory of poetry, it cannot be ignored. It runs as follows:

Bien que je te prie de servir de parrain aux *Fleurs du Mal*, ne crois pas que je sois assez perdu, assez indigne du nom de poëte pour m'imaginer que ces fleurs maladives méritent ton noble patronage. Je sais que dans les régions éthérées de la véritable Poésie, le Mal n'est pas, non plus que le Bien, et que ce misérable dictionnaire de mélancolie et de crime peut légitimer les réactions de la morale, comme le blasphémateur confirme la religion. Mais j'ai voulu . . . rendre un hommage profond . . . à l'auteur d'*Albertus*, de *la Comédie de la Mort* et d'*España*, . . . dont je me déclare . . . le plus dévoué . . . des disciples.[1]

In this dedication, Baudelaire appears to apologize for, and to that extent to condemn his poems, in the name of a poetic doctrine which both he and Gautier uphold. We may discard the possibility that Baudelaire really believed his poetry to be inferior poetry on account of its connections with problems of morality. It therefore becomes necessary to define the extent of his insincerity by defining the extent of his disagreement with Gautier on the subject of the relation of poetry to morality.

[1] FM, p. 408.

Gautier had evidently come to believe by this time that the best way of avoiding confusion between purely artistic values in poetry and the extraneous value of morality, was to exclude from poetry, as far as possible, subject-matter which directly invited moral judgements. Many of his *Émaux et Camées*, published five years earlier than *Les Fleurs du Mal*, may be regarded as attempts to put the theory into practice. As will presently be shown, Baudelaire was almost certainly willing, in 1857 (before 1852 he might not have been), to admit the legitimacy of such a step. He did not however alter his own practice and it is highly significant that *Émaux et Camées* is absent from the list of works which he attributes in the dedication to the author whose devoted disciple he is. The omission might well be a smiling reminder that he gives to Gautier of the difference which is so neatly and tactfully glossed over in the earlier part of the dedication. Like Edgar Allan Poe, Baudelaire did not consider that Gautier's step was essential. What is more, even while he granted its legitimacy, he almost certainly considered that it tended to impoverish poetry, and that for him personally it was, in a sense, impossible.

For unlike later poets and critics who wrongly claim him as an ally in this respect, Baudelaire does not normally stress the freedom of the poet-craftsman to do what he wills in the domain of his art. As is so often the case, this admirer of extremes strikes an admirable balance in his criticism. He fully recognizes the necessity for the craftsman's approach to poetry, as advocated by Poe in *The Philosophy of Composition*, and in his notes for a preface to *Les Fleurs du Mal* he uses Poe's theory of the complete detachment of the artist from his

6419 D

subject to counter the charge of immorality. He nevertheless
sees the theory for the half-truth that it is, and he remains
very much aware of an element of determinism which seems
to him to govern artistic activity—a determinism of temperament or passion.[1] Individual differences of temperament and
passion, reflected in the widely different types of subject-
matter preferred by individual poets, suggest that the subject
of poetry is unimportant; and so it is, in the sense that good
poetry can apparently be written on any subject. What
impresses Baudelaire is the fact that individual poets cannot
do so—or rather that every poet must treat a given subject in
his own way, which, strictly speaking, will make of it a new
subject within his personal range of expression. Thus understood, the subject becomes of the greatest importance relative
to the individual poet: as Baudelaire himself remarked, 'le
sujet fait pour l'artiste une partie du génie'.[2] If the artist is to
give of his best, he must treat the subject best suited to his
temperament in the manner best suited to his temperament.
And in Baudelaire's own case, it seems that his temperament
itself led him inevitably to the kind of subject-matter which
raised moral issues in a glaringly obvious way. Nor could he
subscribe to any theory of poetry which contradicted his own
deepest feelings, as well as the practice of countless generations of poets.

What then can Baudelaire mean when he states: 'Je sais que
dans les régions éthérées de la véritable Poésie, le Mal n'est
pas, non plus que le Bien'? Marcel Ruff gives the following
answer: 'Il est permis de penser que Baudelaire ... ne croit
pas déchoir de la "véritable Poésie" en renonçant aux

[1] CE, pp. 89–90, p. 111, p. 197, pp. 444–5.   [2] CE, p. 345.

"régions éthérées" '.[1] So Baudelaire really means: 'I know of regions of true Poetry, other than your celestial ones, where Good and Evil do exist, and these are the ones which I prefer.' Marcel Ruff regards the statement as 'une concession de courtoisie, ou, si l'on préfère, de flatterie.' But it might be thought that the reference to the 'régions éthérées', on which Baudelaire turns his back in somewhat cavalier fashion, comes perilously close to being a jibe in the worst possible taste, and, as such, is out of character and out of place in the dedication of a serious work of art. This objection, however, is a minor one in comparison with the other difficulties that are raised by so unorthodox an interpretation of a central point in Baudelaire's theory. The dedication is by no means the only place where Baudelaire makes statements of this kind and they cannot all be explained by assuming that he means something quite different from what he says. Acceptance of Marcel Ruff's interpretation therefore entails some measure of acceptance of the view advanced by L. J. Austin, when he writes: 'tantôt Baudelaire dira que sa poésie n'a rien à voir avec la morale et la religion, tantôt il criera qu'il y a mis "tout son coeur" et "toute sa religion". Poe lui a bien plutôt appris à déraisonner qu'à "raisonner" sur ce point'.[2] Against such verdicts Baudelaire must be allowed an eternal right of appeal. It could indeed be argued that neither singly nor together, do the principal texts referred to here (the *Projets*

---

[1] *Op. cit.*, p. 101.

[2] *Op. cit.*, pp. 167–8. This dismissal of an essential feature of Baudelaire's aesthetic is all the more surprising in view of the later statement: 'De part et d'autre, ce que l'on retient, c'est le contenu conceptuel de l'oeuvre, les propositions que l'on croit pouvoir en déduire. Mais ces analyses seraient justes, qu'elles ne nous diraient rien sur la valeur poétique de cette poésie' (*Op. cit.*, p. 338).

de Préface and the letter to Ancelle of February 1866) constitute 'déraison'. As has already been suggested, they could be complementary half-truths, since all poets must be concerned with poetry both as an impersonal problem of technique and as a personal problem of self-expression. Moreover, it may be that this question, which is one of fact, has been confused in the above quotation with one of aesthetic theory. Although one may personally prefer a different view of poetry, it is not unreasonable for a poet to state that 'tout son coeur' and 'toute sa religion' is in his poetry, and yet affirm that it is not as morality or religion that his work is poetically valuable. Baudelaire is hardly likely to have said that '*sa* poésie n'a rien à voir avec la morale et la religion': the subject-matter of his poems is there to prove the contrary. He might well have said: '*la* Poésie n'a rien à voir avec la morale et la religion', using the word 'Poésie', complete with capital, in the abstract sense of 'poetic value'. It is so used in the dedication when he speaks of 'les régions éthérées de la véritable Poésie'.

There is no lack of texts in Baudelaire's writings which clarify the matter. The following passage from his article on Auguste Barbier, published in 1861, is his last word:

Tel poëme est beau et honnête; mais il n'est pas beau *parce qu'*il est honnête. Tel autre, beau et déshonnête; mais sa beauté ne lui vient pas de son immoralité, ou plutôt, pour parler nettement, ce qui est beau n'est pas plus honnête que déshonnête. Il arrive le plus souvent, je le sais, que la poésie vraiment belle emporte les âmes vers un monde céleste; la beauté est une qualité si forte qu'elle ne peut qu'ennoblir les âmes; mais cette beauté est une chose tout à fait inconditionnelle, il y a beaucoup à parier que si vous voulez, vous poëte, vous imposer à l'avance un but moral, vous diminuerez considérablement votre puissance poétique.[1]

'. . . ce qui est beau n'est pas plus honnête que déshonnête'! By the same token—'ce qui est honnête n'est pas plus beau que laid'! It is as much a mistake to confuse these judgements in artistic criticism, as it would be for a court of law to give preference to the more eloquent advocate of a cause—and no more easy to avoid doing so, as the history of literary criticism shows. Just as in the ethereal regions of true Morality, aesthetic Beauty and Ugliness are irrelevant values, so 'dans les régions éthérées de la véritable Poésie, le Mal n'est pas, non plus que le Bien'. It seems to me that L. J. Austin illustrates the matter on the level of practical criticism in an admirable comment which he makes on the following lines from *Un Voyage à Cythère*:

> Je sentis, à l'aspect de tes membres flottants,
> Comme un vomissement, remonter vers mes dents
> Le long fleuve de fiel des douleurs anciennes;

The comment runs: '. . . l'horreur de l'idée est vaincue par la perfection de la forme, mais . . . la beauté de l'effet prend une immense résonance de la violence initiale de la passion qu'elle enchaîne et qu'elle enchâsse'.[2] It is true that the 'beauté de l'effet', by which is meant the feelings to which we attach poetic value, is in this case affected by the 'violence de la passion', if not the 'horreur' itself. It is none the less true that poetic value itself (that part of the 'effet' which is a constant, the elusive quality which is both 'la perfection de la forme' and the perfection of *content considered as form*)

[1] AR, pp. 319–20.   [2] *Op. cit.*, p. 219.

cannot be conditional either upon violence of passion or upon
the horror of ideas. It could be said that: 'la Poésie n'a rien
à faire avec l'horreur', and Baudelaire has said it—with
reference to the early poems of Théophile Gautier:

C'est un des privilèges prodigieux de l'Art que l'horrible,
artistement exprimé, devienne beauté et que la *douleur* rhythmée
et cadencée remplisse l'esprit d'une *joie* calme.[1]

The distinctions between the horrible and beauty, and between
'la *douleur*' and 'une *joie* calme', are identical with that made in
the dedication between Good and Evil and true poetic value.

One final point may be made in connection with this important question which will be raised again in Chapters III
and IV. In the dedication, as in the passage from the article
on Barbier and in countless other texts to be quoted later,
poetry is said to raise one, through its emotional effect, 'vers
un monde céleste'. As will be shown in detail in connection
with the poems on Beauty, Baudelaire's conception of that
'monde céleste' (described in the important but neglected
essay *De l'essence du rire*) tallies with his conception of the
effect of poetry. There is no 'Bien' because there is no 'Mal'.

One need not necessarily conclude from this view of poetry
that matters of morality or religion are better left out of the
content of poetry. Poe himself had written in one of the
essays which seem finally to have reconciled Baudelaire to this
amoral theory of poetic value after his doubts of 1851:

It by no means follows ... that the incitements of Passion, or
the precepts of Duty, or even the lessons of Truth, may not be
introduced into a poem, and with advantage; for they may sub-

[1] AR, p. 172.

serve incidentally, in various ways, the general purpose of the work.[1]

As interpreted by Baudelaire, Poe's theory seemed exactly fitted to his needs. It seemed to place no restriction on the expression of his temperament and passions, moral or otherwise. And not only did the basic distinction between Beauty and the non-artistic values of Goodness, Truth and Passion strike him as logically necessary, but it also provided him with a rational defence against the charges of immorality that he now knew would be made against him.

Thus, when he came to write his dedication, Baudelaire both knew that he could not exclude moral issues from his poetry and believed that they need not detract from the poetic or artistic value of his poems. This belief is the total measure of his disagreement with Gautier—clearly not a serious one because of the agreement on the general principle. And Baudelaire's tactful failure to state this belief is the sum total of his insincerity—if one excludes the conventional expressions of modesty. He says neither that moral issues should be treated in poetry, nor that they should be omitted. He states instead that the moral value of the content of poetry is not relevant to its poetic value, thus giving Gautier a double assurance. He assures him firstly that he agrees with the basic principle of the doctrine of Art for Art's Sake; he assures him secondly that his principal aim in writing *Les Fleurs du Mal* was to write the best poetry of which he was capable (which does not of course exclude the possibility that his poetry might subserve a moral end also). For the

[1] *The Poetic Principle; The Works of Poe*, edited by John H. Ingram, London, A. and C. Black, 1901, Vol. IV, p. 205.

rest, he defers to Gautier, with a trace of humour rather than of servility, in appearing content that his treatment of moral questions should be considered a blemish. He is a 'blasphémateur' not only as regards the religion of public morality, but also as regards the doctrine of Gautier, the high priest of art: it is for the sake of this second meaning, which would not escape the older poet, that Baudelaire so curiously anticipates and approves the action of those who will later try and condemn him. And Gautier might well be trusted to understand the unexpressed hope that the poems themselves would justify the disciple's theory and practice in the Master's eyes. The greatest liberty that Baudelaire takes, lies in the omission of *Émaux et Camées* from the list of Gautier's works. Yet even this does not prevent the dedication from being, as one might expect, a model of correctness, and indeed of sincerity.

3. *AU LECTEUR*

Nothing is known of *Au Lecteur* until its publication in June 1855 in the *Revue des Deux Mondes*, where it served as an introduction to the seventeen poems published with it. This fact and the internal evidence provided by the poem itself, makes it likely that it was specially composed to serve as an introduction to the first edition of the work. Considered in that light, it is, in a very real sense, an apology for the work. As Marcel Ruff remarks: 'il ne déclare pas seulement une position morale, mais religieuse'.[1] Even while he affirms that evil can and does attract, the poet makes his attitude towards evil as unambiguous as possible.

[1] *Op. cit.*, p. 101.

Baudelaire knew, however, that even if his good faith were accepted he would still be reproached with having uncovered depths of perversity so exceptional as to be scarcely relevant to normal life. The introductory poem is designed to cover this objection also, in the manner most suited both to Baudelaire's temperament and to his convictions. For the poem, which is an apology to the reader, is also and more obviously an attack upon the reader, a sweeping indictment of the universal 'postulation vers Satan' which unites the 'hypocrite lecteur' in an unwelcome fraternity with the poet and the hero of *Les Fleurs du Mal*.

Since the aim of the introductory poem is universality, not particularity, we cannot expect it to have a very close application to the personal tragedy of the hero of *Les Fleurs du Mal*. The first six stanzas nevertheless anticipate the plan of the work by presenting the life of humanity in terms of a repeated cycle of sin, remorse, repentance, sin, where sin corresponds to the hero's more degraded Ideals and remorse and repentance correspond to a form of Spleen. As with the poet-hero, this repeated cycle leads the sinner ever deeper into sin. In stanzas 1 and 2, the sinner is at the stage of deluding himself with promises of eventual reform. In stanza 3, as his will to virtue weakens, and as he begins to become conscious of the 'postulation vers Satan' as such, his 'esprit enchanté' is still under the impression that sin will offer him unalloyed pleasure, pleasure with no mixture or aftermath of pain. The music of the stanza is softly and voluptuously caressing as the vital operation is painlessly performed. But in stanzas 4 and 5 the sinner is brought face to face with a pleasure that is nakedly disgusting, and he does not recoil, but clings to it. The dissolution of the will has allowed the sado-masochistic complex to develop in the direction of recognized evil, and line 2 of stanza 4 reveals it as the same vice which causes the poet-hero's tragedy in the volume: 'Aux objets répugnants nous trouvons des appas'. It is not merely that the objects are attractive *and* repugnant from another point of view; it is in large measure *because* they are repugnant that they attract. An earlier and more subtle reference to the same curious fact of human nature is obscured by the irony of 'nos aimables remords' in stanza 1. The word 'aimables' must be understood seriously as well as ironically, for, as Baudelaire warns us in section IV of *Le Poëme du Haschish*, '... le remords lui-même, dans ce drame diabolique ... peut agir comme excitant et réchauffer puissamment l'enthousiasme du coeur.' Once the taste for painful pleasure has been aroused there can seemingly be no escape, and, like the poet-hero— 'Chaque jour vers l'Enfer nous descendons d'un pas.'

Stanza 7 anticipates the shocked objection of the 'hypocrite lecteur' and answers it with the help of an idea borrowed from the *Soirées de Saint-Pétersbourg* (3e *Entretien*), or else from La Rochefoucauld's celebrated saying: 'Si nous résistons à nos passions, c'est plus par leur faiblesse que par notre force.' Our apparent lack of resemblance to Baudelaire's portrait of the sinner in general is not necessarily a proof of virtue, but more likely to be a proof of spinelessness, cowardice, lack of energy. The 'hélas!' of the last line of this stanza implies agreement with La Rochefoucauld's dictum that 'Il y a des héros en mal comme en bien' and suggests an actual preference for the great criminal over the petty, surreptitious sinner. It places Baudelaire in the tradition of nineteenth-century writers which includes Stendhal and Leconte de Lisle and leads to Nietzsche. And it brings into the introductory poem itself a trace of heterodoxy which will become still more evident in the volume. For the hero of *Les Fleurs du Mal* differs from the 'hypocrite lecteur', not in his psychology, but simply in the superior energy which drives him to extremes and gives him something at least of the prestige of a fallen angel ('*Satan*,—à la manière de Milton'). In so far as Baudelaire, the creator of this hero, may be thought to prefer him morally, as well as aesthetically, to less adventurous humanity, his moral values conflict with those of the Christianity which has a special tenderness for the lamb or sheep. They are in fact the moral values which conflict with conventional ones in the aesthetic of tragedy, where energy itself is a value, irrespective of the use to which it is put.

Although the oratorical and poetical climax of the poem is still to come, stanza 7 marks the climax in respect of the boldness of the poet's assault on the reader's complacency. For all the poetic excellence of the personification of Ennui, the 'monstre' is the development of an easily recognizable commonplace and provides a more easily acceptable familiar for the 'hypocrite lecteur' than the 'Satan Trismégiste' of the earlier stanzas. This is not to say that the poem ends weakly. A certain moderation in the strength of the final accusation was necessary in order that it, and by implication the preceding ones also, might be thrust right home with the delicate, insinuating irony of the last two lines. And the 'monstre' himself, for all his commonplace origin and associations, gives plenty of food for thought. His name, in fact, is an understatement of the idea which he represents, just as his physical passivity and impassibility are an under-statement of his potential violence and evil. He represents a more negative and more generalized form of Spleen than any which the poet-hero will express, inasmuch as he has no apparent splenetic emotions and appears to be emotionally empty: it is in the vain hope of arousing a flicker of excite-ment or life within himself that he turns to sadistic dreams of 'échafauds'. Whereas the poet-hero's Spleen is that of a man with an unquenchable thirst for the infinite, this Ennui suggests a deficiency of energy, not an excess, and it is there-fore a more appropriate weakness to attribute to humanity at large.

Nevertheless, as a form of Spleen, it holds the dangers of Spleen, and Baudelaire classifies it as a vice. It is not easy to see why it should be a vice in itself but one may suppose that it results from a perverse refusal of normal, healthy interests, and so testifies to a yielding to the 'postulation vers Satan'. It is also suggested that Ennui-Spleen closes the circle of vice, in the sense that it may be both the result of sin—the bored oriental monster is surely a voluptuary—and the cause of more sin. But it is the causal function only that is clearly expressed in these stanzas. It may assist the development of the sado-masochistic complex in which Baudelaire sees the root of all sin, and may lead it to the extremes of gratuitous des-tructiveness envisaged in the images of the last stanza but one:

> Il ferait volontiers de la terre un débris
> Et dans un bâillement avalerait le monde.

Au Lecteur, considered purely as an introduction, fulfils a triple purpose. It defines the moral attitude of the poet towards the tragedy. It prepares that tragedy by indicating in advance something of its structural plan together with the nature of the flaw or vice in the hero which will bring about his downfall. And it does so in a manner that claims for the vice, the hero and the tragedy alike, not the truth of exception but universal truth. This claim, too, has seemed to verge on unreason but discussion of its merits must be reserved for later chapters of this study.

III

THE ASPIRATION

I. THE IDEALS OF GOD AND ART (POEMS I–VI)

THE first group of poems in *Spleen et Idéal* introduces the reader to a poet who is taking stock of the nature of his vocation. First, in the two complementary poems, *Bénédiction* and *L'Albatros*, he considers the problem faced by the poet or artist as a human-being living in society but distinguished by his special talent and function. For the most part Baudelaire is content to give an original and effective treatment to the commonplace Romantic view that poetic genius, like all divine gifts, dooms the recipient to incomprehension and suffering on earth. The splendid hymn that forms the second part of *Bénédiction* derives more from De Maistre than from Romanticism, for it attributes to suffering, considered as a divine punishment and remedy for our sins, a religious merit which is normally attributed to virtue itself.

The principal function of *Bénédiction* within the architecture is to establish the fact of the poet-hero's initial aspiration towards the ideal of God. The tragedy starts at what is actually the peak of the hero's spiritual and moral development. In no other poem will this aspiration express itself so directly and with such fervour. It may even be said that the process of degrading the hero's ideal begins with the very next poem, in so far as the poet there concerns himself, not with the ideal of God, but with the associated ideal of poetry and art. What is more, such is the innocence of the 'Poëte' of *Bénédiction* that despite the persecution of the mother, the wife and the world at large, he is a stranger to Spleen and hence to the 'postulation vers Satan'. That is because he accepts all suffering as a blessing from God and so converts it into fresh ardour for his Ideal.

Thus far it has been assumed that the poet-hero of the volume is the 'Poëte' who is spoken of in *Bénédiction* in the third person. But the 'Poëte', who has both an individual and a generic significance, cannot really be separated from the writer of the poem. That being so, it must be admitted that his temperament is more complex than the description of the 'Poëte' suggests. Analysis of the emotional attitudes expressed by the poem reveals this very clearly. The stanzas which convey the sadistic hatred of the mother and the wife indicate in the writer himself feelings of fascinated repulsion, similar to those in *Au Lecteur*. Only 'le goût de l'horreur', only a relatively well-developed sado-masochistic complex, could satisfactorily explain those elements in the narrative which constitute, in relation to the didactic purpose, an overstatement, and so endanger the balance and poetic value of the poem as a whole. And if the writer's attitude towards what is manifestly unpleasant in his poem reveals this complexity and ambiguity, so also does his attitude—and that of the 'Poëte' as well—towards what is manifestly pleasant—the ideal of God and Paradise envisaged in the hymn which ends the poem. Even this ideal and the joy of the aspiration towards it, contain an admixture of pain. The 'saintes voluptés' are

seen only through the veil of 'la souffrance' and 'la douleur'
which is 'la noblesse unique . . .' In a very real sense the hymn
is an aspiration, not towards God, but towards 'la douleur'
itself, or—to be more exact—towards the *kind* of pleasurable
pain which the 'Poëte' associates with the ideal of God. It is
a highly moral expression of the sado-masochistic complex,
but an expression of it none the less, and, as such, in harmony
with future developments.

Whether Baudelaire himself intended the ending of
Bénédiction to contain quite so much dramatic irony, is of
course far from certain. It is probable that when he wrote the
poem, the irony of the aspiration towards pain and suffering
was masked for him by the fact that it was his own temperament he was expressing, his own incurably tragic view of the
beautiful and the desirable, and his own fervent hope if not his
settled belief. It is possible, however, that when he came to
look at the poem more impersonally, in the process of elaborating the architecture, he saw and welcomed the tragic irony
of the fact that in the initial poem, the poet-hero should express his complete willingness to receive from God the suffering which will be accorded him in greater measure than he
knows, which will lead him to Satan, and which will deprive
him, at least in this world, of any hope of return to the ideal
of God. The optimistic hope of salvation expressed here
may certainly be that of the poet Baudelaire at any moment of
his life. It cannot however be thought to convert the ending
of the poet-hero's *Voyage*—and hence the entire journey—
from a tragic to a happy and successful one. The tragedy
ends, and ends completely, before the poet-hero's death.

Bénédiction was followed in the first edition by *Le Soleil*, which was transferred in the second edition to the *Tableaux parisiens*. As the second poem of *Spleen et Idéal*, *Le Soleil* provided a less impersonally expressed view of the function of a poet, and established an analogy between it and the function of the sun. The tranquil, charitable tone fitted in perfectly with the description of the 'Poëte' given in *Bénédiction*, whilst contrasting effectively with the impassioned 'élévation' of the hymn to God, and with the ecstatic 'élévation' of the mood of the poem which bears that name and is placed third in both editions. Nothing in *Le Soleil* makes it unsuited to its original position and Baudelaire's reason for moving it was probably the need to fill the new and important book of *Tableaux parisiens*, coupled perhaps with the availability of *L'Albatros* and its undoubted merits as a replacement.

L'Albatros echoes the theme of suffering and persecution and is, to that extent, complementary to *Bénédiction*. It also distinguishes, by means of the allegory, between the capabilities of the poet as a poet and his capabilities as a man in ordinary life. He can 'fly' but he cannot 'walk'. From the didactic point of view, the poem is a touching apology for the artistic *inadapté*, a claim that his inadequacy in the affairs of normal, social life is the inevitable price that he must pay for his powers in his own special sphere of activity. The poem is also a proud affirmation of these powers, the 'ailes de géant', and this feature makes it a perfect introduction to the following poem which, though the albatross-image is of course abandoned, depicts the poet as quite literally 'in flight'.

Élévation is the first poem to give clear proof of Baudelaire's extraordinary mastery of the imagery and rhythms of motion, a department of poetry in which most Romantics and post-Romantics excel. The title is the most obvious example to be found in the first three poems of the gift which may be thought to contain the essence of the poet's art—that of conferring upon words the quality of polyvalency, the maximum richness of meaning consistent with the expression of a single but complex mood. Thus 'élévation' has the physical sense illustrated by the imagery of the poem, the emotional and aesthetic sense in which Baudelaire uses it in his prose when he speaks in the *Notes nouvelles sur Edgar Poe* of 'cette extraordinaire élévation . . . qu'Edgar Poe exige de la Muse',[1] and lastly the physical and religious sense in which the word is used to describe the most sacred moment of the ritual of the Mass (for although the poem itself does not develop the analogy between the uplifting of a poet's heart and that of the Host, the association of ideas would be inevitable for a Catholic and perfectly in keeping with the poet-hero's state of mind at this point and the mystical view of poetry and art which he may be presumed to share with Baudelaire).

Whereas *Bénédiction* indicates in emotionally ambiguous terms the Ideal at which the poet-hero aims in the hereafter, *Élévation* presents in terms of pure exhilaration the Ideal which he can, and evidently does attain to, in the here-and-now. Such is the importance of this privileged emotional state in the context of the tragedy, that reference must be made to the passages in Baudelaire's prose-writings which throw more light upon his understanding of it.

The most generalized form in which he envisages it is that described in the *Poëme du Haschish*, the opening chapter of

[1] NHE, p. xxi.

which bears the title of *Le Goût de l'Infini* (the word 'infini' is synonymous for Baudelaire with the word 'idéal'). As presented here, the Ideal is an intense feeling of well-being accompanied by heightened sensory and intellectual perception. It owes its generality to the fact that it is not associated with any specific kind of activity and not necessarily the result or reward of any conscious effort on the part of the subject. To quote Baudelaire:

... ce qu'il y a de plus singulier dans cet état exceptionnel de l'esprit et des sens, que je puis sans exagération appeler paradisiaque, si je le compare aux lourdes ténèbres de l'existence commune et journalière, c'est qu'il n'a été créé par aucune cause visible et facile à définir.[1]

Baudelaire is therefore prepared to consider it, in this its most generalized and purest form, as 'une véritable grâce, comme un miroir magique où l'homme est invité à se voir en beau, c'est-à-dire tel qu'il devrait et pourrait être; une espèce d'excitation angélique, un rappel à l'ordre sous une forme complimenteuse'.[2]

On the primary level of meaning, *Élévation* clearly stands for an experience of just this kind. But the surrounding poems, as well as one meaning of the title, relate the poem to the experience characteristic of poetic activity. Here too, reference to the prose-works is of interest. For example, in the essay on Banville published in 1861, Baudelaire characterizes the spirit of this poet's work by saying that it represents

[1] PA, p. 4. The importance of *Le Poëme du Haschish* for an understanding of *Les Fleurs du Mal* was pointed out by Alison Fairlie in *Some Remarks on Baudelaire's 'Poëme du Haschish'* in *The French Mind, Studies in Honour o Gustave Rudler*, Oxford, Clarendon Press, 1952.

[2] PA, pp. 4–5.

these same 'belles heures de la vie', 'ces sortes d'impressions, si riches que l'âme en est comme illuminée, si vives qu'elle en est comme soulevée'.[1] And he adds, using the same image that is developed in *Élévation*: 'Tout l'être intérieur, dans ces merveilleux instants, s'élance en l'air par trop de légèreté et de dilatation comme pour atteindre une région plus haute.'

Although this characteristic of Banville is identified with 'une manière lyrique de sentir', it is evident that all poetry cannot and does not reflect this privileged mood in its subject-matter. Poems which express the mood of *Élévation* are extremely rare in Baudelaire's work. And it appears from his prose-writings that the art of poetry is connected with this Ideal in a deeper, more intimate way than is offered by the mere expression of such a mood. The relevant texts are those in which Baudelaire paraphrases Poe's description of the Poetic Sentiment—'that pleasurable elevation, or excitement, *of the soul*', as Poe himself calls it. Here is the passage as given in the major article on Gautier:

> Ainsi le principe de la poésie est, strictement et simplement, l'aspiration humaine vers une Beauté supérieure, et la manifestation de ce principe est dans un enthousiasme, un enlèvement de l'âme; enthousiasme tout à fait indépendant de la passion, qui est l'ivresse du coeur, et de la vérité, qui est la pâture de la raison. Car la passion est chose *naturelle*, trop naturelle même pour ne pas introduire un ton blessant, discordant, dans le domaine de la Beauté pure; trop familière et trop violente pour ne pas scandaliser les purs Désirs, les gracieuses Mélancolies et les nobles Désespoirs qui habitent les régions surnaturelles de la Poésie.[2]

This 'enthousiasme' or 'enlèvement de l'âme' is the specifically poetic (or artistic) form of the ideal state of mind or 'infini'

[1] AR, pp. 353–4.   [2] AR, pp. 159–60.

which is portrayed in *Élévation* and repeatedly referred to in
Baudelaire's works in prose. To enjoy it, the poet has no need
to *express* it, to make its characteristic exhilaration the mood
or the subject of his poem. Since it is 'le principe de la poésie',
this enthusiasm must be communicated by all genuine poetic
activity and all genuine poems, however gloomy or unpleasant or horrible the mood expressed may be. It is in fact the
emotional equivalent of the abstract idea of poetic value
which was discussed in the previous chapter. But here we
see that it must be distinguished, not only from moral,
religious and philosophic values, but also from the very mood
or emotion that a given poem expresses—that is, from what
Baudelaire refers to as 'passion' in the quotation given above.
It is not the expressed passion or mood of a poem, but it
manifests itself as that passion or mood subtly transformed
into the more serene and specifically artistic pleasure which
Baudelaire denotes by the expressions *'purs* Désirs, ...
gracieuses Mélancolies . . . *nobles* Désespoirs'. Considered in
themselves, the moods and passions which we find in his
poems are very seldom pure, gracious or even noble. Yet
they may be felt as such when his poems are appreciated as
poetry. As he himself remarked in the essay on Gautier:
'C'est un des privilèges prodigieux de l'Art que l'horrible,
artistement exprimé, devienne beauté, et que la *douleur*,
rhythmée et cadencée, remplisse l'esprit d'une *joie* calme'.[1]
He believes the transformation to be analogous to that
which takes place in the feelings of the hashish-taker in
the state of *Kief*, as may be seen from the following passage:

[1] AR, p. 172.

Ce n'est plus quelque chose de tourbillonnant et de tumultueux; c'est une béatitude calme et immobile, une résignation glorieuse . . . La douleur et l'idée du temps ont disparu, ou si quelquefois elles osent se produire, ce n'est que *transfigurées par la sensation dominante*, et elles sont alors relativement à leur forme habituelle *ce que la mélancolie poétique est à la douleur positive*.[1]

It is analogous also to the transformation which occurs in the sister art of the sculptor as the following passage from the *Salon de* 1859 testifies:

De même que la poésie lyrique ennoblit tout, même la passion (hence the 'purs Désirs . . . gracieuses Mélancolies . . . nobles Désespoirs' of the article on Gautier), la sculpture, la vraie, solennise tout, même le mouvement; elle donne à tout ce qui est humain quelque chose d'éternel et qui participe de la dureté de la matière employée. La colère devient calme, la tendresse sévère, le rêve ondoyant et brillanté de la peinture se transforme en méditation solide et obstinée.[2]

Like the generalized form of the experience, the state of mind which represents the specifically poetic and artistic ideal is a temporary realization of what man 'devrait et pourrait être'.[3] It is also a foretaste and a promise of 'les splendeurs situées derrière le tombeau'.[4] It therefore enables the poet and artist to see man and his environment in terms of perfected creatures and a perfected environment. To quote Baudelaire himself in the essay on Gautier: 'C'est cet admirable, cet immortel instinct du Beau qui nous fait considérer la Terre et ses spectacles comme un aperçu, comme une *correspondance du Ciel*'.[4] This means that the Ideal, which is essentially an emotional state and an emotional experience, presents itself

[1] PA, p. 41.
[2] CE, pp. 349-50.
[3] PA, pp. 4-5.
[4] AR, pp. 159-60.

also as a cognitive experience. The objects of normal sense-perception are transformed by an intuitive certainty that they represent some hidden and higher reality of which they are the symbol. It is cognitive experience of this nature which is indicated by the last two lines of *Élévation* where those who have attained to the heights of the Ideal are said to have an effortless understanding of 'Le langage des fleurs et des choses muettes!' In this way *Élévation* introduces the next poem *Correspondances* and another controversial section of the poetic theory common to Baudelaire and his poet-hero.

The difficulty does not lie so much in the poem *Correspondances* as in the prose-writings of Baudelaire which are used to elaborate on its meaning. These supporting texts have been thought to point to two substantially different theories, one of which cannot be fully reconciled with Baudelaire's poetic practice.

The two theories may be understood both in terms of Georges Blin's distinction between the so-called 'analogie verticale' and 'analogie horizontale', and in terms of L. J. Austin's distinction between 'la Symbolique' and 'le Symbolisme'. 'La Symbolique', or supernatural symbolism, aims at discovering 'vertical analogies', by which are meant relations between the natural world and a supernatural world. For example, bread, according to Swedenborg, is the earthly symbol of the food of the angels—spiritual good. 'Le Symbolisme', or natural symbolism, is concerned only with 'horizontal analogies', relations between such natural things as the flight of an albatross, and the activity and accompanying *état d'âme* of a poet. Baudelaire's poems have seemed to critics to contain little more than natural symbolism. Some of his prose-writings, on the other hand, seem to claim for all poetry the mystical value of a 'Symbolique'. Thus Jean Prévost has been led to emphasize the aesthetic aspect of the doctrine at the expense of the mystical.[1] Marcel Ruff, who dissociates Baudelaire as far as possible from purely aesthetic aims and doctrines, prefers to emphasize the mystical aspect of the theory and the poem.[2] L. J. Austin agrees in some measure with Prévost, but thinks that Baudelaire may have started with a supernatural symbolism (a poetic based on the belief that nature is a symbol of divine reality), and, finding that reality was satanic, not divine, eventually turned in disappointment to natural symbolism.[3] The theory certainly allows, as Prévost's does not, for the fact that Baudelaire does relate the theory of *correspondances* to the supernatural. And in its insistence on the value of Baudelaire's natural symbolism, it is a most welcome reaction both against more or less veiled implications that Baudelaire was a mystic, and against the tendency—evident in Guy Michaud's *Message poétique du Symbolisme*—to criticize him and his poetry because he was not. Unfortunately Baudelaire's prose-writings give little support for the chronological basis of the theory. Amongst those which are most 'supernaturalist' in character are works published as late as the chapters on the imagination in the *Salon de* 1859, the introduction to *Richard Wagner et Tann-häuser* of 1861, and the passage on 'l'universelle analogie' in the essay on Victor Hugo. L. J. Austin admits that here 'Baudelaire ... retombe dans la théorie de la symbolique

---

[1] *Baudelaire*, essai sur l'inspiration et la création poétiques. Paris, Mercure de France, 1953, pp. 74–75.
[2] *Op. cit.*, pp. 103–4. [3] *Op. cit.*, pp. 53–55.

traditionnelle', but is obliged to conclude that he does so 'sans s'en rendre compte' and that in doing so '(il) dépasse sa propre pensée'.[1] Examination of the chronology of the poems is no more helpful and one is reminded that the order in which they appear in the volume invites a very dangerous confusion between the biography of Baudelaire and the spiritual itinerary of his hero. Nor is it clear why a reader of Swedenborg should not be fully prepared, from the start, to find that the world is as much a reflection of Hell as it is of Heaven: Baudelaire's apparent predilection for the infernal variety of supernatural symbolism is more likely to result from a combination of temperament and artistic choice than from the replacement of a youthful optimism by a mature pessimism. Nevertheless the major objection to this approach, as far as Baudelaire himself is concerned, lies in the possibility that the distinction between a 'symbolique' and a 'symbolisme' was simply not a valid one at all in his eyes, and that this is by no means an unreasonable point of view. To what extent Baudelaire himself may actually have believed in the supernatural regions of which he speaks, is not of course a matter on which anyone but Baudelaire can pronounce with much authority. We can say only whether in his writings he does or does not relate them to poetic analogy.

The idea of supernatural symbolism lends itself to an unfortunate ambiguity, in that it may presumably be found either in the work of a mystic or in that of a non-mystic—nor is the ambiguity lessened by the difficulty of distinguishing between the two. The fact that it is found in the work of Swedenborg proves nothing as to his mystic powers. It may

[1] *Ibid.*, p. 165.

be doubted whether there is any feature of his supernatural symbolism—or of his accounts of his adventures—which could not have been invented by a poet who consciously sought for new 'correspondances' between his knowledge of the natural world and his knowledge of exisiting religious cosmology and religious symbolism. If that is so, the distinction between supernatural symbolism and natural symbolism is reduced to a difference in the nature of the subject-matter treated: it does not necessarily involve a distinction between mystical and non-mystical modes of knowledge. But even this distinction between types of subject-matter is difficult to uphold. Belief in the supernatural necessarily involves belief in a fusion of the supernatural with the natural, with the result that the *clear* distinction between the two is ultimately reduced to the idea of a geographical Heaven, and possibly a Hell, as opposed to the visible universe. When Swedenborg says that bread is the symbol of the food of angels, he is in the realm of supernatural symbolism. But what of the poet who gives symbolic expression to the idea that bread is to the body what the love of good is to the soul? To the agnostic, this may be natural symbolism. To a Christian who believes that the soul comes from God, and that through goodness and the bread that is the body of Christ, it may return to God, the symbolism may be as much supernatural as natural. In the view of Swedenborg himself, the spirit-world and the natural world are not even separate: 'Man is so created as to be at the same time, in the spiritual world and in the natural. The spiritual world is the abode of angels, and the natural of man.'[1]

---

[1] *Compendium of Swedenborg's Theological Writings*, London, The Swedenborg Society, 1939, p. 23.

In his *Divine Love and Wisdom* he records a fascinating conversation between the shades of Sir Hans Sloane and Martin Folkes, two Presidents of the Royal Society, in which it is established beyond all doubt that the species originated in the spirit-world, where affections or lusts still take on visible form as animals, birds or plants. These need only to be filled with matter to become identical with the creatures visible to us in the natural world, and their natural counterparts still correspond to the original spiritual affections and lusts.[1] To compare a woman to a gentle dove or a man to a rapacious eagle, is to comment on the spirit-world as well as on this one, and the very idea of *correspondances* implies that it is impossible to do otherwise. But it was not necessary for Baudelaire to follow Swedenborg so far beyond the bounds of ordinary Christian belief, in order to find a view of the natural which confuses it with the supernatural, and so denies a distinction which, from other points of view, is obviously valid and necessary.

Baudelaire did not claim that the 'instinct du Beau' or poetic state of which he speaks in the article on Gautier, gave him direct mystical knowledge of another world in the sense that he could describe it, as Swedenborg has done. In this respect, the cognitive experience stopped short at the intuitive certainty that 'la Terre et ses spectacles' *was* 'une correspondance du Ciel'—the very fact that it was based on an ecstatic 'enthousiasme', quite distinct from 'passion', overrode but did

---

[1] *Angelic Wisdom*, London, The Swedenborg Society, 1931, pp. 133–134. Baudelaire himself wrote to Toussenel in 1856: 'Votre livre réveille en moi bien des idées dormantes,—et à propos de *péché originel*, et de *forme moulée sur l'idée*, j'ai pensé bien souvent que les bêtes malfaisantes et dégoûtantes n'étaient peut-être que la vivification, corporification, éclosion à la vie matérielle, des *mauvaises pensées* de l'homme. Aussi la *nature* entière participe du péché originel.' (CORR, I, p. 370.)

regard, sa tristesse, sa douceur, sa joie éclatante, sa haine répulsive, son enchantement ou son horreur; enfin, en d'autres termes, tout ce qu'il y a d'humain dans n'importe quoi et aussi tout ce qu'il y a de divin, de sacré ou de diabolique.[1]

This is the 'langage des fleurs et des choses muettes' of which Baudelaire speaks in the last line of *Élévation*. It is not a matter of knowing what the celestial (or infernal) equivalent of a flower may be or look like. It is a matter of seeing the analogy between the appearance or situation of that flower and some aspect of the human condition, which is in turn related to the supernatural as 'naturally' as joy may be related to God and suffering to Satan. That Baudelaire takes for granted the relation between the human and the supernatural (which includes the diabolic as well as the divine) is fairly evident in the last sentence of the quotation.

A question arises here as to whether the finding of such analogies is creation or discovery. Baudelaire's answer, given in the essay on Victor Hugo and the chapters on the *Reine des facultés* in the *Salon de* 1859, appears to be that it is both. From the human point of view it is creation: from the divine point of view it is discovery. It is creation in the sense that each individual poet is a new being whose task it is to 'illuminer les choses avec (son) esprit'[2] and establish relations or analogies between them and his own moral and spiritual life which will produce 'la sensation du neuf'.[3] To use another of Baudelaire's images, he will arrange words selected from the dictionary of Nature, just as he does those selected from the dictionary of language, to form new lines of poetry. But from the divine point of view, this is discovery—discovery of the

[1] AR, p. 304.   [2] CE, p. 284.   [3] AR, p. 305.

possibilities inherent in the dictionary when God created it, presumably with all possibilities in mind. To be sure, all possibilities are not equally good; there is poetic error just as there is moral error and neither corresponds to the divine intention. But thanks to the analogy between the imagination of the Creator and the imagination of the poet, it can be said that 'Chez les excellents poëtes, il n'y a pas de métaphore, de comparaison ou d'épithète qui ne soit d'une adaptation mathématiquement exacte dans la circonstance actuelle, parce que ces comparaisons, ces métaphores et ces épithètes sont puisées dans l'inépuisable fonds de l'*universelle analogie*'.[1]

Baudelaire's view of the poet's function therefore seems to demand no more than that the poet should concern himself with natural symbolism, the relations between man and the things of the visible universe. But if his language is any guide to his beliefs, Baudelaire sees man and the visible universe as meeting-points for the conflicting supernatural forces of God and Satan, Heaven and Hell. He appears to believe that whether or not a poet is aware of it, his work will symbolize supernatural reality also, and, to that extent, will have the value of a 'symbolique'. In the case of *Les Fleurs du Mal*, the poet is well aware of it, and as L. J. Austin remarks, his work abounds in symbols of the infernal if not of the divine.[2] Unless one refuses to accept the infernal aspect of the supernatural as a subject for art, which is not a very reasonable attitude, it is hard to see how Baudelaire could have done more to implement his theory. Had he been the mystic that he never claimed to be, and that nothing in his theory required him to be, he might, unlike Swedenborg, have preferred silence.

[1] AR, p. 305.   [2] *Op. cit.*, p. 92.

One final feature of the theory remains to be explained. As Baudelaire's prose-writings and poems both go to show, the supernatural reality which the poet discovers in man or the visible universe is as likely to be diabolic as it is to be divine. God's 'dictionary', which is Creation, has indeed been wrongly used, but since errors have been committed, errors have become part of the truth. The error of evil may therefore quite legitimately figure in the subject-matter of poetry. But if poetry can depict 'la Terre et ses spectacles' in their satanic aspect, how can Baudelaire write of 'cet immortel instinct du Beau qui nous fait considérer la Terre et ses spectacles comme un aperçu, comme une *correspondance* du Ciel'? The answer must of course be sought in the power of poetry and art to transform its materials. Evil itself can be so transformed, and as Baudelaire says in his *Projets de Préface* his aim was precisely to 'extraire la beauté du Mal' (the ambiguity of the word 'beauté' will be explained in Chapter IV). This proves again how essential to his theory was the distinction between Beauty (the value of poetry) and all non-poetic values which might be found in, or demanded from, the subject-matter of poems. The only possible exception to the rule is the value of mystical truth which attaches to the revelation of the spiritual in the material and of the supernatural in both, thanks to an unerring choice from the 'universelle analogie'. But as the relevant passage from the essay on Hugo serves to show, this power is so completely identified, in Baudelaire's view, with the mere power of metaphorical expression, the essential poetic gift of conferring polyvalency on words, that no confusion can possibly result. Good poetry, whatever its avowed subject, means true mystical insight; bad poetry means false final tercet is to 'expand' the suggestions of the part to the proportions of the whole, and to point at the same time, not merely to the ecstasy of the lover of perfumes, but also to that of the poet-mystic who is so familiar with 'l'universelle analogie' that his fingers, inspired by the scent, can 'courir *avec agilité* sur l'immense clavier des *correspondances*'.[1]

The first quatrain is remarkable for the poetic use that has been made of ideas which, in themselves, are banal. The verse, sober, strong and controlled in tone, invests the visible world with a solemn, grandiose mystery, thanks to the fusion of three images—Nature itself, a temple with its pillars, which in turn suggest the trees of the 'forêts de symboles'. The temple is not the puny one made for God by man, but the one made for man's habitation by God himself. The supernatural is not however directly referred to; it is simply 'present' in the natural, in the temple which is Nature, in the strange 'paroles' and 'regards' (vertical and horizontal analogies alike) of decorated pillars, trees, and every object in the visible universe.

The second quatrain deepens the sense of supernatural mystery, still without leaving the realm of the natural. The temple, pillars, trees, words and looks of the first stanza, did, for all their strangeness, recall the sights and sounds of life. Here they disappear—or are resolved into the elementary sensations which are the immediate form in which we apprehend the natural world. Here there is nothing solid, nothing formed; the universe is an infinity of perfumes, colours and sounds. This already is a reduction of multiplicity and a step towards the perception of 'une ténébreuse et vaste unité', which, 'vaste comme la nuit et comme la clarté', embraces

[1] CE, p. 222.

both the visible universe and the unfathomable mystery which surrounds and penetrates it. But what fully establishes the unity of the whole, which is nothing less than the cosmos, is the underlying unity of these seemingly disparate sensations, the unity of their 'echoes' in the human sensibility.

The phenomenon referred to here is certainly that which is now called synaesthesia. There is, however, no reason to suppose that Baudelaire made any clear distinction between synaesthesia and *correspondances* in general. His writings indicate that the analogies between sensations were placed by him on exactly the same level as all other analogies that went to form 'l'analogie universelle'. His policy had much to recommend it as far as poetic theory is concerned, for in this respect the notion of synaesthesia has come to enjoy a not altogether deserved prestige in the eyes of poets and critics. Some consideration of this development is indeed necessary if the references to synaesthesia in *Correspondances* are to be seen in something like their true historical perspective.

The artistic importance of the fact of synaesthesia is so immense that we can scarcely begin to understand it. The value of everything in the arts that inclines towards the abstract, seems to involve and depend upon its working at subconscious or semiconscious levels—not, to be sure, in quite such spectacular and possibly unusual forms as that of the coloured audition which preoccupied the Symbolists. It is granted to few to see notes of music as red or black and to fewer still to smell them, but well-nigh all can see them, or feel them, as high or low, moving up and down, carrying greater or less weight with a better or worse sense of balance. Without the aid of such normal forms of synaesthesia music would presumably be meaningless sound and the music of poetry would likewise lose its value. But synaesthesia proper must not be confused with the record of synaesthetic experience found in language and literature. Prior to quoting Paul Souriau's statement that the painter wishes to render 'le toucher soyeux de cette étoffe, le velouté de ce fruit et jusqu'à sa saveur fondante ...', S. Johansen remarks: 'il parle de la peinture, mais ses paroles s'appliquent aussi bien à la poésie'.[1] This assumption, which is nowhere qualified, may be the source of a strange confusion. The literary and linguistic synaesthesia that we find in the subject-matter and language of poetry, is not, like the colours of the painter or the auditive music of poetry, a means whereby actual experiences of synaesthesia are induced in those who appreciate the work. Nor does it necessarily imply synaesthetic experience in the poet, who may simply be imagining such kinds of experience or using and elaborating on the habits of thought and speech to which normal synaesthesia has given rise since the earliest times. It is not impossible that some of the prestige enjoyed by the notion amongst poets and critics alike, is due to a confusion of reality with the idea of reality, which is all that is given by the meaning of words and all that need pre-exist them in the mind of the poet.

The principal factor in that prestige remains the ambiguity of the term, an ambiguity recognized by Victor Ségalen as early as April 1902 in the article entitled *Les Synesthésies et L'Ecole symboliste*, published by *Le Mercure de France*. In its primary sense (and only proper sense?) the word refers to the case that arises when a sensation which can be ascribed to a

---

[1] *Op. cit.*, p. 30.

normal external cause, is itself the sole apparent cause of a
sensation of a different order. Whatever physiological ex-
planations of the occurrence may be advanced, it will, if it is
not sufficiently normal to be taken for granted, seem inex-
plicable, in so far as no conscious *mental* process of association has linked the first sensation to the second. But Ségalen
points to a wider meaning of the word: '... la sensation-
Echo peut simplement être *pensée*, n'exister qu'à l'état
d'Idéation, et sa relation avec la Primaire est faite d'*analogie*,
plutôt que de réelle évocation.' Here, a mental process of
association is involved and the secondary sensation is weakened to the idea of a sensation. Distinctions in such matters
can never be clear-cut: there must inevitably be a considerable
overlap between the two types of experience. But some danger
may lie in making no distinction at all.

As it is, the broader meaning attached to the word 'synaesthesia' has allowed it to cover the association of different
kinds of sensation and their appropriate objects in the infinity
of cases where there is a good and obvious reason why they
should be associated, as when the sound of the wind evokes
the idea or visual image of a mournful ghost. When one
considers how easy it is to reduce any experience at all to its
basic sensations, one can appreciate the size of the field which
is opened up for the study of 'synaesthesia'. The word even
covers the tendency, no less evident in the novel than in
poetry, to mention several different sensations in order to
describe an experience as completely as possible, as Baudelaire
does in the 'vers synesthésique' of *Harmonie du Soir* quoted
by S. Johansen:[1] 'Les sons et les parfums tournent dans l'air

[1] *Ibid.*, p. 28.

du soir' (it is not clear whether the use of the verb 'tournent' is regarded as an additional element of synaesthesia or not). Thus, what is called synaesthesia and identified almost exclusively with a late nineteenth-century movement in poetry, has come to occupy a vast amount of territory which has been familiar ground to poets of all ages. This would not matter if synaesthesia had not been treated as a new development in poetic technique and so allowed to obscure the function of traditional technique in the work of the innovators. There is nothing technically new about a line such as: 'Les sons et les parfums tournent dans l'air du soir'. The verb 'tournent' is just a particularly felicitous way, in this particular context, of rendering the commonplace analogy between sounds and perfumes (not to mention a feeling of mental vertigo) and visible things that move (and in this instance 'waltz') through space. It also brings out the possibly relevant fact that synaesthesia can be translated into poetry only by ceasing to be synaesthesia and becoming analogy. The poet does not and cannot present us with the primary sensation only, and leave it to suggest the secondary one by synaesthesia: he gives us both at once (the kinaesthetic 'turning' as well as the sound and perfume). All we are left to do is to find and appreciate the suggested link between them, which is exactly what we do with the terms of any analogy and, indeed, with any pair of juxtaposed words. The basis of that link may be a form of synaesthesia so commonplace and so rooted in habits of thought and language as to be instinctively recognized. But in poetry it should be strengthened by an association of ideas with a definite emotive colouring, for, as Mallarmé said, '. . . si, véritablement, les pierres précieuses of proving the permanent or temporary irrationality of the person concerned). We cannot but believe that in the good poem the thread of poetic reason will always be present. It is not always easy to discover, but fortunately the words of poets prove to be less mute under persistent interrogation than do the sensations of the hallucinated. One can only hope they tell the truth.

It is in any case unlikely that Baudelaire regarded synaesthesia in the same light as his modern critics. He may not have given us just cause to use the second quatrain and tercets of *Correspondances* as a basis for a distinction between synaesthesia and *correspondances*, and to follow up by rebuking him for a change of subject of which he was no doubt quite unaware. The *correspondances* which exist between sensations are not mentioned in order to provide a sub-heading for the exposition of the doctrine. Inasmuch as the visible universe presents itself in and through sensations, their fundamental unity is the most striking proof that 'Dieu a proféré le monde comme une complexe et indivisible totalité'.[1] There is no change of subject between the first quatrain and the second, merely a change from an objective view which admits a degree of multiplicity, to a subjective view which reduces Nature to an almost perfect unity.

In the tercets the poet begins his explanatory excursion into the web of relations which connects both sensations and the objects of sensation. He does not however remain upon the level of sensation, and the fact is further proof of the unity he is demonstrating. The 'parfums frais comme des chairs d'enfants' present an analogy based on numerous relations. In this

[1] AR, p. 206.

position, with its possible meaning of 'cool', the word 'frais' reminds us that Baudelaire definitely wants to evoke the idea of synaesthesia for the purpose of his demonstration, for the sake of the strangeness of the phenomenon, and also to classify himself, the poet, as a hypersensitive subject. But he does no more than evoke, in passing, the idea that someone might smell perfume and feel cool. The line of poetry itself does not represent such an experience, it merely hints at one in the course of presenting an ordinary analogy based on an association of ideas. The hint depends on the position of 'frais', but the boldness is tempered by at least three factors. In the first place, 'frais' could denote the cool sensation produced by scent in contact with the skin; secondly 'frais' can and does also have the more banal sense of 'fresh' as opposed to 'stale' (as in Victor Hugo's *Booz endormi*); thirdly 'frais' can and should appear also as a transferred epithet belonging to 'chairs d'enfants' and largely explained by this expression from which 'parfums' and 'frais' together force the maximum of meaning. Within this meaning may be found other relations between the two terms of the analogy. The simile yields not only the physical sensations of coolness and the fresh sweet smell of the skin of some infants, but also vague ideas of youth, health, a mild pleasantness or 'douceur', and finally an impression of innocence, although this is not fully brought out until one reaches the contrasted perfumes and the word 'corrompus'. In addition to sensations properly so called the analogy involves what Baudelaire calls in his essay on Hugo 'sensations morales'.[1] The importance of these impressions in poetry cannot be exaggerated. They provide the

[1]AR, p. 304.

indispensable link, which is generally suggested rather than expressed, not only between the sensations involved in analogies, but also between them and the *état d'âme*. As is so often the case with Baudelaire, the 'sensations morales' in these tercets are moral in more than one sense and actually have an ethical colouring.

The 'sensations morales' attached to the first image in the tercets, are strengthened by the two following similes in which this class of perfumes is compared to the auditive mildness and sweetness of oboes, and the visual mildness and freshness of green fields. The position of 'verts', in particular, shows once again how the delicate hint at the possibility of a most extraordinary kind of synaesthesia is conveyed by a transfer of the epithet which the reader can almost instinctively restore to the 'prairies'. But in this case, the painstaking reader may also be forced to seek in colour-symbolism a direct relation between the 'mood' of the colour green and that appropriate to the perfumes. This is not synaesthesia but an effort to rationalize or poeticize a juxtaposition of words which would suggest an abnormal case of synaesthesia more strongly if the following simile were not there ('verts comme des prairies') to indicate a normal association of ideas, and perhaps even of scents.

The perfumes of the second group are related directly to the 'sensations morales' by the epithets 'corrompus, riches et triomphants'. Why 'corrompus'? Baudelaire may well be conscious of the fact that ambergris and musk are more or less corrupt secretions of the glands of the whale and musk-deer. Possibly they are not 'pure', like the other scents mentioned, because their stimulation is based on their power to irritate

rather than to soothe, and in strong concentrations they are
of course thoroughly unpleasant. But above all, perhaps,
Baudelaire is conscious of the fact that these perfumes which
have such strong biblical, religious and spiritual associations,
are also powerful stimulants of the animal system in man.
These appear to be the artificial scents as opposed to the
natural scents. They are the perfumes which 'correspond' to
the nature of the 'type idéal du Dandy',[1] and the three epithets together, coupled with the idea of perfume, anticipate
the extremely complicated 'sensations morales' which will be
evoked by the figure of the female Dandy who is the black
Venus.

The first line of the second tercet, strengthened by the
enjambement, provides another example of Baudelaire's power
to work with words on several levels of meaning at once. In
this case it is the nondescript, abstract word '*expansion*' which
is transfigured. The scents 'expand' in the same sense as the
'grain d'encens' in *Un Fantôme* (Poem XXXVIII), 'qui rem-
plit une église.' This expansion, a kinaesthetic sensation, is
compared to the apparent expansion—a purely visual phenomenon—of such 'choses infinies' as the sea, of which 'six ou
sept lieues représentent pour l'homme le rayon de l'infini'.[2]
At the same time, these scents produce an effect of 'expansion'
within the sensibility and mind of a human-being that is
analogous to that produced by contemplation of such things
as the sea. That is to say, through normal kinds of synaesthesia and association, they activate other senses and stimulate
the imagination, mind and emotions as well, in the manner
already illustrated *à propos* of the other scents, but much more

[1] JOP, II, p. 64.   [2] JOP, II, p. 108.

strongly. Like the sea itself, they present an 'invitation au voyage', for as Baudelaire tells the reader of *Un Hémisphère dans une Chevelure*, '(son) âme voyage sur le parfum comme l'âme des autres hommes sur la musique'.[1] But the identification of 'choses infinies' with the sea, has been made only as a convenient way of illustrating the richness of the ideas that have been condensed into the image, by linking it with a train of thought that Baudelaire himself has developed elsewhere. The expression 'choses infinies' includes the sky and the cosmic infinite of Pascal, envisaged here with a less fearful, more enraptured form of his vertigo. In the final line the verb 'chantent' is a curious example of the manner in which the *theme* of synaesthesia can be evoked by a single word and so give added interest to a metaphor which, as always, is more than justified by normal associations, for it is natural that these 'triumphant' scents should be personified, and song is the obvious, but none the less effective choice for their mode of expression. The primary sense of *'transports'* hints in passing at the theme of the imaginary journey, while its secondary meaning presents the idea of the emotional Ideal and the poetic state, to dominate the unity of the three main faculties of man ('les transports de l'esprit et des sens').

The significance of the poem within the architecture of *Spleen et Idéal* is substantially the same as its significance within the poetic theory of Baudelaire. Having represented in *Élévation* the ecstasy which is the emotional Ideal, particularly when it appears as the principle of poetry or the poetic state, the poet-hero goes on to clarify his attitude towards Nature (as distinct from humanity) considered as a source of the

[1] PPP, p. 51.

experiences which he seeks both as a man and as a poet. He
expresses a conception of Nature which, through its insistence
on unity and its suggestions of the supernatural, is quite in
keeping with the spirit of *Bénédiction*. And this view can obviously serve as the basis for a poetic theory though it is not
presented as such.

One point only may conflict with the knowledge already
gained of the poet. It is the insistence on, and even the seeming
preference for the class of perfumes that he himself describes
as 'corrompus'. The force of the word is not altogether balanced by the devotional associations of the scents themselves.
In the absence of knowledge of the sequel, it will appear no
more than strange. But considered as a preliminary suggestion
of what is to come, it is illuminated in a remarkable fashion
by the following quotation from *Le Poëme du Haschish*:

> Hélas! les vices de l'homme, si pleins d'horreur qu'on les suppose,
> contiennent la preuve (quand ce ne serait que leur infinie expan-
> sion!) de son goût de l'infini; seulement, c'est un goût qui se
> trompe souvent de route.[1]

Amongst the 'choses infinies' of *Correspondances*, with their
infinite expansion, is vice. It has not yet been clearly detected
by the poet-hero. But in his pursuit of the infinite represented
by 'les transports de l'esprit et des sens', he will take the wrong
road and will find it.

In Poem V, we pass from Nature considered as a source of
emotional and poetic inspiration, to humanity considered in
the same light. This is a curious poem and probably an early
one, but it fits perfectly well into the architecture. The first
fourteen lines present an ideal of humanity which is identified

[1] PA, p. 6.

with Classical times and which is characterized by energy, health, happiness and a moral innocence that goes hand in hand with a certain sensuality. As a whole, this part of the poem strengthens the impression that we receive of a poet whose Ideal is pure and healthy in all respects. By contrast, the next fourteen lines represent the Spleen inspired in the poet by modern life, a similar Spleen to that mentioned in stanzas 3 and 4 of *Élévation*, and the first part of *Bénédiction*. It is not a Spleen for which the poet-hero himself is in any way responsible. Then in lines 29 to 32, comes what is the most important part of the poem in view of the following tragedy:

> Nous avons, il est vrai, nations corrompues,
> Aux peuples anciens des beautés inconnues,
> Des visages rongés par les chancres du coeur,
> Et comme qui dirait des beautés de langueur.

These lines detect and admit a kind of beauty or attraction in what the poet has just condemned as ugly and repulsive. It is not the attraction of pity, although it might conceivably pass as such if it were considered only in the context of this poem. Although another ideal of human beauty has been preferred to this one in the poem, it is a foretaste of what the poet-hero's ideal will soon become. As in the case of the 'parfums corrompus' of *Correspondances*, we have a suggestion of the poet-hero's sado-masochistic complex, his tendency to be pleasurably stimulated by what he recognizes as basically unpleasant —and stimulated for that reason.

The lines have a bearing also on the formation of Baudelaire's own theory of a relative and specifically modern beauty. The question is relevant to the poems on Beauty and will be touched on there.

Les Phares concludes the first group of poems. Having considered a number of general problems connected with his vocation, the poet pays tribute to a group of painters and sculptors who are eternal examples to all artists. The last three stanzas justify the title, reaffirm the beliefs set forth in *Bénédiction*, and deduce from them the duties of the artist on earth. The artist's task is firstly to speak to and for his fellow-men by expressing their '*Te Deum*', their ecstasies, but above all, it would seem, their suffering, not excluding their blasphemies. This expression will serve as a 'divin opium' for mankind, not a means of forgetting, but a means of conquering pain. At the same time, the artist speaks for mankind to God, bearing witness to the fullness of the suffering which was accepted in *Bénédiction* as 'la noblesse unique'. And once again Baudelaire's mastery of the kinaesthetic image and its appropriate rhythms is admirably illustrated by—

> . . . cet ardent sanglot qui roûle d'âge en âge
> Et vient mourir au bord de votre éternité!

Neither of the two views of the artist's function which are expressed here, are developed at any length in Baudelaire's critical writings, but his critical writings certainly do not contradict them. The deeply tragic nature of these views accords with his tragic aesthetic and as far as the architecture of the volume is concerned they bring out once more the exemplary nature of the Ideal which is before him at the outset of his career—whilst hinting at future 'malédictions' and 'blasphèmes'.

2. THE HEART OF A POET (POEMS VII–XVI)

Poems VII to XI form the second group of poems. Whereas hitherto the poet has spoken with a degree of impersonality, he now considers his personal problems as a poet and so introduces the reader to himself.

After the splendour of *Les Phares*, recalling, as it does, some of the greatest of artists, there is a certain humility and pathos about the poet's first address to his *Muse malade* (Poem VII). This poor poet cannot even control his own inspiration.

Within the poem itself, there is a contrast which recalls Poem V, '*J'aime le souvenir . . .*' On the one hand there is the desire for a healthy poetic inspiration, at once Classical and Christian. On the other hand, the beauty of the Muse herself is, as depicted here, an unhealthy modern beauty, that which was described in the earlier poem as 'des beautés de langueurs'. This sonnet is important as the first indication of a source of Spleen within the poet himself, the first sign of a fatality which prevents him from realizing in his poetry, and presumably his inner life also, the pure Ideals towards which he aspires. He is drawn, it seems, to the unhealthy, the morbid, the painful, and must seek his pleasure and his inspiration there.

In *La Muse vénale* (Poem VIII), Spleen is again present, but related to external circumstances, poverty and the financial necessity to prostitute genius. It does not seem necessary to interpret the line: 'Chanter des *Te Deum* auxquels tu ne crois guère' as L. J. Austin does when he writes: 'Non, Baudelaire ne croit plus guère aux *Te Deum*; et son expérience de l'art, de la beauté et de l'amour ne fera que confirmer son pessimisme grandissant'.[1] Even when one considers the poem without reference to the architecture, the '*Te Deum*' appear to be no more than a secular use of a religious image and certainly do not suggest a loss of faith—which appears remarkably sudden if the architecture is consulted. It is true that *La Muse malade* introduces a new series of poems distinct from *Les Phares*, but in *La Muse malade* itself the poet expresses the seemingly sincere wish: 'que ton sang chrétien coulât à flots rhythmiques'. Is the wish the first sign of a loss of religious faith? If so, a very important development—for which not the slightest reason is given—has been effectively hidden in two sonnets which appear to be concerned purely with poetic inspiration and public taste. The falling away from the ideal of God, which does not imply a loss of religious *faith*, is better considered as a gradual and indeed unconscious process.

In the three remaining poems of the group, *Le Mauvais Moine*, *L'Ennemi* and *Le Guignon*, it is again the feeling of artistic impotence which is to the fore and it is closely connected with suggestions of some deep and mysterious grief and unrest. The character of the hero is beginning to resemble the curious ideal of male beauty that Baudelaire defines in *Fusées*:

... cette tête contiendra aussi quelque chose d'ardent et de triste,—des besoins spirituels, des ambitions ténébreusement refoulées,—l'idée d'une puissance grondante et sans emploi ... quelquefois aussi,—et c'est l'un des caractères de beauté les plus intéressants,—le mystère, et enfin ... le *malheur*.[2]

As a whole, this group of poems presents the reader with the elements of a conflict. The career and personal happiness

[1] *Op. cit.*, p. 101. [2] JOP, II, p. 64.

of a highly idealistic poet are jeopardized by a Spleen dependent not only on his material environment but also on certain obscure features of his own temperament. Prominent amongst these is a tendency to dwell on his own impotence and misfortune, a tendency to be attracted towards what is sombre, unhealthy and painful in his own situation and that of others. It is the first sign of the 'postulation vers Satan' making itself felt at a time when the poet wants no more than to give himself up to the 'postulation vers Dieu'. This series of poems gives the first clear indication of the dramatic basis of the volume.

The next group of poems is less easy to fit into the architecture. They must be taken as a group since the first poem, *La Vie antérieure*, has no apparent connection with the vocation-theme of the preceding group, and the last poem, *Châtiment de l'Orgueil*, certainly has none with the following group of poems on Beauty. But it is not easy to see either how the group fits in with the surrounding groups or what connection these five poems have amongst themselves. We should therefore be justified in suspecting that Baudelaire chose this point at which to insert a number of early poems that did not lend themselves very well to his overall design. But other suggestions can be made.

According to Marcel Ruff, *La Vie antérieure* and the two following poems present 'le chant de l'évasion'.[1] The poet attempts here to escape from his gloom. This may well be the intention, but one might think also in terms of the requirements of an exposition and in particular of the advisability of giving the reader a somewhat fuller introduction to

[1] *Op. cit.*, p. 105.

the character of the poet-hero than has been possible in preceding poems. From the poet-hero's point of view, this group of poems might represent no more than preliminary exercises on themes other than his personal problems as a poet, and to some extent, therefore, an escape from his gloom. But from the point of view of Baudelaire, the author of *Les Fleurs du Mal*, these poems might be chosen with a view to underlining certain important features of the poet-hero's character which are reflected in the poetry however impersonal its content may seem. The link between the ostensible themes is as casual as one would expect in a set of exercises. Yet when one looks more closely at these themes and the poems which develop them, one can see a pattern of psychological elements that together suggest a type of personality, and this must be assumed to belong to the poet-hero himself. This is the legitimate use which Baudelaire may have found for a number of poems that were not well suited to those parts of the architecture which fulfil a more obviously useful function.

The previous poems have introduced the reader to a poet whose soul is highly idealistic, yet strangely sombre, restless and dissatisfied. In *La Vie antérieure* we find him seeking a somewhat different form of the Ideal in a dream of a past existence. It is a predominantly sensuous ideal which recalls the sensuous aspect of the sonnet of *Correspondances*. Like *Élévation*, the first poem to do so, it represents an imaginary journey (in this case through time as well as space), but the destination and accompanying feelings are different. The 'voluptés calmes' mentioned in line 9, define the mood of the poem and they are due above all to the mingled profusion

of colours, sounds and odours in an extraordinarily vague
architectural and natural setting. They are due also to the
privileged passivity of the poet himself. Considered as an
ideal existence, it may fairly be called a less elevated ideal
than any previously envisaged by the poet. Moreover, it is
made to seem a strong probability that an essential ingredient
of the 'voluptés calmes' is pain—the pain of the mysterious
'secret douloureux' referred to in the final line. This appears
to harmonize with the 'voluptés' rather than to conflict with
them. It is an echo of the 'délectable mélancolie' of René,
the melancholy which tells of an insatiable soul and brings its
own consolation in awareness that it is, like the sufferings of
the martyr, a badge of distinction. It is an echo of the 'douleur morale' that Baudelaire noted and admired in the eyes of
the women of Delacroix, an element of beauty as well as an
ingredient in 'volupté'. And once again the reader should be
made conscious of the complexity of the poet-hero's nature,
in which pleasure and pain are not mutually exclusive. If
'évasion' there is, the escape is not intended to reach an ideal
of pure pleasure; the ideal itself contains an admixture of the
pain of Spleen and in this case it has not the religious justification that it had in *Bénédiction*. Perhaps because of this, *La
Vie antérieure* is the first poem which creates in full measure
the atmosphere that is characteristic of many of Baudelaire's
finest lyrics. He has defined it for us in *Fusées* in the following
note which concerns his plans for a 'roman sérieux':

Noyer le tout dans une atmosphère anormale et songeuse,—
dans l'atmosphère des *grands jours*. Que ce soit quelque chose de
berçant,—et même de serein dans la passion. Régions de la Poésie
pure.[1]

[1] JOP, II, p. 72.

If we interpret 'passion' in this quotation as a combination of 'volupté' and suffering (this is justified by the outline of the projected work) and vary the relative proportions in which these two elements appear, the description may be applied to a large group of poems including *Recueillement*, *Le Balcon*, *Invitation au Voyage*, *Tristesses de la Lune*, *La Mort des Amants*, as well as *La Vie antérieure* itself.

Bohémiens en Voyage is thought to be inspired by the engravings of Jacques Callot. The picture of these nomadic gypsies vainly searching for their 'chimères absentes' in space and in *future* time, can nevertheless be seen as an allegorical expression of the same temperament that is seen in *La Vie antérieure*. For all the apparent impersonality of the poem, the poet's interest in the subject is surely largely due to the analogy which he sees between the eternal wanderers and his own restless, dissatisfied soul with its vague nostalgic yearnings—yearnings that the ideals of God and even of art, do not seem able to appease.

The thematic link between *Bohémiens en Voyage* and *L'Homme et la Mer* is tenuous but not invisible. If gypsies do not suggest the sea, wanderings may do so. Above all, the rebellious freedom of the life that gypsies lead, together with the mystery that the poet has found in their nature, leads him to see an analogy between these human qualities and the attributes of the sea. 'L'Homme' of the title, is amended in the first line to 'Homme libre'. There is a sense in which the analogy is universally valid, but it is particularly valid in the case of the gypsies and the poet who resembles them in having and wanting no more ties than the ocean wave with its 'déroulement infini', and in possessing for an inner nature 'un gouffre amer'.

Marcel Ruff suggests that the remaining two poems of the group represent 'un effort d'évasion par l'orgueil'.[1] It is indeed in terms of pride that both poems should be understood, though a trifle difficult to apply the notion of attempted escape.

Don Juan aux Enfers is not a gratuitous transposition of art, if it is one at all. The poem has a point which is implicit in its original title, *L'Impénitent*, and is of far more interest to Baudelaire than it might seem at first sight. Don Juan is pictured at a moment when he realizes, after a life of sin, that there is such a thing as eternal justice and retribution. The point of the poem lies in his complete imperturbability. This is all, but for Baudelaire it establishes Don Juan as a dandy and invests him with the beauty that attaches to this type. For, we are told in *Le Peintre de la Vie moderne*: 'Le caractère de beauté du dandy consiste surtout dans l'air froid qui vient de l'inébranlable résolution de ne pas être ému'.[2] This is what constitutes for the poet the beauty of the figure of Don Juan in the poem. But what, if any, is the bearing of the poem on the architecture?

It is possible that the theme of the dandy which appears in *Don Juan aux Enfers* is intended to link up with the previously developed theme of the 'homme libre' and the 'beau ténébreux', for the dandy is both these types and more. The dandy represents 'ce qu'il y a de meilleur dans l'orgueil humain, . . . ce besoin, trop rare chez ceux d'aujourd'hui, de combattre et de détruire la trivialité'; he is 'le dernier éclat d'héroïsme dans les décadences'.[3] He is, then, a man of intense feeling who, finding only triviality about him instead of the ideals that he

[1] *Op. cit.*, p. 105. [2] AR, p. 92. [3] AR, p. 91.

seeks, withdraws contemptuously into himself, masks his sensitivity with an air of indifference and disdain and devotes himself exclusively to the cult of his ego—'C'est une espèce de culte de soi-même'.[1] It is as certain as it can be that Baudelaire adopted for a time a similar attitude in his personal life and never altogether lost his sympathy for it. It is possible that he wished to suggest this development in his poet-hero in a series of poems which form a transition between the reader's first introduction to him and to his problems as a poet, and the beginning of the story of his pursuit of Beauty. The group of poems as constituted is far from adequate to that purpose, but there are undoubtedly many parts of the architecture that Baudelaire would have strengthened if he could. *Don Juan aux Enfers* suggests no more than a certain admiration on the part of the poet-hero for the type of the dandy. And to judge by *Châtiment de l'Orgueil* he is aware, as Baudelaire himself is, that the dandy tends to substitute the worship of self for the worship of God. His nature appears more complex than ever when he recognizes and condemns a satanic pride which was admired in the 'calme héros' of the previous poem.

Having surveyed some of the major problems presented by his vocation, his own poetic talent and temperament, the poet turns to the problem of Beauty. It is in the complex idea of Beauty that all the paths which lead from Spleen to the various forms of the Ideal seem to him to meet.

[1] AR, p. 89.

IV

THE TEMPTATION

THE IDEAL OF BEAUTY (POEMS XVII–XXI)

In the second edition of *Les Fleurs du Mal* the poems on Beauty (XVII–XXI) form one of the most clearly defined subdivisions of *Spleen et Idéal*. Baudelaire has stressed its unity by the very titles which he gave to the first and last of its poems, *La Beauté* and *Hymne à la Beauté*. But although the existence of this aesthetic cycle is not in doubt, commentators who have considered it from the point of view of the 'architecture secrète' have not been impressed with its value. Even Marcel Ruff, who reveals so much meaning in neighbouring cycles, apparently finds no necessary connection between them and this one, and apologizes for its seeming lack of inner coherence by reminding us that we are dealing with poems, not a treatise on aesthetics.[1]

The key to the matter lies in the problem which is raised by the initial poem, *La Beauté*. It has proved difficult to interpret because critics cannot reconcile it with Baudelaire's own aesthetic. Jean Prévost admits the difficulty when he says: 'Tout s'explique si l'on admet que ce n'est pas vraiment le poète qui parle, ni sa Beauté, mais qu'il laisse parler une statue grecque, qui l'a séduit pour un moment à son idéal purement

[1] *Baudelaire, l'homme et l'oeuvre*, Paris, Hatier-Boivin, p. 105.

olympien et à sa tranquillité marmoréenne'.[1] Marcel Ruff
advances the same theory of momentary—and seemingly
reprehensible—seduction, and states that the sonnet 'sera
démenti, non seulement par l'ensemble des *Fleurs du Mal*, mais
par l'oeuvre entière de Baudelaire, si on voulait y voir une
profession de foi'.[2] And he remarks earlier: '*Allégorie*, poème
de la même époque, ressortit à la même esthétique; mais aussi
Baudelaire le placera dans le chapitre *Fleurs du Mal*, c'est-à-
dire celui des erreurs criminelles'.[3] Alexis François, however,
has reconciled the poem with Baudelaire's sculptural ideal if
not with his poetic theory.[4] It is chiefly with poetic theory that
Pierre-Georges Castex concerns himself in his more recent
article, and he goes so far as to conclude: '*La Beauté* ne doit
plus nous apparaître comme une profession de foi isolée et
bientôt dépassée'.[5] But it appears to be only as a 'Fleur du
Mal' that *La Beauté* can be restored to its place in Baudelaire's
poetic theory—from which Prévost and Ruff have banished
it as a Flower of culpably pagan, impassive and Parnassian
purity.

Although the poems on Beauty need not necessarily be
expected to correspond exactly with the principal trends in
Baudelaire's thought on aesthetics, some consideration of the
meaning—or rather the *meanings*—which he attaches to the
word 'beauté' in his other work, would seem to be a necessary
preliminary to interpretation of the poems. Here is a relevant
passage dating from 1846:

[1] *Baudelaire*, Paris, Mercure de France, 1953, p. 182.
[2] *Op. cit.*, p. 105.   [3] *Ibid.*, p. 27.
[4] *Le Sonnet sur 'la Beauté'* in *Le Mercure de France*, 1er Juin, 1954.
[5] *La Beauté—Fleur du Mal* in *La Revue des Sciences humaines*, Juillet-
Septembre 1959.

Toutes les beautés contiennent, comme tous les phénomènes possibles, quelque chose d'éternel et quelque chose de transitoire,— d'absolu et de particulier. La beauté absolue et éternelle n'existe pas, ou plutôt elle n'est qu'une abstraction écrémée à la surface générale des beautés diverses. L'élément particulier de chaque beauté vient des passions, et comme nous avons nos passions particulières, nous avons notre beauté.[1]

And here is another passage written about 1860, nearly fourteen years later:

C'est ici une belle occasion, en vérité, ... pour montrer que le beau est toujours, inévitablement, d'une composition double, bien que l'impression qu'il produit soit une; car la difficulté de discerner les éléments variables du beau dans l'unité de l'impression n'infirme en rien la nécessité de la variété dans sa composition. Le beau est fait d'un élément éternel, invariable, dont la quantité est excessivement difficile à déterminer, (there is evidently less doubt about its 'existence' in 1860!) et d'un élément relatif, circonstanciel, qui sera, si l'on veut, tour à tour ou tout ensemble, l'époque, la mode, la morale, la passion. Sans ce second élément, qui est comme l'enveloppe amusante, titillante, apéritive, du divin gâteau, le premier élément serait indigeste, inappréciable, non adapté et non approprié à la nature humaine. Dans l'art hiératique, la dualité se fait voir au premier coup d'oeil; la partie de beauté éternelle ne se manifeste qu'avec la permission et sous la règle de la religion à laquelle appartient l'artiste. Dans l'oeuvre la plus frivole d'un artiste raffiné appartenant à une de ces époques que nous qualifions trop vaniteusement de civilisées, la dualité se montre également; la portion éternelle de beauté sera en même temps voilée et exprimée, sinon par la mode, au moins par le tempérament particulier de l'auteur. La dualité de l'art est une conséquence fatale de la dualité de l'homme. Considérez, si cela vous plaît, la partie éternellement subsistante comme l'âme de l'art, et l'élément variable comme son corps.[2]

[1] CE, p. 197.   [2] AR, pp. 52–53.

It follows that the word 'beauty' may have three meanings. It may denote: (1) the absolute and eternal element, or absolute beauty; (2) the relative and transitory element; (3) the combination of both elements.

Baudelaire's theory of absolute beauty figures far more prominently in his aesthetic than seems to have been realized. What in fact happened was that he very naturally came to identify the absolute beauty which first appeared to him in 1846 as a predominantly intellectual abstraction, with that other abstraction which is aesthetic or poetic emotion, the 'Poetic Sentiment' of Poe and the 'principe de la poésie' defined by Baudelaire himself in the following passage:

> Ainsi le principe de la poésie est, strictement et simplement, l'aspiration humaine vers une Beauté supérieure, et la manifestation de ce principe est dans un enthousiasme, un enlèvement de l'âme; enthousiasme tout à fait indépendant de la passion, qui est l'ivresse du coeur, et de la vérité, qui est la pâture de la raison. Car la passion est chose *naturelle*, trop naturelle même, pour ne pas introduire un ton blessant, discordant, dans le domaine de la Beauté pure, trop familière et trop violente pour ne pas scandaliser les purs Désirs, les gracieuses Mélancolies et les nobles Désespoirs qui habitent les régions surnaturelles de la Poésie.[1]

In the word 'passion' which is a synonym for relative beauty, and in the expressions 'Beauté supérieure' and 'Beauté pure' which are synonyms for absolute beauty, one may see the fusion of the two abstractions and the two theories. It is equally obvious in the preceding remarks on *Mademoiselle de Maupin* which the passage quoted is designed to clarify.[2] The poetic enthusiasm which is the sign of absolute beauty is itself an absolute and may be experienced *à propos* of any true work

[1] *Ibid.*, p. 159. [2] *Ibid.*, pp. 156–7.

of art. It is necessarily independent therefore of any and all moods that such works *express*: it may best be thought of (as Jean Prévost suggests[1]) as a serenely joyful way of experiencing any expressed emotion, and whether the expressed emotion itself is serene or not, it must never be confused with the way of feeling that Baudelaire believes to be the sign of absolute beauty.

It follows that expressed emotion can rank only as 'passion' or 'relative beauty'—which brings us to the second possible meaning which the word 'beauty' can have for Baudelaire. It can be used as he uses it in the expression 'notre beauté', to isolate the relative and variable element in all beautiful things, that which constitutes the particular, tangible 'body' of a work of art as opposed to its eternal, intangible 'soul', and which is referred to by Baudelaire not only as 'nos passions particulières' but also as 'l'époque, la mode, la morale'. As these terms suggest, the notion of relative beauty is capable of unlimited extension. So far from being restricted to artistic activity, it may include any experience which is 'beautiful' in the sense that it arouses pleasurable excitement ('passion') in any given person, people or age, and such experiences may range from murder and arson to eating sweets. Baudelaire's personal conception of relative beauty which he has defined in a celebrated passage of *Fusées*, leads him to prefer the tragic beauty of '*Satan,*—à la manière de Milton'.[2]

A question arises here which is not fully covered by Baudelaire's pronouncements though his final answer is

---

[1] *Op. cit.*, p. 355. ('L'émotion poétique n'a donc pas son domaine séparé: elle est une manière d'être de toutes les émotions.')

[2] JOP, II, p. 64.

clear enough. Can the element of relative beauty exist apart
from the element of absolute beauty? At first sight it would
seem that the answer should be an unqualified affirmative, to
avoid the absurd necessity of attributing absolute beauty
to the activities of murder, arson and eating sweets, not to
mention bad works of art which may contain any given
person's idea of relative beauty. But the matter is not so
simple. To judge by Baudelaire's reference, in the quotation
given above, to 'tous les phénomènes possibles', he is prepared to believe that there is an eternal element (a Platonic
or Hegelian Idea?) even in such activities as murder or eating
sweets, just as it may be held that there is an immortal soul
even in the worst or most childish of mortals. An explanation
of this belief is suggested by the *Salon de* 1846. It indicates
that what an artist sees in his model, whatever it may be, is
not only relative beauty but some degree of absolute beauty
also, an absolute beauty which is no more, at first, than the
rudiments of a harmony of corresponding parts (both physical and moral, in man, his actions, and the décor alike) that
must be perfected by ordering them around a '*dominante*' determined partly by the characteristics of the model and
mainly by the artist's ideal of relative beauty, his 'passions'.
If absolute beauty is simply this harmony, it will indeed be
present everywhere in life in some slight degree, though
only in art will it be manifested in nearly perfect form. Thus
while the notion of relative beauty may cover as many kinds
of pleasurable activity as Stendhal's notion of 'une promesse
de bonheur', the combination of relative beauty with absolute
beauty (which is meant by the expression 'toutes les beautés')
is made manifest only in art, and no doubt in the less imper-

fect creations of Nature also. Baudelaire does not accept
Stendhal's definition of beauty without qualification.[1] He
retains part at least of the Classical conception of an absolute,
eternal beauty and superimposes it on Stendhal's Romantic
conception of relative beauty. The result is a narrower, more
satisfactory definition which provides a third meaning of the
word 'beauty'—one which denotes the presence of the
absolute element and the relative element together as they
are found in a true work of art (the word 'true' simply implies
that experts accord it a substantial amount of the value which
Baudelaire calls 'absolute beauty').

Which of the three possible meanings of the word 'beauté'
best fits the title and principal theme of the sonnet, *La Beauté*,
in *Les Fleurs du Mal*? There can be but one answer, and it
will be found to solve all difficulties including those related to
the architecture. The 'Beauté' of the sonnet is absolute and
eternal beauty, and, as such, she is no more Parnassian or
Classical than she is Romantic, Realist or Symbolist. All these
terms, in fact, are connected with relative beauty. In particular
they serve to denote the nature of the particular 'passions'
which serve a given artist or set of artists as subject-matter
('le corps'), and which the great artist ennobles,[2] however
base or lofty they may be *in themselves*, by endowing them
with the element of absolute beauty ('l'âme'), thanks to the
alchemy of artistic expression. Far from being a particularized
earth-bound statue, *La Beauté* is merely *compared* with 'un
rêve de pierre' and is quite literally 'above' all schools: '(elle)
trône dans l'azur' and never was a sphinx more misunderstood
than Baudelaire's goddess of absolute beauty.

[1] AR, p. 53.   [2] CE, pp. 349–50.

That she is none other is clearly proved by her own description of herself. Reference has several times been made to Baudelaire's belief that 'la poésie vraiment belle emporte les âmes vers un monde céleste'.[1] From Baudelaire's description of the inhabitants of that world it is clear that they bear a remarkable resemblance to the Beauty of the poem. In the relevant passage of *De l'essence du rire*, he speaks, it is true, of the 'paradis *terrestre*', but he goes on to give the term an infinite extension which permits it to cover any paradise and also, we may suppose, 'les splendeurs situées derrière le tombeau' which are glimpsed in and through poetry, 'le domaine de la Beauté pure', 'les régions surnaturelles de la Poésie',[2] 'les régions éthérées de la véritable Poésie',[3] 'Régions de la Poésie pure'.[4]

Il est certain, si l'on veut se mettre au point de vue de l'esprit orthodoxe, que le rire humain est intimement lié à l'accident d'une chute ancienne, d'une dégradation physique et morale. Le rire et la douleur s'expriment par les organes où résident le commandement et la science du bien et du mal: les yeux et la bouche. Dans le paradis terrestre (qu'on le suppose passé ou à venir, souvenir ou prophétie, comme les théologiens ou comme les socialistes), dans le paradis terrestre, c'est-à-dire dans le milieu où il semblait à l'homme que toutes les choses créées étaient bonnes, la joie n'était pas dans le rire. Aucune peine ne l'affligeant, son visage était simple et uni, et le rire qui agite maintenant les nations ne déformait point les traits de sa face. Le rire et les larmes ne peuvent pas se faire voir dans le paradis de délices. Ils sont également les enfants de la peine, et ils sont venus parce que le corps de l'homme énervé manquait de force pour les contraindre. Au point de vue de mon

[1] AR, p. 319.   [2] *Ibid.*, p. 159.
[3] FM, p. 408.   [4] JOP, II, p. 72.

philosophe chrétien, le rire de ses lèvres est signe d'une aussi grande misère que les larmes de ses yeux.[1]

A similar idea is expressed in the article on Théodore de Banville:

> Or, je me souviens qu'en trois ou quatre endroits de ses poésies, notre poëte, voulant orner des femmes d'une beauté non comparable et non égalable, dit qu'elles ont des *têtes d'enfant*. C'est là une espèce de trait de génie particulièrement lyrique, c'est-à-dire amoureux du surhumain. Il est évident que cette expression contient implicitement cette pensée, que le plus beau des visages humains est celui dont l'usage de la vie, passion, colère, péché, angoisse, souci, n'a jamais terni la clarté ni ridé la surface.[2]

It is this serenity of innocence, of a world where 'le Mal n'est pas, non plus que le Bien',[3] of the 'Éden perdu' towards which 'tout poète lyrique, en vertu de sa nature, opère fatalement un retour',[4] which Baudelaire has rendered in the sonnet in terms of colour (white—a synthesis in which conflicts of colour disappear), immobility (a pose which, suggestive of graceful movement only, resolves kinaesthetic conflicts) and impassiveness (a state of mind which is not the absence of feeling but is simply above the conflicts of passion). That the content of this 'coeur de neige' might actually be the '*joie* calme' which even 'l'horrible' and 'la *douleur*' can produce when they are artistically expressed,[5] is

---

[1] CE, pp. 373-4. Cf. Swedenborg's ideas on laughter: 'The affection of good . . . does not express itself by laughter, but by a kind of joy, . . . for in laughter there is commonly something which is not so good'. (*Compendium of Swedenborg's Theological Writings*, p. 156.)

[2] AR, p. 355.   [3] FM, p. 408.

[4] AR, p. 355.   [5] AR, p. 172.

made to seem extremely likely by another passage of *De l'essence du rire*:

> Mais il faut bien distinguer la joie d'avec le rire. La joie existe par elle-même, mais elle a des manifestations diverses. Quelquefois elle est presque invisible; d'autres fois, elle s'exprime par les pleurs. (. . .) La joie est *une*. Le rire est l'expression d'un sentiment double, ou contradictoire; et c'est pour cela qu'il y a convulsion.[1]

Finally, what of Beauty's eyes? Theirs is not the blank serenity of a statue's sightless orbs. The 'clartés éternelles' which they reflect are those of the same 'monde céleste', those of the 'pure lumière' of *Bénédiction,*

> Puisée au foyer saint des rayons primitifs,
> Et dont les yeux mortels, dans leur splendeur entière,
> Ne sont que des miroirs obscurcis et plaintifs!

But the 'clartés' reflected by Beauty's eyes are also those of the pure poetry that is referred to in the following passage:

> Comparant, ainsi que nous en avons le droit, l'humanité à l'homme, nous voyons que les nations primitives . . . ne conçoivent pas la caricature et n'ont pas de comédies (les livres sacrés, à quelques nations qu'ils appartiennent, ne rient jamais), et que, s'avançant peu à peu vers les pics nébuleux de l'intelligence, ou se penchant sur les fournaises ténébreuses de la métaphysique, les nations se mettent à rire diaboliquement du rire de Melmoth; et, enfin, que si dans ces mêmes nations ultra-civilisées, une intelligence, poussée par une ambition supérieure, veut franchir les limites de l'orgueil mondain et s'élancer hardiment vers la poésie pure, dans cette poésie, limpide et profonde comme la nature, le rire fera défaut comme dans l'âme du Sage.[2]

---

[1] CE, pp. 382–3. Elsewhere in the same article Baudelaire writes: 'J'ai dit: comique absolu; il faut toutefois prendre garde. Au point de vue de l'absolu définitif, il n'y a plus que la joie' (CE, p. 385).

[2] CE, p. 380.

The subject-matter of *Les Fleurs du Mal* is filled with the satanic laughter of Melmoth. But 'la dualité de l'art est une conséquence fatale de la dualité de l'homme', and of the duality of Nature. *La Beauté*, the absolute beauty which is the artistic soul of the entire book, is therefore not a *Fleur du Mal* in the eyes of Baudelaire. It is a *Fleur du Ciel*. The poem expresses the 'aspiration humaine vers une Beauté supérieure' in which Baudelaire sees the principle of poetry.[1]

Descending to the level of relative beauty, we may find amongst the feelings expressed in the sonnet, several of the recognized 'passions particulières' of Baudelaire. One such passion is for women or goddesses who exhibit the insensibility, the coldness, the aloofness of the female dandy.[2] Such is the power of the 'passion particulière' that this very personal and relative taste colours and compromises the white serenity of Baudelaire's goddess of absolute beauty. Like other dandies the goddess of beauty possesses also the quality of mystery—something else to which Baudelaire is attracted. And in the feelings of the poets who worship her and try in vain to render the absolute beauty which they glimpse in her eyes, we may find the painful yearning which is still another important element in Baudelaire's personal ideal of relative beauty and which constitutes the characteristic attitude of the poet-hero whose adventure is narrated in *Les Fleurs du Mal*. This also tends to compromise the serenity of pure poetic enthusiasm and absolute beauty, by giving it the tragic colouring which is evident in Baudelaire's belief that—'quand un poëme exquis amène les larmes au bord des yeux, ces

---

[1] AR, p. 159. [2] JOP, II, p. 64, p. 66, p. 72.

larmes ne sont pas la preuve d'un excès de jouissance, elles sont bien plutôt le témoignage d'une mélancolie irritée, d'une postulation des nerfs, d'une nature exilée dans l'imparfait et qui voudrait s'emparer immédiatement sur cette terre même, d'un paradis révélé'.[1] But the tears, like laughter, are distinct from the absolute beauty represented by the goddess. They express a longing for the serenity of her joy.

Like Mallarmé's 'azur' and indeed all ideals, Baudelaire's goddess of absolute beauty can torment as well as inspire. Yet as far as his art was concerned, as distinct from his life, Baudelaire's aspirations were not carried to impossible lengths. It never occurred to him, as it did to Mallarmé, to attempt the impossible task of eliminating relative beauty from poetry altogether—which would entail the elimination of subject-matter itself, the tangible 'body' of the work to which the 'soul' must be attached! Far from reducing him to sterility and silence, Baudelaire's goddess allowed him the greatest possible freedom of expression by assuring him that 'toutes choses'—the most mundane of things—could be made 'plus belles' by the powers common to all true poets in all ages. Baudelaire's theory, as distinct from his temperament, was no more conducive to artistic impotence than those of the most conscientious artists among his contemporaries and predecessors.

Interpreted in this way, *La Beauté* fits perfectly well into the framework of Baudelaire's aesthetic theory. What is no less important is that it fits perfectly well into the architecture of *Spleen et Idéal*. Despite numerous indications of disturbing depths in the nature of the poet-hero, the first sixteen poems

[1] AR, p. 159.

of the volume testify to a fervent desire on his part to escape from Spleen towards a very high and pure Ideal in which religious and aesthetic values are closely associated. The principal means of escape is to be the practice of the art of poetry in which his vocation lies. Appropriately enough, therefore, the initial movement of aspiration is made to culminate in poem XVII where the poet-hero personifies as a celestial goddess the austerely Platonic ideal of absolute beauty which he sees as the goal of all his efforts.

But, as the first of the group of five poems ending with the *Hymne à la Beauté*, this same sonnet marks the beginning of a new and critical phase in the poet-hero's development. It is this progression that must now be examined by comparing the opening poem of the group with those that follow and particularly with the last.

Poem XVIII, *L'Idéal*, provides a contrast with *La Beauté* which must surely be deliberate. There is no trace here of the goddess of the previous poem and the austerely pure emotion which she helped to express. In *L'Idéal* it is a very different kind of ideal which is envisaged as the poet-hero expresses distaste for the insipid 'beautés d'hôpital' of Gavarni and explains the fascination held for him by Shakespeare's Lady Macbeth and Michaelangelo's statue of Night. The theme is still that of beauty and beauty with feminine associations. But it is not the same kind of beauty. The poet has turned from the first meaning of the word (absolute beauty) to the second (relative beauty). Nothing could be more relative to the poet's personal taste in passion than the reasons—for reasons they surely are—which he gives to explain his preference for the tragic character and statue:

Ce qu'il faut à ce coeur profond comme un abîme,
C'est vous Lady Macbeth, *âme puissante au crime*,
Rêve d'Eschyle éclos au climat des autans;

Ou bien toi, grande Nuit, fille de Michel-Ange,
Qui tords paisiblement dans une pose étrange
Tes appas façonnés aux bouches des Titans!

Two main features are distinguished in the beauty of Lady
Macbeth. The first is that of unusual energy, a common attribute of tragic heroes and heroines. By most people it is either
admired or deprecated according to the morality of the use to
which it is put. By others it is found beautiful in itself from a
frankly amoral point of view. But for the poet-hero of the
Fleurs du Mal, energy, already beautiful in itself, can clearly
appear more beautiful for being deliberately directed towards
evil. Its attraction for him can be strengthened by the addition
of an element of fascinated repulsion which accompanies
recognition of moral evil, just as it accompanies recognition
of those other forms of evil called ugliness and pain. Thanks
to this sado-masochistic complex, moral evil joins with energy
to provide the two main elements in the beauty of Lady Macbeth. Nothing less could justify the poet's claim to unusual
emotional depths.

In the statue of Night, the quality of energy can only be
dormant, but it cannot be wholly dissociated from the mere
'grandeur' for which Baudelaire professes his unfailing admiration in a passage of his *Salon de* 1859:

Car il faut, mon cher, que je vous fasse un aveu qui vous fera
peut-être sourire: dans la nature et dans l'art, je préfère, en suppos-
ant l'égalité de mérite, les choses *grandes* à toutes les autres, les
grands animaux, les grands paysages, les grands navires, les

grands hommes, les grandes femmes, les grandes églises, et, transformant, comme tant d'autres, mes goûts en principes (this would be tantamount to confusing a 'passion particulière' with absolute beauty: Baudelaire is always conscious of the danger), je crois que la dimension n'est pas une considération sans importance aux yeux de la Muse.[1]

In addition to the statue's size, there is some suggestion of mystery in its very name, its 'pose étrange' (at once twisted and peaceful, it satisfies Baudelaire's need for a synthesis of Romantic and Classical opposites), and in the evocation of the absent Titans. Finally, there is a strong suggestion of sensuality and 'volupté' to add to the attributes which recommend the statue to the poet and which are constant features of his ideal of relative beauty.

The contrast between *La Beauté* and *L'Idéal* is not a contradiction and the transition from one to the other is perfectly logical. After affirming his faith in the ideal of absolute beauty, the poet-hero proceeds to examine his taste in relative beauty, in passion. For it is this that he must use as a means of attaining absolute beauty. It is relative beauty of one kind or another that must provide the 'body' of his poems, to be endowed through artistic expression with the 'soul' of absolute beauty. This is the feat that he seeks to accomplish in *L'Idéal* itself, in so far as it is a poem and not the mere presentation of a particular subject or passion. It is also the feat that he sought to accomplish in *La Beauté*. There he took absolute beauty as his subject, but the fact alone was no guarantee that his poem would attain to absolute beauty (true artistic value). Far wiser than Poe in this respect, Baudelaire and his poet-

[1] CE, pp. 312-13.

hero are well aware that all subjects *qua* subjects are on exactly the same level—the level of relative beauty which, in itself, is of no artistic value whatever. They know that even subjects and passions which most people find ugly can serve the artist's purpose as well as others, for, to quote Baudelaire, 'c'est un des privilèges prodigieux de l'art que l'horrible, artistement exprimé, devienne beauté, et que la *douleur*, rythmée et cadencée, remplisse l'esprit d'une *joie* calme!' The serenity of absolute beauty which is the subject of *La Beauté* can just as well be achieved with the aid of the very different subject used in *L'Idéal*. It follows that the true importance of subjects *qua* subjects lies in their suitability or lack of suitability for particular poets, and Baudelaire's theory of 'naïveté' or 'tempérament' is based on the conviction that artists will treat best those subjects which best satisfy the emotional needs of their nature, their tastes in passion or relative beauty.[1] His theory of 'la beauté moderne' is an application of the same idea to particular ages instead of particular artists. Baudelaire's poet-hero in *Les Fleurs du Mal* evidently subscribes to the same beliefs and that is why he begins, in *L'Idéal*, to take stock of his 'passions particulières' in a more conscious and deliberate fashion than before. As we shall see, their nature and implications bring him face to face with the central problem of his life.

The same qualities of energy and size, voluptuous sensuality, and an air of mystery, are all to be seen in the beauty of the young giantess who gives the following poem its title. The transition from the statue of Night, with her attendant Titans, to this new figure, could not be neater. Here, however, the

[1] CE, p. 64, p. 110, p. 193.

poet's exploration of his tastes in relative—and indeed feminine—beauty broadens out into a phantasy in which he himself plays a part. The theme is no longer the simple idea of
literary characters or statues, but the idea of the poet's existence alongside the giantess he has himself called into being.
This existence itself has certain definable qualities which make
up its beauty in the poet's eyes. The outstanding quality here
is the opposite of the energy that the poet admires in the
giantess and others. It is passivity or idleness, already familiar
to the reader thanks to the earlier phantasy of *La Vie antérieure*. Together with this passivity goes a curious cerebral
sensuality: like the cat to which he compares himself, the poet
is a privileged, protected spectator, yet, just as in *La Vie
antérieure*, this is sufficient to give him sensuous fulfilment and
the 'volupté calme' which was defined as such in the earlier
phantasy and which is the emotion characteristic of this ideally
beautiful existence. This wider aspect of the poet's ideal of
relative beauty reappears in many of the later poems, particularly those with an exotic setting. *L'Invitation au Voyage* is a
last attempt to realize it in the midst of Spleen, and it is ironically answered across the intervening poems by the *Voyage
à Cythère* and finally by *Le Voyage* itself.

The full significance of the way in which the poet-hero
presents his ideal in *La Géante* emerges very clearly from the
first edition of the *Fleurs du Mal*. There, *La Géante* is immediately followed by *Les Bijoux*, the initial poem of the cycle of
the 'Vénus noire'. The implication is that the poet-hero has
exchanged imaginary forms of his ideal of relative beauty for
real existence alongside an ideal of flesh and blood. The
existence depicted in *Les Bijoux* reveals several analogies with

that imagined in *La Géante*. But in *Les Bijoux* a conflict is
already suggested between the sincere desire of the poet for
detached artistic enjoyment (or passive cerebral sensuality)
on his 'rocher de cristal', and an incipient carnality which
owes much of its strength to the thrill of conscious wrongdoing. His spiritual path does in fact follow a descending
curve which runs from such morally pure forms of the ideal
as that of absolute beauty, through the somewhat equivocal
ideal of relative beauty envisaged in *L'Idéal* and *La Géante*, to
a thoroughly degraded form of the same ideal which is represented by the black Venus in her satanic aspect. In the
second edition of the volume, the addition of two new poems
to the cycle of Beauty postpones full understanding of the
implications of *La Géante*. But it remains to be seen whether
the change has not added to the overall significance of the
cycle and provided an even better transition to the next. Let
it be said at once that Baudelaire would have been pained to
think that editions of his work would be published in which
Les Bijoux has been restored to its position next to *La Géante*
and has thus come to occupy the centre of a cycle to which it
has never belonged.

Le Masque is usually interpreted in terms of the reference
made to Christophe's statue in Baudelaire's *Salon de* 1859.[1]
The passage, however, brings out only that part of the poem's
significance which is summed up in the philosophic conception of 'le masque universel', and this idea is not relevant to
the principal themes of *Les Fleurs du Mal* save through its
connection with the ideal of the dandy and hence with Baudelaire's ideal of relative beauty. If the 'architectural' significance

[1] CE, p. 360.

of the poem is to emerge, it must be considered in relation to this latter ideal, which is, after all, the subject of the cycle.

Le Masque continues the poet's exploration of his personal tastes. The familiar quality of energy is repeatedly distinguished in Christophe's statue by such words as 'musculeux', 'la Force', 'divinement robuste'. It is combined here with a quality taken for granted hitherto, that of 'élégance' or 'grâce'. Inasmuch as it may be equated with the general quality of coherence or harmony (a close relation or conformity between parts, including the different stages of a movement), grace is a quality very closely connected indeed with artistic value. It is not, however, a prominent feature of Baudelaire's ideal of relative beauty. His taste tends towards a baroque complexity which, outside his poetry, cannot always be reconciled with perfect coherence. Grace and muscularity can and do at times conflict.

The second stanza of the poem associates this physical and moral energy with the inevitable 'volupté', for the expression on the statue's face is described as one of sensual ardour, challenge, triumph. The remainder of the poem adds three further qualities. The face is found to be a mask: the real face expresses intense suffering. The woman's beauty is thus enhanced by mystery, which may be taken to include 'bizarrerie' and surprise. It is enhanced also by the admiration which the poet feels for the stoical fortitude and apparent insensibility of the dandy: the woman of the mask is a sister of the Don Juan depicted in Poem XV. And here also, brought out unmistakably for the first time, is the quality of suffering itself. The poet has already associated it with 'saintes voluptés' in *Bénédiction*, with the strange beauty of modern life in '*J'aime le*

Le Masque therefore takes us close to the heart of the ideal of relative beauty which Baudelaire's poet-hero evidently shares with his creator. And in the following poem, *Hymne à la Beauté*, this ideal reappears in a form which can hardly fail to make the reader aware that it raises a problem which is at once aesthetic and moral:

> Viens-tu du ciel profond ou sors-tu de l'abîme,
> O Beauté? ton regard, infernal et divin,
> Verse confusément le bienfait et le crime . . .

The reader should find himself prepared to meet Beauty in her heavenly aspect: he will already have met her in the person of the goddess depicted in the opening sonnet of the cycle. But he may not at first recognize her infernal counterpart despite the latter's earlier appearance in the shape of Lady Macbeth and, less obviously, in the statue of Night, the giantess and the lady of the mask.

The image of an infernal beauty arises quite naturally from the distinction made by Baudelaire and his poet-hero between absolute beauty, which is by definition spiritually pure, and relative beauty, which may be pure but may equally well be corrupt. Satanic beauty is an extreme form of relative beauty. It corresponds to the extreme form of the tendency to be pleasurably attracted by what repels—the extreme form of what Baudelaire calls elsewhere 'le goût de l'horrible'[1] 'cette dépravation du sens de l'infini',[2] 'la postulation vers Satan'.[3] So, if we limit its application to the realm of aesthetic theory, the word 'Beauté', as used in the *Hymne*, plays quite deliberately upon three meanings. The concept of relative

[1] *Ibid.*, pp. 6–7.   [2] PA, p. 6.   [3] JOP, II, p. 93.

beauty provides two meanings: beauty that is spiritually pure (as when a poet expresses none but pure passions in a poem), and beauty that is corrupt. The third meaning is provided by the concept of absolute beauty. It allies itself with the pure form of relative beauty and combines with it in the image of the divine beauty which comes from the 'ciel profond'. But it must not be forgotten that this absolute beauty is, so to speak, above the quarrel which divides the pure and corrupt kinds of relative beauty. It actually resolves, on the plane of aesthetic experience, the apparent antithesis between morally pure and morally impure kinds of subject-matter. It ensures that even the most bloody, repulsive and evil tragedy can fill us with a 'joie calme' which is strictly beyond morality but can still be classified as spiritually pure.[1] Art, as Valéry said with reference to the horrors of tragedy, 'nous fait des regards qui peuvent tout considérer'.[2] And one can only disagree with Marcel Ruff when he casts doubts on the sincerity of Baudelaire's words in the original dedication of *Les Fleurs du Mal*: 'Je sais que dans les régions éthérées de la véritable Poésie, le Mal n'est pas, non plus que le Bien ....'.[3]

[1] AR, p. 172.
[2] *Oeuvres complètes*, Paris, Bibliothèque de la Pléiade, t.1, 1957, p. 1089. Valéry remembers the strange beauty with which the crystalline medium of sea-water endowed the horrible mass of entrails and viscera that the fishermen of Sète used to throw back into the Mediterranean. And he continues: 'Puis ma pensée se reporta vers ce qu'il y a de brutal et de sanglant dans la poésie des anciens. Les Grecs ne répugnaient pas à évoquer les scènes les plus atroces ... Les héros travaillaient comme des bouchers. La mythologie, la poésie épique, la tragédie sont pleines de sang. Mais l'art est comparable à cette limpide et cristalline épaisseur à travers laquelle je voyais ces choses atroces: il nous fait des regards qui peuvent tout considérer.'
[3] FM, p. 408.

Even on the plane of relative beauty, the antithesis presented in the *Hymne* is not a real one for aesthetics. The distinction which has been made between two kinds of relative beauty is a moral distinction only. It is simply not justified by aesthetics, which coincides, for once, with mere appetency: all relative beauty is beautiful for the same reason that all pleasure is pleasurable, whether it be morally pure or morally corrupt. So although it arises from aesthetic considerations, the real antithesis involved is one of morality, and it concerns aesthetics only because aesthetics contradicts morality in the same way as appetency—by not recognizing that any such conflict of values exists. Therein, as we shall see, lies the problem of the poet-hero: his natural appetite and his aesthetic nature run counter to his moral nature.

Seen in more detail, the problem is this. The poet-hero is fully aware of the nature of the true beauty of art (*La Beauté*): it is a beauty distinct from the passions which may attach to the subject-matter of any particular work, yet dependent on them, as on every other tangible element in the work, for its existence. To attain to this absolute beauty, he must use in his poems subject-matter which will be beautiful only in the sense that it provides the kind of emotional excitement best suited to his temperament and talent. Exploration of his tastes has led him from the pure, serene goddess of *La Beauté* to such creatures as Lady Macbeth, Night, his own giantess and the lady of the mask. In the *Hymne à la Beauté* his taste in relative beauty is shown to lead him further still, to the extreme which Baudelaire himself had reached in the continuation of the passage from *Fusées* already quoted:

... je ne conçois guères (mon cerveau serait-il un miroir ensorcelé?) un type de Beauté où il n'y ait du *Malheur*.—Appuyé sur—d'autres diraient: obsédé par—ces idées, on conçoit qu'il me serait difficile de ne pas conclure que le plus parfait type de Beauté virile est *Satan*,—à la manière de Milton.

The transition from the first idea to the second is quite logical. If one can find pleasure in misfortune and its attendant suffering (evil in the widest sense) one will inevitably find it, and find it perhaps in its most intense form, in moral or spiritual evil. The 'Prince du Malheur' is also the 'Prince du Mal'. This is in effect the same transition that we find in the poems between the lady of *Le Masque* with her 'beautiful' misfortune and suffering, and the satanic beauty of *Hymne à la Beauté* with her 'beautiful' sinfulness. It is clear that this is the critical point in the volume, the moment at which the poet of *Spleen et Idéal* finds himself on the verge of becoming the poet of *Les Fleurs du Mal*.

It is also clear that the poet is very well aware of the direction in which his taste is leading him and of the dangers of his position. The first five stanzas of the *Hymne*, so often dismissed as a regrettable example of 'bas Romantisme', are as lucid as they are impassioned. In addition to her significance in terms of aesthetic theory, the poet's satanic beauty stands for all possible incarnations of Lilith or 'la Circé tyrannique' of *Le Voyage*, that may be seen in legend, art or history. Particular illustrations are Lady Macbeth and her companions in the preceding poems, and above all the black Venus whose entry upon the scene in the very next poem is here foreshadowed. And the poet uses this formidable generalized figure to state or suggest what is surely no more than the truth. 'Beauty' can indeed be associated with horror, death and evil of all kinds, both literally and figuratively: literally in the sense that man's desire to possess 'beauty' results in these evils in real life; figuratively in the double sense that these evils can serve as material for producing the absolute beauty of art, and that contemplation of them, or even participation in them, can be 'beautiful' in a relative sense when it arouses pleasurable excitement—as the thought of these horrors appears to do in the poet himself.

Fully aware then of the immorality of his tendency to be attracted towards evil—no less because it repels him than because it is intrinsically attractive—it occurs to the poet that a choice might be made. He can continue to pursue the ideal of absolute beauty using for his poetry, and seeking in his life, only such material as is morally pure or contains a minimum of the dangerous fascination possessed by things that repel. Alternatively he can refuse to choose, and continue to pursue the same ideal using any material, any form of relative beauty however impure it may be. Refusal to choose will not only provide him with a wider and more original range of material for his art, but it will also increase the number of forms of relative beauty in which he can seek an escape from Spleen in everyday life—with the excuse that he is doing so for the benefit of his art. As the last stanzas of the poem show clearly, he does refuse to choose, though his reasons for doing so are not consciously immoral except in so far as he feels it immoral to adopt the amoral attitude of 'De Satan ou de Dieu, qu'importe?' Nor is it perhaps for deliberately immoral reasons that he exchanges imaginary realizations of his ideal of relative beauty for actual existence alongside a living one—

as we see he has done in *Parfum exotique*, the first poem of the
next cycle. Nevertheless, by the refusal to choose, to which
the *Hymne* bears witness, he assumes complete moral responsibility for his subsequent tragedy. He takes the right
course as a poet, but the wrong course as a man. And like
the conventional tragic hero, he is at once innocent and guilty.
What is happening is that he is beginning to yield to the
temptation of Satan, of whom it is said in *La Destruction*
(Poem CIX):

> Parfois il prend, sachant mon grand amour de l'Art,
> La forme de la plus séduisante des femmes,
> Et, sous de spécieux prétextes de cafard,
> Accoutume ma lèvre à des philtres infâmes.

Baudelaire undoubtedly believed that the personal conception of relative beauty which he outlined in Poems XVIII
to XXI, was in harmony with the general trend in modern
taste that held the greatest significance for art. In the passage
from *Fusées* quoted earlier, Baudelaire's confession that 'le
malheur' is an essential feature of his ideal of relative beauty,
is prefaced by the words: '. . . pour que j'aie le courage d'avouer
jusqu'à quel point je me sens moderne en esthétique'.[1] This
anticipates Baudelaire's later defence, in the *Projets de lettre à
Jules Janin*, of 'Byron, Tennyson, Poe et Cie':

> Ciel mélancolique de la poésie moderne. Étoiles de première
> grandeur. Pourquoi les choses ont-elles changé? . . . Pourquoi
> donc toujours la joie? . . . Pourquoi la tristesse n'aurait-elle pas sa
> beauté? Et l'horreur aussi? Et tout? Et n'importe quoi?[2]

It is the same conception of relative beauty, and an understandable sympathy for natures akin to his own, which lead

---

[1] JOP, II, p. 63.   [2] JOP, I, p. 230.

him to exalt 'ces sublimes défauts qui font le grand poëte: la mélancolie, toujours inséparable du sentiment du beau, et une personnalité ardente, diabolique, un esprit salamandrin'.[1] It would however be quite wrong to think that these expressions of a preference for melancholy over a facile and vulgar joy (as this might be expressed in the *subject-matter* of poetry) contradict Baudelaire's pronouncements on the subject of the pure poetic enthusiasm that is the principle of poetry, and the *'joie* calme' that all great art can give when properly appreciated, irrespective of the nature of the passions it presents. The poems on Beauty, and the important section of the architecture which they embody, are a perfect illustration of Baudelaire's belief that 'la dualité de l'art est une conséquence fatale de la dualité de l'homme',[2] and that 'l'artiste n'est artiste qu'à la condition d'être double et de n'ignorer aucun phénomène de sa double nature'.[3] The duality of man consists of a body and a soul, a body which predisposes him towards evil and Satan, just as the soul predisposes him towards goodness and God. The duality of art consists of absolute beauty and relative beauty. Absolute beauty corresponds to the soul, is perfectly pure and is a foretaste of heavenly bliss. Relative beauty is of the body and the passions of the body. As such it is likely (though this is not necessarily the case) to partake of evil and be, in fact, satanic, as it is with the poet-hero of *Les Fleurs du Mal* and with his creator. It is this conception of universal dualism which gives unity to Baudelaire's aesthetic, religious and ethical thought, as well as providing the basis of the tragedy which is outlined in *Les Fleurs du Mal*.

---

[1] *Ibid.*, p. 232.   [2] AR, p. 53.   [3] CE, p. 396.

V

THE FALL

THE *Hymne à la Beauté* ends the exposition and *Parfum exotique* presents the beginning of the action proper which coincides with the appearance of a second character. Originally the second poem of the black Venus cycle, it was moved to first place in the second edition after *Les Bijoux* had been banned. The *Hymne à la Beauté* may well have been written with *Parfum exotique* in mind, since the transition from the first poem to the second is admirably smooth. Thanks to the perfume and the exotic associations of the woman, the 'porte d'un Infini' does swing open for the poet in exact accordance with the prayer of the last two stanzas of the *Hymne*. In the manner suggested earlier in *Correspondances*, the poet explores within himself the power of expansion of a scent and is transported by it into an imaginary world which 'corresponds' with the woman, in the sense that it is the kind of setting appropriate to her physical and moral nature, and which 'corresponds' with his own nature, in the sense that it represents what he conceives to be an ideal form of existence. *Parfum exotique* brings out what is barely suggested in *Correspondances* itself—the relation between the theme of *correspondances* and synaesthesia considered as a means of attaining the Ideal, and the theme of *le voyage* in all its forms. It also relates both these themes to the theme of Woman, but the latter, for the moment, is subordinate to them. Woman is at first envisaged as a fund of *correspondances* which spring from her physical attributes, her perfume, her hair, the glitter of her eyes and the rhythm of her movements. She provides the ideal or infinite which can be reached through the *correspondances* and *voyages* which these qualities suggest. Later she will oust them and will herself provide the ideal or infinite of conscious sensual vice.

It is important to observe this connection between the earlier poems and the first poem devoted to the theme of Woman, if one is to understand the full meaning of the architecture at this point. Although the poet's Ideal is already much less exalted than the religious, semi-mystical ideal which informed the opening poems, it is not yet by any means corrupted. Woman, as she first appears in *Parfum exotique* and *La Chevelure*, is primarily a magnificent illustration of the poet's theory of *correspondances*. The infinite or ideal of sensuous and intellectual delight which she offers is primarily an artistic ecstasy, and *Parfum exotique* in particular is the poem of an artist, not the poem of a sensual lover. It is true that the starting-point is a sensation, and a sensation traditionally regarded as belonging to a lower, not to say bestial order.[1] What is clear from the poem is that sensation does not remain upon the level of sensation as it might be supposed to do with the brute. It is at once transformed and becomes memory, imagination and intelligence, the kind of total experience which is proper to art. In the poem itself, the

[1] See the interesting remarks of L. J. Austin, *op. cit.*, p. 201.

presence of the woman is barely mentioned, for the only three words which concern her are: 'ton sein chaleureux'. She is a pretext for an experience which transcends her; passion and sensuality are dormant or absent. The first appearance of the black Venus could not be more quietly and more discreetly made, and in view of the fact that she is an incarnation of satanic beauty who will bring about the catastrophe in the poet's life, this entry is dramatically most effective. It is less spectacular than that provided for her in the first edition by the banned poem, *Les Bijoux*. But the indication given in *Les Bijoux* that the poet would presently succumb to sensuality, if not to the toils of a sado-masochistic complex, weakens irony, surprise and the effect of gradation which is achieved in the second edition.

Both technically and considered in terms of atmosphere and aspiration towards an ideal, *Parfum exotique* must be grouped with *La Vie antérieure* and *La Géante* which are also dream-phantasies and imaginary journeys in time and space. In *Parfum exotique* both the journey and the destination give the usual impression of 'volupté calme', of dreamy, languorous, nostalgic serenity, and complete sensuous fulfilment. Here, as in *La Géante*, there is no pain, unless it be the delicate one that attaches to dreams of what is not. There is the familiar energy present in the human-beings encountered by the poet, and the familiar passivity in the manner in which the poet himself is drawn along without effort amongst these sights, sounds and odours. The sonnet ends, like *Correspondances*, 'inside' the poet's mind with a mingling of sensations that frequently accompanies realization of the emotional ideal.

La Chevelure, one of the poems added to the second edition, forms a transition between *Parfum exotique* and Poem XXIV. The theme is similar to that of the previous poem: expansion of the sensibility under the influence of the scent of the woman's hair becomes a voyage in space and the destination is again exotic. But the tone of dreamy nostalgia and 'volupté calme' changes to one of controlled triumphant passion. The poet is no longer passively carried along on the tide of sensation; he is very much in command of the situation. The dreamy 'Je vois se dérouler . . .' of *Parfum exotique* gives place to the energetic, passionate, masterful exclamations of *La Chevelure*: 'Je la veux agiter . . .', 'J'irai là-bas . . .', 'Je plongerai ma tête . . .'

The same triumphant energy is present in some of the splendid images and audacious analogies which the rhythm itself sustains:

> Fortes tresses, soyez la houle qui m'enlève!
>
> · · ·
>
> Un port retentissant où mon âme peut boire
> A grand flots le parfum, le son et la couleur;
> Où les vaisseaux, glissant dans l'or et dans la moire,
> Ouvrent leurs vastes bras pour embrasser la gloire
> D'un ciel pur où frémit l'éternelle chaleur.

The very use of this five-line stanza with its extra line, gives the same impression of an inspiration which is stronger than usual, the impression of *souffle*.

Lastly the poem is more passionate in the sense that the poet stays closer to the source of his inspiration and ecstasy. He repeatedly renews its strength by returning to the woman herself. The change is surely significant. In the following

poems the woman herself takes the centre of the stage. She
ceases to be a means of attaining an imaginary aesthetic ideal.
She herself becomes the sexual ideal, with curious consequences.

The next three poems, XXIV, XXV and XXVI (*Sed non
satiata*), record the first descent into evil. They show a
progression from a love that is linked with and subordinated
to artistic ecstasy, to a sensual love that is linked with feelings
of disgust and hate.

The first stanza of Poem XXIV, *Je t'adore à l'égal de la
voûte nocturne*, is written in a conventional tone of adoration,
though a peculiarity of this poet may be noticed in the fact
that an element of beauty in the beloved is sadness ('O vase
de tristesse'). The other element which fits the analogy established between the woman and the 'voûte nocturne' (or
the moon—it is not clear which it is), is her inaccessibility,
and that appears highly conventional, at least at first sight.
All the more striking, therefore, is the second stanza with its
mingling of emotional opposites:

> Je m'avance à l'attaque, et je grimpe aux assauts,
> Comme après un cadavre un choeur de vermisseaux,

Sensual desire and disgust at sensual desire are both expressed
in these two lines.

> Et je chéris, ô bête implacable et cruelle!
> Jusqu'à cette froideur par où tu m'es plus belle.

Contempt and hatred mingle with desire in the concluding
lines which add two more elements to the beauty of the
beloved: cruelty and coldness. The sequel makes it clear that

they are not to be understood in the sense which they have in Renaissance love-poetry.

This stanza reveals in miniature the pattern of the architecture in the following poems, expressing, as they do, alternating attitudes of love and hate, desire and disgust, a defiant acceptance of sin and a horrified recoil from sin. The tragedy is narrated, not in terms of incidents, but in terms of an analysis both of the qualities in the woman which attract and repel the poet-hero, and of his own varying reactions of attraction and repulsion.

Poem XXV repeats the charge of cruelty made against the woman and extends it to woman in general. To it is added the charge of impurity. Woman is regarded as 'la reine des péchés' and here disgust and hate dominate the poet's attitude.

In Poem XXVI, on the other hand, he affirms in unmistakable terms the attraction which this 'reine des péchés' can hold for him even when he envisages her in all her libertine sensuality and sinfulness. It is here that the reader may begin to realize that the qualities of cruelty and coldness to which the poet has referred have nothing to do with modesty or virtue. They appear to be due to a fundamental incapacity for the feelings of tenderness and sympathy which are part of normal human love. The black Venus is presented as a creature without a heart, who can offer her lover nothing but the crudest of sensual pleasures and who is completely lacking in the sense of sin which the poet himself possesses to an abnormally high degree. In the mood expressed by Poem XXV the poet is horrified and disgusted, both by the woman for being what she is, and with himself for finding her attractive. And he is all the more horrified because, in moods

such as that which is expressed in *Sed non satiata*, her evil
and his own repulsion are important elements in the overall
attraction which she exerts. She is no longer merely an artistic
ideal; she is no longer merely a sexual ideal in the normal sense
of the word; she has already become an ideal of vice, a source
of the pleasurable thrill that is due to the mingling of feelings
of repulsion and pain with those of desire, and is characteristic
of the sado-masochist. Marcel Ruff has rightly recalled, in
connection with these poems, 'la célèbre formule de *Fusées*:
"Moi, je dis: la volupté unique et suprême de l'amour gît dans
la certitude de faire le mal" '.[1] But Ruff greatly underrates
the importance of this development for the architecture,
when he suggests that in this cycle 'le bien l'emporte sur le
mal'. The poet-hero has begun to enjoy what Baudelaire
calls, in his essay on *Tannhäuser* (which reads in places like a
commentary on his own intentions in *Les Fleurs du Mal*):
'les délices du crime'.[2] The poet-hero resembles Tannhäuser
in that, 'saturé de délices énervantes, (il) *aspire à la douleur*! cri
sublime que tous les critiques jurés admireraient dans Corneille,
mais qu'aucun ne voudra peut-être voir dans Wagner'.[3] The
poet of *Bénédiction* is indeed aspiring to a satanic form of 'la
douleur'. And he will need no journey to the Pope in Rome
to be informed of 'le caractère irréparable de son crime', to
make him feel 'le sentiment presque ineffable, tant il est
terrible, de la joie dans la damnation', and to persuade him to
seek once again 'les grâces de l'enfer auprès de sa diabolique
épouse'.[4]

---

[1] *Op. cit.*, p. 108.   [2] AR, p. 222.   [3] *Ibid.*, p. 223.

[4] *Ibid.*, p. 226. Albert Feuillerat forgets this poem when he suggests (with
reference to *Le Possédé*) that the 'caractère démoniaque' of this love is a
peculiarity of the second edition (*op. cit.*, p. 294).

This is the development of which *Sed non satiata* marks the true beginning. The imagery of the poem is appropriately infernal and even the very doubtful poetic taste of the analogy 'Je ne suis pas le Styx pour t'embrasser neuf fois', is not out of keeping with the mood of the poem—a highly ambiguous mood, since the plaintive plea for pity covers the harsh iconoclastic joy of an 'aspiration à la douleur' which is no less insatiable in its way than the appetite of the 'démon'. The final analogy established between the poet and Proserpine has given rise to much speculation. Jacques Crépet and Enid Starkie have seen in it a possible suggestion that Jeanne Duval was a Lesbian,[1] but the context ('Pour briser ton courage et te mettre aux abois') surely contradicts the idea as far as the poem is concerned. Proserpine appears to be merely a symbol of purity which serves the additional purpose of identifying the black Venus with Pluto, the Classical Satan.

The poet's descent into the ideal of vice does not follow a perfectly regular curve. After the conscious acceptance of sin in *Sed non satiata*, there follow two poems which reveal less sombre and more specifically artistic aspects of the ideal of the black Venus. In poem XXVII, which ranks with the finest poems in the cycle, a number of analogies are established to link the moral coldness with certain of her physical attributes. The first of these provides the content of the two quatrains and it can only be described as 'rhythm'. The rhythm of her movement is compared first with the swaying movement of the snake, which seems physically attached to the waving wand of the charmer, then with the rhythm of undulating

---

[1] FM (Crépet), p. 344 and *Les Fleurs du Mal*, edited by Enid Starkie, Oxford, Basil Blackwell, 1947, p. 203.

desert-sands and the undulating sea. Snakes, sands and seas are all 'cold' in the sense that they seem devoid of feeling, 'insensibles à l'humaine souffrance'. All therefore prepare the revelation of the moral coldness of the beautiful woman. The second aspect of her physical attraction, which provides the content of the tercets, is that of glitter or brilliance, related particularly to her eyes. It is the glitter of sexless, sterile, mineral things. It can be found in the earlier images of the sea, the sand, the eyes of the snake, as well as in the precious metals, precious stones, and the 'astre inutile' referred to in the lines which relate it directly to the moral coldness—'la froide majesté' of the sterile woman.

In this poem the poet is clearly attracted to this strange unnatural beauty. Both the physical appearance of coldness and the moral coldness make the woman 'plus belle' (cf. Poem XXIV) in the eyes of the poet for reasons that are not hard to explain. In the first place the absence of tender emotions associated with maternity and love gives to the woman an artificial quality as opposed to naturalness, a bizarre, enigmatic quality, an air of mystery, that are well brought out in the lines of the first tercet:

> Et dans cette nature étrange et symbolique
> Où l'ange inviolé se mêle au sphinx antique …

This same cold inscrutability is also connected with Baudelaire's ideal of the dandy. There is a passage in *Fusées* presenting a scene from a projected novel, possibly the one with the title of *La Maîtresse vierge*,[1] which illustrates the point. The scene describes a reconciliation between lovers, and in refer-

[1] JOP, III, p. 15.

ring to the woman, who is clearly modelled on Jeanne Duval, Baudelaire speaks of 'son dandysme de femme froide'.[1] The black Venus is another female dandy and this is a further reason why the poet—at least in this mood—finds her so attractive. Lastly, when the idea of sterility is insisted on, as it is in the last two lines of the sonnet, this same coldness in the woman acquires a touch of pathos, a faint suggestion of 'le Malheur', thanks to the suggestion that she is destined to go through life without knowing what it is to give the warmth of life or love. All these attributes, in this poem and others, are presented as elements in the attraction which the black Venus holds for the poet. But in other moods, as preceding poems have shown, her coldness and consequent 'cruelty', her complete inability to give the tenderness that converts a sexual relationship into love, may be seen in conjunction with her sensuality and lasciviousness and may excite either the poet's contempt, disgust and hatred which is the form of Spleen appropriate to the ideal of sexual vice, or the sado-masochistic desire and excitement which is the ideal of sexual vice itself.

Poem XXVIII, *Le Serpent qui danse*, is linked by its title with the preceding poem, and by its content with all the less sombre and more aesthetically pleasing aspects of the ideal of the black Venus, particularly those envisaged in *Parfum exotique* and *La Chevelure*. By contrast, the next three poems (the next four, if one includes the banned poem *Le Léthé*) carry the reader back into the realms of vice and tragedy.

It is difficult to agree with Barbey d'Aurevilly and Maurice Barrès that *La Charogne* is a poem in which the realism is contained and conquered by a pure idealism or 'spiritualism'. The

[1] JOP, II, p. 72.

ely writing flat poetry in order to underline from the start
the cruelly ironic mood of the poem. The same technique may
be employed in the simile of the third stanza and again in the
last two lines of stanza four where even the rhythm is impossible:

> La puanteur était si forte, que sur l'herbe
> Vous crûtes vous évanouir.

But whether or not the bad poetry is deliberate, the opening
invocation to the beloved undoubtedly has the effect of identifying her with the rest of her sex in the simile given in line one
of stanza two ('Les jambes en l'air comme une femme lub-
rique'), and hence with the carcass itself, in a way that is
deliberately and disgustingly insulting Nor is it only the
woman who is insulted, but love also, for love is similarly
identified with lubricity, physical decay and death. The same
identification is made in the last and most 'idealistic' stanza by
means of an image which is in such extraordinarily bad taste
that it must surely be designed to be so. The worms are
promoted to the status of the rivals of the human lover.
Poem XXIV expressed the idea as a simile; here, it is clearly
suggested:

> Alors, ô ma beauté! dites à la vermine
> Qui vous mangera de baisers,
> Que j'ai gardé la forme et l'essence divine
> De mes amours décomposés!

A claim of the kind made in the two concluding lines is, by
tradition, illustrated and proved by the poem in which it is
made. What is there in the poem that could illustrate and prove
it? If we take the claim seriously, the answer must lie, and lie

exclusively, in the epithets applied to the beloved. They are: 'âme', 'étoile de mes yeux', 'soleil de ma nature', 'mon ange et ma passion', 'la reine des grâces', 'ma beauté'. And when they are examined in this light, they may indeed appear to denote an effort to extract an 'essence divine'. But their poetic and philosophic effect must be weighed against that of the identification of the beloved and love with the 'charogne' and its cohorts of assorted 'vermine', aided and abetted by the bitch (another graceful compliment to the sex?) which is disturbed at its meal. It must be weighed against the extraordinary degree of sympathetic understanding and self-sacrificing heroism which the poet—and idealistic commentators—confidently expect of the beloved: for the sake of a dubious immortality as one of his 'amours décomposés' (the plural and the witty play on abstract and concrete meanings are both significant), she is presumably expected to share his enthusiasm for her role in the 'victory' to be won over death by the human spirit, by love, and of course the poetic genius of her lover, as easily consoled as he is idealistic. In the light of these harsh realities and curious implications, every one of the epithets applied to the beloved can appear as platitudinous and cruelly ironic. It will then be evident that the 'forme' and 'essence divine' which the poet will retain on the woman's death, will differ very little from the corrupt substance submitted to the caresses of the worms—all, in short, that he has truly *represented* in the poem.

To the extent that the poet loves the woman, and there is every reason to suppose that he does, the epithets applied to her are sincere and will conserve part of her essence. If we regard her as 'une fleur du Mal', they will conserve the essence

of the 'fleur'. But there remains the 'Mal'—and the fact that
we are faced with an ambiguity of meaning in the poem that
cannot be other than deliberate. Its very existence tells against
the purely idealistic interpretation and argues strongly in
favour of the ironic. To take the poem as a sincere expression
of love and idealism is to do it not a service but a disservice, by
rendering it ludicrously inept in conception and execution
alike. Yet it will have considerable poetic value if the mood is
interpreted as one of amorous hate, controlled by a savage
yet caressing irony. The poet loves, but in this mood he is in
revolt against his love and the beloved. He does not, as he did
in Poem XXV, take revenge on the woman in the name of a
high moral ideal. Having sunk much lower himself, he does
so by indulging his taste for the horrible and his mental
sadism. Revenge becomes a source of the same corrupt excitement as does surrender to a sexual desire that is felt as
sinful. The Ideal itself is here being degraded to the level of a
Spleen which differs from the Ideal only in being felt as depression instead of excitement: the nature of the feelings,
hatred, disgust, repulsion, may be virtually the same in both.

It is a milder form of Spleen which dictates the following
poem, *De profundis clamavi*. After the sadistic revolt against
the black Venus comes an appeal to her pity and a renewed
affirmation of love. A similar contrast occurs in the first
edition in the poems addressed to the white Venus. The out-
rageously sadistic *A celle qui est trop gaie* preceded *Réversibilité* in which the poet pleads for the lady's prayers. This
second example, together with the suggestions of the original
title (*La Béatrix*) and the fact that Baudelaire frequently
mingles the sacred and the profane—here for a good and

themselves and others untold moral and material suffering—
from which they can find or can *want* no escape save a return
to the vice which has become their corrupt ideal. This is
precisely the situation of the poet-hero with regard to his
own sado-masochistic vice which consists of finding pleasurable excitement in a sexual relationship, not so much for the
sake of sexual pleasure itself, as *because* he recognizes it as
sinful. That is why his sense of sin, horror, disgust and hate
do not force him to break the bond. Feelings of repulsion
though they are, they nevertheless give the bond its unbreak-
able strength. They make him pay a terrible price for his
corrupt pleasure in the genuine anguish expressed in this
poem. They none the less force him to return to his 'vampire',
if not for an orgy of horrified excitement, at least for the escape
of bestial oblivion that is envisaged in *Le Léthé*. These two
poems are the first to develop the important theme of
L'Héautontimorouménos, the idea that the sinner is his own
tormentor.

Poems XXXII to XXXIV have a common theme which
was neatly introduced in the first edition by the reference in the
last lines of *Le Léthé* to the breast of the black Venus 'Qui
n'a jamais emprisonné de coeur'. It is the theme of heartless-
ness, coldness and cruelty, revived here not in any mood of
satanic frenzy or Spleen, but with a reflective regret that is
almost tender. This is particularly true of Poem XXXII in
which the poet seeks forgetfulness 'près d'une affreuse Juive'
but cannot efface the memory of the black Venus—

> Car j'eusse avec ferveur baisé ton noble corps,
> Et depuis tes pieds frais jusqu'à tes noires tresses
> Déroulé le trésor des profondes caresses,

Si, quelque soir, d'un pleur obtenu sans effort
Tu pouvais, seulement, ô reine des cruelles!
Obscurcir la splendeur de tes froides prunelles.

For the first time in the cycle, we find here a suggestion of a love, on the part of the poet, which includes tenderness or the need for tenderness. It will reappear in a more definite form in *Le Balcon*, and no doubt corresponds to an aspect of the relationship between Baudelaire and Jeanne Duval. On the other hand it would be unwise to attach so much importance to it as to let it conjure up visions of a peaceful domesticity that might have been, for one must always reckon with the Baudelaire for whom 'la candeur et la bonté sont dégoûtantes',[1] and remember that to long for what is not, does not necessarily imply a real desire that what is not should be. The coldness which he seems to regret here (the precautionary word 'seems' is necessary in view of the fact that he can enjoy 'la douleur') can combine with the woman's sensuality to make her an object of horrified, consciously sinful desire. The fact remains however that the tone of tenderness adds considerably to the richness of the symphony.

The same absence of tender feelings in the woman offers the most likely explanation of *Remords posthume*, a poem which is distantly related to *La Charogne*, though more subdued and more subtle. The black Venus is to all intents and purposes buried alive in this sonnet, since she is credited with consciousness and fear even though depicted in her grave. And the idea is developed with a deceptively soft and caressing cruelty. For example, the expression of endearment in the

[1] CORR, I, p. 331.

first line, 'ma belle ténébreuse', serves the added purpose of suggesting the woman's dark beauty and thereby fitting her for her future black marble monument and her equally dark 'alcôve et manoir'. The same caressing cruelty is present in the idea of the 'charmant nonchaloir' which will prevent her from moving beneath the weight that oppresses her 'poitrine peureuse'. The ending is deliberately enigmatic:

> ... Que vous sert, courtisane imparfaite,
> De n'avoir pas connu ce que pleurent les morts?

Interpreted in the light of previous poems, this could mean that what the woman has never known, and what the dead weep for, are the feelings implied by the tears that *she* cannot shed—tenderness, sympathy, love. She is a 'courtisane imparfaite' because even a courtesan should have a heart. The woman is emotionally cold, like the cat to which she is compared in Poem XXXIV.

Out of the remaining five poems of the cycle, three were written specially for the second edition, *Duellum*, *Le Possédé* and *Un Fantôme*. Two of the three are poems of 'l'amour maudit' and have the effect of strengthening the end of the adventure by insisting on the poet's vice.

The best commentary on *Duellum* is to be found in Baudelaire's essay on *Tannhäuser* in the passage dealing with the overture to the opera:

Aux titillations sataniques d'un vague amour succèdent bientôt des entraînements, des éblouissements, des cris de victoire, des gémissements de gratitude, et puis des hurlements de férocité, des reproches de victimes et des hosannas impies de sacrificateurs, comme si la barbarie devait toujours prendre sa place dans le drame de l'amour, et la jouissance charnelle conduire, par une logique satanique inéluctable, aux délices du crime.[1]

Placed as it is between *Duellum* and *Le Possédé*, *Le Balcon* provides yet another of the striking contrasts of which Baudelaire is so fond. In retrospect, if not in reality, he attains to a love based on tenderness and sympathy, and, in doing so, recaptures 'l'atmosphère des grands jours'. *Le Possédé*, on the other hand, reaffirms the poet-hero's vice and puts the finishing touch to the tragic aspect of the adventure with the black Venus. The attitude expressed here is one of complete acceptance of the beloved including the evil that she represents ('O mon cher Belzébuth je t'adore!'). Baudelaire's probable intention in this poem and in the entire cycle of the black Venus is admirably expressed in still another passage of the essay on *Tannhäuser*:

Tout à l'heure, en essayant de décrire la partie voluptueuse de l'ouverture, je priais le lecteur de détourner sa pensée des hymnes vulgaires de l'amour, tels que les peut concevoir un galant en belle humeur; en effet, il n'y a ici rien de trivial; c'est plutôt le débordement d'une nature énergique; qui verse dans le mal toutes les forces dues à la culture du bien; c'est l'amour effréné, immense, chaotique, élevé jusqu'à la hauteur d'une contre-religion, d'une religion satanique … Nous ne voyons pas ici un libertin ordinaire, voltigeant *de belle en belle*, mais l'homme général, universel, vivant morganatiquement avec l'idéal absolu de la volupté, avec … l'indestructible et irrésistible Vénus.[2]

The last two poems of the cycle end it on a note of tragic pathos instead of violence, as the black Venus fades out of the poet's life and is veiled by the past. *Un Fantôme*, written for

[1] AR, p. 222.   [2] *Ibid.*, pp. 223-4.

the second edition, is designed to echo (much as *Le Serpent qui danse* does earlier) some of the principal aspects of the ideal of the black Venus which have helped to enrich, rather than degrade, his life and his poetry. In '*Je te donne ces vers . . .*' Baudelaire deliberately sets out to rival the long line of great poets who have promised immortality to their loves, and he surely succeeds as much in the two quatrains where the stately movement, vocabulary and images have a Renaissance grandeur, as in the tercets where the 'Être maudit . . .' at once sounds the note that Baudelaire has made his own. What is indeed extraordinary is the manner in which the maledictory theme in the poem has been harmoniously combined with the traditional 'Ave' into a fraternal farewell which is, by virtue of the serenely tragic honesty and dignity to which it attains, a true poetic redemption of the sordid, sinful past, and worthy to rank with the finest poetry of its kind.

From the point of view of the architecture, the same suggestion of malediction should serve to remind the reader that there is no happy ending to this cycle, no facile 'forgiving and forgetting'. Evil has been done which cannot be undone and the following cycle shows its effects.

VI

'PLAISIRS CLANDESTINS'

I. THE WHITE VENUS (POEMS XL–XLVIII)

THE traditional interpretation of the cycle of poems addressed by Baudelaire to Mme Sabatier, invites us to regard it as an attempt at spiritual redemption through the guiding influence and intercession of the white Venus. Whilst accepting this view to the extent of referring to the cycle as 'le cycle de l'amour spirituel', Marcel Ruff makes certain reservations as to the biographical truth of the interpretation. 'On a peine à croire', he remarks, 'qu'un esprit aussi lucide ait pu se faire illusion sur une belle et bonne fille dont la "chair spirituelle" connaissait, il ne pouvait l'ignorer, toutes les faiblesses de la matière. Il est fort possible qu'il ait simplement fixé sur elle le rêve d'un amour parfait, c'est-à-dire échappant à la malédiction du péché. On ne saurait dire qu'il refuse l'incarnation, mais il ne la subit qu'avec répugnance, il aspire à s'en évader'.[1] The biographical basis of this cycle does indeed present a far greater problem than that of the cycle of Jeanne Duval or the black Venus, and the probability that most of the poems were written for Mme Sabatier to read must be taken into account in any attempt to assess their role in the architecture of the volume.

[1] *Op. cit.*, p. 109.

To deal with biographical probability in the first place, Marcel Ruff is surely correct when he concludes that neither the letters nor the poems point to a genuine 'passion amoureuse' on the part of Baudelaire. Such as it was, the affair existed principally in the imagination of the poet and he was apparently content that it should remain there. On the other hand it would be advisable to qualify the statement that Baudelaire '(a) simplement fixé sur elle le rêve d'un amour parfait, c'est-à-dire échappant à la malédiction du péché'. The qualification would affect both the idea that the association of the dream with Mme Sabatier was purely accidental or arbitrary, and the idea that the dream was one of a perfectly pure love.

There was undoubtedly some foundation for this dream though it is obviously not the foundation that appears in the more exalted poems on the theme of spiritual salvation. Marcel Ruff goes so far as to suggest that Baudelaire may have been influenced by 'les étranges théories des Enfantin et des Flora Tristan, selon lesquelles la femme, plus ou moins intermédiaire entre l'homme et Dieu, tiendrait un rôle de messie'.[1] Although Baudelaire at one period of his life was prepared to have a certain Mariette as 'intercesseur' along with Edgar Poe,[2] it is not easy to associate him with this particular form of heresy, despite the example set him by Gérard de Nerval. If he was unlikely to be blind to the less moral aspects of Mme Sabatier's good-nature, he, of all men, was even less likely to accept as a theological doctrine the idea that woman could be the saviour of man. And even if we ignore this improbability, we are still left with the awkward task of explaining why, of

[1] *Ibid.*, p. 109.   [2] JOP, II, p. 84.

all women, Baudelaire should have chosen Mme Sabatier on whom to fix his dream.

A more satisfactory answer to these problems may be found if we begin to look for it on the psychological rather than on the religious and spiritual level. Time and again in the poems, it is made clear that what Mme Sabatier means to Baudelaire is, above all, psychological health as opposed to psychological sickness. Whatever her morals, whatever her attitude to religion and the state of her soul, Mme Sabatier was evidently a creature of light and joy who possessed happiness as a birthright and was glad to give of it generously. For her, pleasure was measured by freedom from pain, in herself and those around her, and in that sense her nature was perfectly pure. Such psychological purity, though strictly speaking distinct from moral and spiritual purity, is none the less the natural basis for virtue. And it is quite possible that Baudelaire saw in it the antithesis of the vice—the predominantly imaginative sado-masochistic vice—which he undoubtedly shared with the poet-hero of *Les Fleurs du Mal*. This psychological purity, this uncomplicated naive capacity for pure pleasure, was the source of the attraction which Mme Sabatier exerted upon his better nature. It pointed to the direction in which he himself would need to return if his future were to be one of light and not of darkness. So, to provide an added source of strength for his good resolutions, he made Mme Sabatier herself the recipient of his anonymous confidences and confessions. By one in the toils of a predominantly religious form of sado-masochistic vice, Mme Sabatier's capacity for a healthy pagan joy might easily be associated with a state of spiritual purity and grace. Such hyperbole would in any case come naturally to a poet of the period, particularly one who admired Poe, and the fact that he had already used it in the mysterious letter to Marie,[1] renders its sincerity somewhat suspect in the case of Mme Sabatier. The first sign of it can be seen in *Réversibilité*, the poem which followed the initial confession of sado-masochistic vice contained in *A celle qui est trop gaie*. But it was not until the beginning of 1854, more than a year later, that Baudelaire fully developed the theme of spiritual salvation to be won through 'l'ange gardien, la Muse et la Madone'. As will presently be suggested, the idea may have had from the start an unpleasantly ironic aspect, but in so far as Baudelaire was genuinely in sympathy with Apollonie, it was a deliberate affectation, an 'enfantillage', less surprising than it seems when attempts are made to use it as the basis for an explanation of the relationship between Baudelaire and Mme Sabatier. The explanation already given seems to accord far better with the eminently reasonable and sober remarks made by Baudelaire himself in the letter of August 18, 1857, written when the affair terminated: 'Supposez un amalgame de rêverie, de sympathie, de respect, avec mille enfantillages pleins de sérieux, vous aurez un à peu près de ce quelque chose très sincère que je ne me sens pas capable de mieux définir ... Vous êtes plus qu'une image rêvée et chérie, vous êtes une *superstition*'.[2]

Amongst the 'enfantillages pleins de sérieux' may figure those elements in the letters and poems alike which suggest

[1] CORR, I, pp. 99–104. Cf. in *La Fanfarlo*, Samuel Cramer's sonnets for Madame de Cosmelly 'où il louait en style mystique sa beauté de Béatrix, sa voix, la pureté angélique de ses yeux, la chasteté de sa démarche, etc.' (PA, pp. 262–3.)

[2] CORR, II, p. 88.

that the dream was not one of a perfectly pure relationship 'échappant à la malédiction du péché'. Their nature may be summed up by saying that both letters and poems are designed to show that the poet is very conscious indeed, and conscious in a definitely sensual and sexual way, of the physical charms of the chosen Madonna. And it is unlikely that either the expressed feelings or the salaciously ambiguous manner of their expression would be classed as free from the taint of sin by Baudelaire, for all that they were a commonplace form of flattery in the circle of 'la Présidente'.[1] They therefore conflict with his supposed aim of psychological convalescence as much as with that of spiritual salvation, and require some further explanation. They may be referred in part to a kind of inverted 'pudeur' in the poet himself, for the greater the degree of sincerity that entered into the desire to use Mme Sabatier as an aid to reform, the stronger would be his impulse to mask his 'weakness' by indulging in the conventional form of flattery which consisted of hinting at a baser aim. Such hints would moreover fit in with his perfectly genuine aim to reform through confession of his vice to the Madonna herself. But the whole affair would be complicated—and complicated in a manner that must surely have appealed very strongly to one of Baudelaire's perversely ironic temperament —by the fact that the vice which was quite sincerely confessed to Mme Sabatier in the character of an ideal of purity, was excited and encouraged by the same Mme Sabatier in the character—the equally appropriate character—of the ideal of sexual vice, 'l'indestructible et irrésistible Vénus'.[2] Nor could

[1] Cf. the letter of May 8, 1854. (CORR, I, p. 276.)
[2] AR, p. 224.

it be said that the hints at baser aims and sexual desires were any less sincere than Baudelaire's expressions of admiration for the lady's temperamental charm and health or his professions of his eagerness to reform. Baudelaire clearly did not want a liaison in *fact*, but a desire is no less sincere and no less real for being confined to the imagination. Nor, finally, could it be said with certainty, in face of such complex motivation, which of the possible motives was the dominant one— the desire for reform, or the desire to indulge in a stimulating and not entirely imaginary adventure (the letters and poems were really sent) with an extremely charming woman who appealed as much to Baudelaire's worst instincts as she did to his best. One can only conclude that the dream was both pure and impure; that it promised satisfaction for Baudelaire's vice as well as for his impulse towards virtue and reform. And one can therefore understand how, in retrospect, he could come to see it in a more ironic and cynical light than when it was in progress. The irony of the adventure did not lie merely in the fact that the attempt at reform was doomed to failure before it started. It lay in the fact that it was started as much in order that it should fail, as in order that it should succeed. Satan, too, might seem to Baudelaire to have given it his blessing.

In his book, *Baudelaire et la Présidente*,[1] François Porché interprets the affair in a conventional way by assuming that the pure Platonic love with which Baudelaire set out on the adventure was gradually corrupted and converted into *l'amour maudit*. But he treats *A celle qui est trop gaie* as if it were the last poem sent to Mme Sabatier, not the first. And he forgets that Baudelaire's is by no means a simple nature.

[1] Paris, Gallimard, 1959, and Geneva, Ed. du Milieu du Monde, 1941.

It is not perhaps irrelevant to recall at this point what Baudelaire had said in 1851 about the effect of hashish on the emotion of love: 'Dans ce suprême état, l'amour, chez les esprits tendres et artistiques, prend les formes les plus singulières et se prête aux combinaisons les plus baroques. Un libertinage effréné peut se mêler à un sentiment de paternité ardente et affectueuse'.[1] As it stands, the remark presents an analogy with feelings expressed in the Marie Daubrun cycle rather than in that of Mme Sabatier. But only the word 'paternité' need be altered. It is not of course suggested that Baudelaire's affection for Mme Sabatier is to be explained by his addiction to a drug! As he himself insists, a drug merely exaggerates natural tendencies, and amongst those on which he dwells in his descriptions of the effect of drugs, we are likely to find some which fit his own 'esprit tendre et artistique'. No less pertinent are the passages in *Le Poëme du Haschish* in which Baudelaire analyses the satanic pleasure that may enter into remorse and repentance: 'nous avons vu que, contrefaisant d'une manière sacrilège le sacrement de la pénitence, à la fois pénitent et confesseur (the sacrilege may be even greater when the confessor is a Mme Sabatier), il s'était donné une facile absolution, ou, pis encore, qu'il avait tiré de sa condamnation une nouvelle pâture pour son orgueil. Maintenant, de la contemplation de ses rêves et de ses projets de vertu, il conclut à son aptitude pratique à la vertu . . . Il confond complètement le rêve avec l'action, et son imagination s'échauffant de plus en plus devant le spectacle enchanteur de sa propre nature corrigée et idéalisée . . . il finit par décréter son apothéose en ces termes nets et simples, qui contiennent pour lui tout un monde

[1] PA, p. 226.

d'abominables jouissances: "*Je suis le plus vertueux de tous les hommes*".[1] We cannot say with certainty that the poems were not actually written with the ambiguity of repentance in mind, and written as much for *Les Fleurs du Mal* as for Mme Sabatier herself.

There can be little doubt that the ironic point of view was the one which Baudelaire wished the reader to adopt towards the cycle of the white Venus in *Les Fleurs du Mal*. Not only is the theme of sensuality and vice clearly expressed in connection with the white Venus herself by *Tout entière*, *A celle qui est trop gaie* (in the first edition) and *Le Flacon*, but a poem, *Semper eadem*, was specially written for the second edition to present the cycle as a form of 'mensonge'. This interpretation does not in any way harm the architecture; it actually strengthens its psychological basis. From the dramatic and psychological point of view, a wholehearted attempt at spiritual regeneration through a pure Platonic love would be quite effective at this point in the volume, if a trifle obvious. But it would be no less effective, much less naive, and much more in keeping with the uncompromisingly tragic outlook of the author, if this adventure were designed to show that the poet-hero is already so far at the mercy of his vice and so far beyond redemption, that he can be tempted to 'contrefaire le sacrement de la pénitence' as much in order to indulge his vice as to savour in imagination the joys of a purity that can no longer be his and that he might not even want except at the feet of the white Venus.

Semper eadem was not amongst the poems sent to Mme Sabatier nor was it included in the 1857 edition. It was either

[1] *Ibid.*, pp. 59–60.

chosen, or specially written, to commence the cycle in the second edition, thus displacing *Tout entière*. It establishes a strong opposition between the temperaments of the poet and a lady who cannot possibly be confused with the sombre 'grand ange' of the preceding poem and the preceding cycle. Wishing, it would seem, to share her joy with the poet-hero, she finds an obstacle in his 'tristesse étrange' and is naturally curious. His attitude towards her is a strange mixture of tenderness, faint contempt for her naïveté, and a certain envy for the uncomplicated joy that accompanies it. Yet it is not precisely that joy that he wants to share with her. He will not let her try to dispel his gloom which is, he says, as natural to him and as inevitable as her joy is to her. All that he wants, all that his temperament will let him want, is the diversion referred to in the enigmatic final tercet:

> Laissez, laissez mon coeur s'enivrer d'un *mensonge*,
> Plonger dans vos beaux yeux comme dans un beau songe,
> Et sommeiller longtemps à l'ombre de vos cils!

There is, then, to be no profound change in him. He does not want it, or regards it as impossible. Without making any genuine effort to escape from his habitual gloom and all it may imply, he will indulge in the sophisticated pleasure of pretending to be cured of his Spleen by his charming companion, hoping perhaps to enjoy the best of both their worlds. On the other hand, the poem does not make it clear that the lie and the dream will necessarily be limited to the pretence of sharing a naive joy. The lie and the dream might be almost anything suggested by the 'beaux yeux'—even a personal drama of psychological convalescence and spiritual redemption in which the lady will be invited to play a role that she could scarcely understand. The meaning of the final tercet is indeed so vague as to make one wonder whether its principal purpose is not to introduce the following poems rather than to conclude this one. It certainly invites us to see the cycle as a whole in terms of this dream indulged in before the eyes which mirror the light and sweetness of the soul of the white Venus. And it warns us (even to the extent of italicizing the word 'mensonge') not to take too seriously the idealized image of himself which the poet will also see in their depths and will duly record in his poems.

The same warning is repeated in a deliberately ambiguous form in *Tout entière*, the poem which, in the first edition, was presumably designed to deliver it unaided. The 'mensonge' consists in the poet's apparently successful effort to persuade himself (if not the demon who visits him and raises the matter) that his love for the white Venus is not rooted in sensual, sexual and therefore sinful desire. Even were it not preceded by any warning, the poem would still appear so crudely suggestive as to mean something other than its ostensible meaning, and the mere fact that the matter is raised at all weakens the case for the poet's innocence. What makes the case collapse altogether, as of course it is intended to do, is the poet's all too tactful reply to the demon that amidst so much harmonious beauty no special feature can be preferred. Despite the remarkable charm of the last two stanzas, which are perfectly innocent in themselves, one remains aware that the demon (Sensuality, by name) has no less reason than the lady herself to be satisfied at the sweeping nature of the compliment which she is paid.

This deliberately transparent 'mensonge' leads on to the greater heights of Platonic love which are reached in the next two poems: *Que diras-tu ce soir ...* and *Le Flambeau vivant*. In the latter poem we may note the reappearance of the image of the 'beaux yeux' which is developed at length in a manner closely modelled on the ending of one of Poe's poems *To Helen*. Derived from the same source is the analogy established between the light of the eyes and the light of the sun, and in following poems this will become an analogy between the white Venus and the sun itself, contrasting effectively with the nocturnal associations of the black Venus.[1] Though they have their place in the architecture, it is not perhaps coincidence that these poems which introduce the theme of 'l'Ange gardien, la Muse et la Madone' and which were amongst the last sent to Mme Sabatier, should also be the least poetically impressive poems of the series.

They were followed in the 1857 edition by the first poem sent by Baudelaire to Mme Sabatier: *A celle qui est trop gaie*. Baudelaire's original intention was clearly to create a strong artistic contrast in moods and to indicate a complexity in his feelings towards the Madonna which would confirm the suggestions of *Tout entière* and constitute a relapse into sado-masochistic vice as well as ordinary sensuality. The fact that the banned poem was not replaced in the second edition by another of similar tone in the same position, may mean that Baudelaire was content to let the cycle read more smoothly and sweetly, no doubt feeling that *Semper eadem* and *Tout*

---

[1] L. J. Austin (*op. cit.*, p. 237) observes that the point is made by Otakar Lévy, in *Baudelaire, son esthétique et sa technique littéraire*, Brno, 1947, pp. 412–13.

entière would suffice to warn the reader that the poet-hero had not really changed. This was certainly the function of *A celle qui est trop gaie* which reveals the hero's vice in an unmistakable form.

The first four stanzas of this poem resemble *Semper eadem* in that they explain the attraction of the ideal of the white Venus without the religious trappings. The attraction lies in her healthy, good-natured, natural gaiety combined with her generous share of good-looks. In the poet's better moods he can apparently surrender to this charm and, in doing so, feel the need for purity in himself and even feel purer himself— a feeling which he renders in terms of religious experience. It is not an altogether uncomplicated pleasure, for self-congratulation and self-abasement go hand in hand, but it is the purest feeling which enters into this complex ideal. In his more characteristic moods of perversity, however, he may choose to feel the woman's healthy joy as an insult to his own sickly gloom, as a form of superiority that is humiliating and not to be borne. As the poem shows, he then revolts against the Madonna (and his own better feelings) and derives pleasurable excitement from thoughts that are sadistic in that pain is inflicted on the woman, and masochistic in so far as the poet horrifies and hurts himself by exhibiting his own cruelty and evil. He is still addicted to the vice which was developed in him during the course of the previous cycle and which expresses itself here in a form that is not as different from the earlier ones as it may seem. The apparent difference is mainly due to the fact that the white Venus is as innocent of evil as the black Venus was (in the poet's eyes) guilty. As a result the poet must supply the evil and suffering himself.

Having been corrupted by a basically evil ideal, he must now adopt a corrupt approach to one that is basically good.

So it is that *A celle qui est trop gaie* reveals the worst aspect which the ideal of the white Venus can assume for the poet. By one of those violent contrasts beloved of Baudelaire, *Réversibilité* reveals the best. Despite the title and the use of the 'Ange', repeated as in a litany, the Madonna-theme with its attendant exaggeration is less obtrusive here than in other poems and the white Venus is again characterized in human terms of 'gaieté', 'bonté', 'santé', 'beauté' and 'bonheur'. The poet himself is in a correspondingly less exalted mood as he confesses to his own 'angoisse', 'haine', 'Fièvres', 'rides', and asks for the lady's prayers. In the first edition, at least, the whole poem acquired added urgency and pathos from its connection with *A celle qui est trop gaie*. This is lost in the second edition, but the poem nevertheless makes the relationship between these two opposite temperaments seem more natural, more understandable and the poet more sympathetically sincere than in other poems.

The same humanizing process is carried a stage further in the lady's own *Confession* which—appropriately enough—follows immediately upon that of the poet. In revealing something of her own secret anguish, the white Venus strengthens the bond of sympathy and quite unconsciously enhances her beauty in the poet's eyes by adding to her joy a precious touch of 'le *Malheur*'.

L'Aube spirituelle restores her to her pedestal and identifies her with dawn and with the sun in preparation, so to speak, for her role in *Harmonie du Soir*, where already she, too, begins to fade into the past. Here in the sad solemnity of an evening that must usher in the night of a future containing death, the poet watches the dying sun and remembers the other sun that still shines in his heart like a monstrance (a synonym for 'ostensoir' is 'soleil'). The poem has been called an 'automatic' and 'over-anthologized' *pastiche*,[1] but anthologies are not always wrong. The fusion of the scenic with the religious imagery, and the fusion of both with the theme of the fear of death and the consoling remembrance of life, light and love, is as perfect as it could be, and considering that the poem is made up of only ten different lines it is as remarkably rich in meaning as it is in verbal music.

Le Flacon is the farewell poem of the cycle and ends it on the note required by the architecture—that of 'l'amour maudit':

> Je serai ton cercueil, aimable pestilence!
> Le témoin de ta force et de ta virulence,
> Cher poison préparé par les anges! liqueur
> Qui me ronge, ô la vie et la mort de mon coeur!

The paradoxes are not a senseless striving for effect but a summing up of the fundamental ambiguity of the whole affair. In so far as condemnation is expressed, it is not condemnation of the white Venus. If she is a poison, it is the poet's vice that makes her so, by the process which he calls, in the title of Poem LXXXI, his 'Alchimie de la Douleur'.

2. THE GREEN-EYED VENUS (POEMS XLIX–LVII)

The cycle of Marie Daubrun or 'la femme aux yeux verts' begins as the cycle of the white Venus ends—with the word 'Poison' to serve as a guide to the general intention. This

[1] P. Mansell-Jones: *Baudelaire*, Cambridge, Bowes and Bowes, 1952, p. 40.

remains the same, even while a certain gradation is apparent, a slight but distinct change of tone. The third cycle of love-poems reveals a more cautious and more disillusioned approach to the ideal of woman. Everywhere present is the consciousness of sin and the knowledge that sin will be paid for in remorseful Spleen. The tone ranges between what Marcel Ruff terms 'une tendresse paternelle ou fraternelle, mais non dépourvue d'une sensualité insidieuse',[1] and the amorous hate of 'l'amour maudit'. But compared with the artistic or carnal ecstasies of the cycle of the black Venus, and the hymns of adoration addressed to the white Venus, the key used here is a minor one and a growing impression of lassitude and disillusionment prepares the transition to the cycle of Spleen.

The centre of the cycle from all points of view is Poem LIII, *L'Invitation au Voyage*. Here the third venture into the ideal of Woman so far succeeds that the poet is once again enabled to escape through the 'porte d'un infini' into still another dream of an ideal existence in a land linked by *correspondances* with the personality of his beloved. He recaptures 'l'atmosphère des grands jours' and feelings of serenity and 'volupté calme' in a poem which marks the end of this most distinguished vein of inspiration save for faint or bitterly ironic echoes of it in later poems.

The poet's immediate answer to *L'Invitation au Voyage* is *L'Irréparable*. In its clear affirmation of a source of constant inner torment, in its absolute negation of hope, the poem is probably the most tragic of all that have been presented up to this point in the volume. It raises very acutely indeed the problem of the poet's nature. The feelings expressed in the

[1] *Op. cit.*, p. 111.

poem are religious and Christian in character, like the imagery itself. The play from which the main images are derived, itself portrayed the victory of a good spirit over Satan. Neither the feeling of remorse, nor that of being damned, can be comprehended unless they are taken to spring from a religious conscience—the same, indeed, that found expression in *Bénédiction* and *Les Phares*. But this fact raises a difficulty that has not perhaps been squarely faced by the majority of commentators. Although remorse is natural to a religious conscience, and although the feeling of damnation may likewise be so, it is not natural that a man should persist in the certainty of damnation without seeking refuge in repentance and the hope of redemption—a hope that religious teaching (not excluding that of Joseph de Maistre) does everything to encourage even in the case of far worse sinners than the poet-hero of *Les Fleurs du Mal* appears to be. There might seem to be some disparity between the gravity of the sins committed and the utter hopelessness of the attitude adopted here and throughout the rest of the volume. Catholic commentators, at least, have not failed to notice the puzzling absence in Baudelaire's work in general of any deep interest in the figure of Christ and even in the doctrine of the redemption of sin.[1] The psychological problem raised here is a literary one also, because the reason for the poet's dogged despair must be clearly understood if the drama is not to lose its logical coherence and universality of interest. It is in essence the problem referred to by L. J. Austin when he remarks on the contradiction between the beginning and end of *Spleen et Idéal*, though the contradiction is so obvious, in

[1] Jean Massin: *op, cit.*, p. 251.

the poems and title alike, that it can hardly be thought to
have escaped the attention of all who have studied the work.[1]
What have not always been clearly brought out are the awkward implications of the apparent contradiction, and this is
the more regrettable because the attempt to explain them could
conceivably clarify the psychology of the poet-hero and with
it the architecture of the volume. The explanation offered in
the present study relates to the very nature of the poet-hero's
vice and can find further support, not only in the extremely
important poems of self-analysis which conclude—and
explain—*Spleen et Idéal*, but also in the poems which follow
L'Irréparable itself.

In the words of Marcel Ruff, the last three poems of this
cycle 'sont d'une sombre violence qui nous ramène à la
condamnation de l'amour entaché de compromis avec la
chair'.[2] The final poem, *A une Madone*, is not however
presented as a condemnation, but as yet another relapse into
a very obvious form of the sado-masochistic vice which is
itself the whole explanation of the poet's inability and positive
unwillingness to reform. Luc Decaunes, reacting against a
widespread tendency to minimize the importance of what is
regarded, with varying degrees of tolerance, as a rather
regrettable aspect of the work, writes as follows: 'Il n'est pas
difficile de voir, dans ce poème, du point de vue psychanalyti-
que, l'éclatante manifestation du complexe sado-masochiste
qui a dominé toute la vie érotique (voire morale et intellec-
tuelle) de Baudelaire ... Tout l'univers mental du poète est
résumé dans *A une Madone*'.[3]

[1] *Op. cit.*, p. 92.   [2] *Op. cit.*, p. 112.
[3] *Charles Baudelaire*, Paris, Seghers, 1952, p. 74.

So, in the poem, having enshrined the green-eyed Venus as another Madonna, the poet finds that his pleasure is not complete. He confirms earlier suggestions of irony and consciously sinful sensuality, by profaning in the second part of the poem what he consecrated in the first—no doubt in order that it might be profaned:

> Enfin, pour compléter ton rôle de Marie
> Et pour mêler l'amour avec la barbarie,
> Volupté noire! des sept Péchés capitaux,
> Bourreau plein de remords, je ferai sept Couteaux
> Bien affilés, et comme un jongleur insensible,
> Prenant le plus profond de ton amour pour cible,
> Je les planterai tous dans ton coeur pantelant,
> Dans ton coeur sanglotant, dans ton coeur ruisselant!

The 'volupté noire' is clearly that '. . . qui gît danِ la certitude de faire le mal', and the 'remords' is proof of the fundamentally masochistic nature of the imaginary sadism. The sadistic 'volupté' depends on awareness of the evil of the act and on sympathy with the victim—that is, on feelings which mingle masochistic pain with sadistic pleasure. It was of course too much to expect that all the 'hypocrites lecteurs' would understand such passages in terms of 'l'optique théâtral' and 'miroirs grossissants' and penetrate to the core of human truth which explains why even the tender-hearted can deliberately hurt the people they love.

The cycle ends with the triumph of 'l'amour maudit' and the poet's vice, which is not by any means limited to the domain of sexual relationships. And inasmuch as the triumph is inevitably followed by Spleen and genuine remorse, this adventure ends, like the others, in failure to find a durable ideal.

This impression was given more forcefully in the first edition by *L'Héautontimorouménos*, which followed *Causerie* and concluded this cycle. In the second edition, *L'Héautontimorouménos* was moved to the end of *Spleen et Idéal* to strengthen the group of poems which analyse the poet's vice, and its place at the end of the Marie Daubrun cycle was taken by the two new poems *Chant d'Automne* and *A une Madone*.

3. THE TRANSITION TO SPLEEN
(POEMS LVIII–LXXIII)

The architecture of the remainder of *Spleen et Idéal* was less carefully planned in the first edition than in the second. The group of Spleen poems was set in the middle of a mixture of poems from the group which now forms the transition to Spleen, from the group of poems of self-analysis, and from what is now the separate book of *Tableaux parisiens*. A trace of that weakness remains in the shape of the poems that separate the cycle of the green-eyed Venus from the cycle of Spleen. First come seven poems addressed to women, but they are clearly different women and the poems have no other feature in common. They are followed by nine poems on a wide variety of subjects, the moon, cats, owls, the poet's pipe, music, a burial, an engraving of a skeleton on horseback, a longing for the grave, and an analogy between hatred and a drunkard with an insatiable thirst. So here again it could be said that the architecture is defective and that Baudelaire has chosen this point in the volume for the insertion of poems that did not fit into his plan. On the other hand, it could be argued that the effect given by these sixteen poems does have significance in the context of the drama. The effect produced is that of an inspiration which becomes more and more haphazard. After the sustained excitement of the previous cycles, these poems seem to reflect a weakening in the concentration and intensity of the poet's inner life. And when one observes that this lack of coherence in the choice of subjects is combined with a certain progression in the mood towards a deepening gloom and unpleasantness, one might justifiably feel that they make an acceptable transition to the hopeless apathy and depression of the poems of Spleen properly so called.

VII

THE HELL OF SPLEEN

1. SPLEEN (POEMS LXXIV–LXXX)

THE Spleen expressed in this group of poems is of a far more
virulent kind than that which appears in the exposition of the
tragedy. Having consciously indulged in the 'postulation vers
Satan', the poet-hero must feel as genuine suffering the effect
of the 'postulation vers Dieu'. Each attempt that he has made
to find an ideal in Woman has led him to the degraded ideal of
sexual vice; each time, he has paid the price in pain which was
felt as pain and not as pleasure. Here we find him left a prey to
that pain without any compensating hope of attaining an
ideal, even the ideal of vice. The pain or Spleen is made up of
feelings similar to those which entered into the corrupt form of
the ideal and in which a horrified sense of his own wickedness
and the repulsive nature of his pleasure, was the principal
factor. The difference is that now his sense of guilt and his
disgust with the past, his hatred for the present and his fear
for the future, are not associated with pleasure but with an
anguished desire to escape from the torment they cause. Yet
—and it is this which characterizes Spleen—no attempt to
escape is actually made. The sufferer seems terribly conscious
of the futility of trying to escape and this sense of impotence
is an important ingredient in the pain of Spleen itself. So it is

that this form of Spleen has been aptly described as 'une violence immobile',[1] violent anguish suffered in a state of inertia. This quality of Spleen determines the form of the poems which express it. The typical poem of Spleen presents the poet alone in his room, suffering and hating, and unable to do anything but intensify his private Hell by projecting his inner torment into every object within range of his senses. Hence the curious mixture of trivial realism and obsessional hallucination which characterizes much of this poetry.

La Cloche fêlée illustrates this pattern despite its deceptively gentle start. The interior scene which is briefly evoked is not unpleasant, nor is the development of the idea of the distant bell into a bold analogy between the bell and an alert old soldier complete with a tent which presumably corresponds to the belfry-tower.[2] The choice of the military profession for the bell, rather than the ecclesiastic, is not incongruous, though what determines it is Baudelaire's wish to make the two parts of the sonnet as symmetrical as possible. The analogy with the soldier prepares and balances the impressive final image of—

> . . . un blessé qu'on oublie,
> Au bord d'un lac de sang, sous un grand tas de morts,
> Et qui meurt, sans bouger, dans d'immenses efforts.

[1] Robert Vivier: *L'Originalité de Baudelaire*, Bruxelles, Palais des Académies, 1952, p. 108.

[2] In the course of an excellent commentary which replies to Robert Vivier's criticism of the poem, L. J. Austin has suggested that the image of the tent is to be explained by the shape of the bell itself (*op. cit.*, p. 293). This interpretation, however, reduces the 'cloche' to the clapper only, the image becomes too precise, and a tent is, after all, a protection against the weather—as the tower would be for the bell. One wonders also if the 'souvenirs' can properly be compared with the 'morts'. For Robert Vivier's criticism, see *op. cit.*, p. 22 note.

The image expresses the essence of Spleen. It is a vivid, concrete expression of a 'violence immobile' which may appear in many forms. The force that makes for immobility—here the pressure of dead bodies—may be identified with a prison or the sky pressing down upon the earth like a lid (as in Poem LXXVIII). The 'immenses efforts' which are frustrated may be the desire to escape from Spleen or the aspiration towards the Ideal. The image represents the tragic conflict which is life as Baudelaire sees it in his poetry. Man is in the grip of forces stronger than he is and his struggles to escape are vain.

The mixture of realism and hallucination which characterizes Spleen is illustrated in remarkable fashion by the first poem with the title of *Spleen*. It takes the form of an enumeration of features of the poet's environment starting with the weather. Nothing could be more conventional than the elements of rain, cold, fog and darkness, yet the quatrain is a strong one with its picture of an irritated 'Pluviôse' venting his own Spleen on a city composed entirely it would seem of dead and dying.

The other features of the poet's environment which are introduced in the remaining lines are less conventional but more trivial—the poet's cat, the sound of the wind, the sound of a distant bell, the noise of a log on the fire, the ticking of a clock and finally a pack of cards. By all the laws of poetry and drama it would seem that the middle and end of the sonnet should be weaker than the beginning. But the enumeration of trivial objects and sensations together with their irritating little maladies produces a surprisingly powerful effect. The physical and the moral combine to produce it: everything is physically tainted, ugly, repulsive, and everything is morally restless, uncomfortable, miserable. The order in which the objects are dealt with is also important. The cat is an animal and truly alive, the sound of the wind is human in so far as it is identified with the voice of the ghost of the old poet. The bell, the log on the fire and the clock are also easily invested with life by reason of the noise they make. The pack of cards is a different matter: cards neither move nor make a noise and their participation in this concert of restless unpleasantness is the most surprising and sinister feature of all. They tell of a vain effort at distraction, an attempt to evade the feelings which find expression in the poem. But the semi-hallucinatory quality of the image attached to them suggests that the feelings are extraordinarily deep. It is not anything that the Jack of Hearts and Queen of Spades might say that is sinister, but the fact that they should say anything at all. So intense is the poet's fascinated horror of his surroundings and himself, that his imagination is getting out of hand.

The cycle may be said to reach its climax in the last of the poems with the title of Spleen (No. LXXVIII, *Quand le ciel bas et lourd . . .*). The prison which is the visible universe with its darkness, dampness, rottenness, frustrated hopes, horrors and suffering, becomes strangely confused in the fantastic imagery with the poet's own skull, the 'crâne incliné', on which 'l'Angoisse' finally plants his black flag.

The two remaining Spleen poems were added to the volume in its second edition. It is with special reference to them and to some of the next group that L. J. Austin remarks on the contradiction between the first part of *Spleen et Idéal* and the second.[1] It may well be, as he so acutely observes, that definite

[1] *Op. cit.*, p. 92.

contrasts are intended between particular poems. Thus the first stanza of *Obsession* ('Grands bois, vous m'effrayez comme des cathédrales') may echo, in a very different spirit, the opening stanza of *Correspondances*. The second stanza of *Obsession* ('Je te hais, Océan! . . .') may similarly recall *L'Homme et la Mer*. And corresponding to the ascending movement of *Élévation*, would be the 'chute' associated with the avalanche in *Le Goût du Néant* and, in *L'Irrémédiable* (Poem LXXXIV), with the fall of the angel from the sky. The 'reversal' of the imagery is of course inevitable, given the 'reversal' of the mood, but these *correspondances* in reverse are nevertheless concrete signs of the strength and coherence of the architecture of *Spleen et Idéal* as a whole. Even in the matter of detail, *Obsession* follows on smoothly from the preceding poem (the imprisoning sky and earth reappear as woods, ocean, and the night-sky with and without stars), and the desire for 'le vide, et le noir, et le nu!' expressed in *Obsession*, leads equally smoothly into the title of *Le Goût du Néant*. What is more, these dramatic monologues which end the group of Spleen poems link up without any apparent break in continuity with the first of the poems of self-analysis. There is neither a change of mood nor an obvious change of form. The change lies in the fact that whereas the Spleen poems express the poet's present feelings, *Alchimie de la Douleur* and the following poems penetrate beneath the present mood to deep-rooted tendencies within the poet's nature that explain his present plight and the course of his tragedy.

2. THE 'PUITS DE VÉRITÉ' (POEMS LXXXI–LXXXV)

Of the five poems in the group which concludes *Spleen et Idéal*, only two were present in the first edition (*L'Héautontimorouménos* and *L'Irrémédiable*), and there they were separated and placed at some distance from the end. The group was therefore specially formed for the second edition, and this, together with its privileged position, is a strong indication of its importance.

Alchimie de la Douleur appears to draw its title and many of its images from De Quincey's *Confessions of an Opium-Eater*. It is none the less presented as a personal confession made by the poet. He points quite plainly to a tendency in his own nature to transform 'le paradis en enfer', to turn pleasant ideas into unpleasant ideas, pleasure into pain. This is the form of alchemy in which he must specialize, apparently whether he wishes to or not.

It is surely a mistake to confuse this alchemy of temperament with the alchemy of art and poetry. To do so is to misunderstand both the tragedy of *Les Fleurs du Mal* and Baudelaire's aesthetic theory. The alchemy of art is the opposite of this. It consists of using this horror, ugliness and evil as materials for the creation of absolute beauty. It is the process described in the unfinished *Épilogue* addressed to the city of Paris:

> Car j'ai de chaque chose extrait la quintessence,
> Tu m'as donné ta boue et j'en ai fait de l'or.

The alchemy of temperament consists in the prior transformation described in *Alchimie de la Douleur:*

> Par toi, je change l'or en fer

It relates not to the poet as an artist but to the poet as a man, a man who cannot help being attracted to certain experiences rather than to others (cf. 'ta boue') and who must interpret any experience in his own way (cf. 'je change l'or en fer'). We should be reminded here, not of Baudelaire's conception of absolute beauty and the principle of poetry, but merely of the conception of relative, tragic beauty which he defines in the celebrated passage of *Fusées*. Here also it is clearly affirmed that the poet is drawn towards things which are unpleasant, evil in the widest sense of the word, and it is further affirmed that when he is presented with something else—a Paradise—he will change it to a Hell of suffering. In this poem, it is true, it is not clearly stated that this is what the poet *wants*, that this is actually his favourite form of relative beauty. That revelation is left to the complementary poem *Horreur sympathique*.

Reminded of his present unhappy state and the prospect of future punishment, the libertine who is questioned in this poem replies that he will not complain at being exiled from Paradise. In this mood, at least, he unhesitatingly chooses Hell in all its forms:

> Cieux déchirés comme des grèves,
> En vous se mire mon orgueil;
> Vos vastes nuages en deuil
>
> Sont les corbillards de mes rêves,
> Et vos lueurs sont le reflet
> De l'Enfer où mon coeur se plaît.

As the title of the poem suggests (*Horreur sympathique*) the poet is temperamentally in sympathy with the horror that

poet-hero, it is assumed that a taste for heavenly bliss is not only an inborn quality but an indestructible one as well. Human sins and even human vices are regarded as transitory evils of the flesh: they may be 'bought' at the price of some suffering on earth and perhaps more suffering in a world to come; once they are paid for and forgiven, the sinner turned angel will be ready to enter the City of God. The implications of Baudelaire's poems point to a very different view. Every sin, every indulgence in vice, is a deliberate choice of a pleasure which is not heavenly. Nor does it leave the taste for heavenly pleasure intact. Whether or not the sinner realizes it, however convinced he may be that he *wants* the joys of Heaven, life itself will have corrupted him to a point at which his inmost nature, his soul itself as distinct from his deeds, will render him totally unfit for the City of God unless he is reborn—and reborn *in spite of himself*. There is no hope of any miraculous rebirth to be found in Baudelaire's poems, where the human will is always regarded as the decisive factor in morality. And though he does not commit himself to any definite view as to what may take place after death, his poet-hero behaves in life very much as if he inclined to the view of Swedenborg that no divine judgement is really necessary because man quite automatically judges and condemns (or redeems) himself by his very tastes in pleasure. The title of *Horreur sympathique* and its indication that man will inevitably seek or create the environment best suited to his temperament, is strongly reminiscent of Swedenborg's belief that Heaven and Hell in the next world are the states of mind characteristic of two extreme classes of beings, and that the spirits find their own level between the two merely by obeying the law that like attracts like.[1] On this view, the sinner would be as unhappy in Heaven as the angel in Hell. Baudelaire takes the same view of life on earth, thus anticipating modern existentialist theories of choice and responsibility. And though the 'hypocrite lecteur' may fail to be impressed by parallels with Swedenborg and Sartre, he would do well to remember that the conception of sin implicit in these poems can claim to be based on elementary psychological principles. The psychological law involved is the simple and familiar one referred to by Baudelaire in *Le Poëme du Haschish*:

Enfin il faut songer ... à un autre danger, fatal, terrible, qui est celui de toutes les accoutumances. Toutes se transforment bientôt en nécessités. Celui qui aura recours à un poison *pour* penser ne pourra bientôt plus penser *sans* poison. Se figure-t-on le sort affreux d'un homme dont l'imagination paralysée ne saurait plus fonctionner sans le secours du haschish ou de l'opium?[2]

The human sensibility may likewise be paralysed by 'l'accoutumance' until it ceases to register pleasure except with the help of pain.

The detailed psychological explanation of the attitude

[1] *Cf. Compendium of Swedenborg's Theological Writings*, p. 319, p. 583, pp. 592–601. According to Swedenborg there are various stages in the life beyond death for those who do not go straight to Heaven or to Hell. In the first, the spirits are capable of hypocrisy, as on earth, but in the second they appear as their real selves: like natures are irresistibly attracted towards each other and the good separated in this manner from the bad. For the bad there is no further stage: they become attracted to the evil spirits and enter Hell. The good receive instruction from angels and are prepared for Heaven. As an example of the voluntary parochialism of the spirits, Swedenborg recalls that he saw a spirit scourged by his associates in Hell because, having a cold in the head and not being able to smell, he had approached some spirits in heavenly odour and had brought back some of their perfume on his garments. (See Signe Toksvig: *Emmanuel Swedenborg*, London, Faber and Faber, 1949, pp. 269–70.)   [2] PA, p. 68.

adopted in *Horreur sympathique* is in fact given in the next two poems. The title of *L'Héautontimorouménos*, denoting, as it does, one who inflicts punishment on himself, may remind us that the poet-hero differs from the 'hypocrite lecteur' in being also his own judge, and in knowing precisely what he is doing. There indeed lies the special irony of his case.

As it stands, the poem is the conclusion of a longer poem which was planned but not finished. In his letter of April 7, 1855 to Victor de Mars, Baudelaire has summarized the introductory portion as follows. A poet addresses his mistress in these words: 'Laissez-moi me reposer dans l'amour.—Mais non,—l'amour ne me reposera pas.—La candeur et la bonté sont dégoûtantes.—Si vous voulez me plaire et rajeunir les désirs, soyez cruelle, menteuse, libertine, crapuleuse et voleuse; et si vous ne voulez pas être cela, je vous assommerai sans colère'.[1] This is the familiar pattern of the poet-hero's vice and a detailed confirmation of the preferences expressed in *Alchimie de la Douleur* and *Horreur sympathique*. If the woman refuses to supply the indispensable element of pain and unpleasantness in the pleasure, the poet will have to do so himself, quite deliberately and in cold blood ('sans colère'). The aim is clearly not so much to hurt the woman for the sake of hurting her, as to hurt himself. If she obeys him, he will be the willing yet angry victim as he was in the cycle of the black Venus. If not, he will degrade himself in his own eyes and cause himself sympathetic suffering by abusing the woman, as he did in the case of the white Venus and the green-eyed Venus. The predominantly masochistic nature of the vice is made even plainer by the poem's title.

[1] CORR I, p. 331.

The first stanza of the poem itself sums up the situation in terms of the second alternative. Stanzas two and three are an admirable expression of the corrupt emotional Ideal, and the echo of the imagery attaching to the theme of *le voyage* serves to underline its relationship with the purer forms of the Ideal found in *Correspondances*, *Parfum exotique* and *La Chevelure*:

> Et je ferai de ta paupière,
>
> Pour abreuver mon Sahara,
> Jaillir les eaux de la souffrance.
> Mon désir gonflé d'espérance
> Sur tes pleurs salés nagera
>
> Comme un vaisseau qui prend le large,
> Et dans mon coeur qu'ils soûleront
> Tes chers sanglots retentiront
> Comme un tambour qui bat la charge.

There is a definite and significant echo of the theme and imagery of *Le Masque* as well:

> Pauvre grande beauté! le magnifique fleuve
> De tes pleurs aboutit dans mon coeur soucieux,
> Ton mensonge m'enivre, et mon âme s'abreuve
> Aux flots que la Douleur fait jaillir de tes yeux!

As this parallel suggests, the poet-hero, in the scene imagined in *L'Héautontimorouménos*, is doing no more than adapt his mistress to his ideal of relative beauty! But the pleasurable excitement of the cruelty and accompanying desire, already dependent, in large measure, on conscious judgement of the acts and feelings as evil, must be followed by the pain of the

unequivocal condemnation contained in the following passage
of *Fusées*: 'Quant à la torture, elle est née de la partie infâme
du coeur de l'homme, assoiffé de voluptés. Cruauté et volupté, sensations identiques, comme l'extrême chaud et l'extrême froid'.[1] Georges Blin's investigations in another connection,[2] show that in the second of these sentences it would
be possible to substitute 'Pitié' for 'Cruauté'. The attitudes
are not wholly distinct in this respect. Cruelty may enter into
the poet-hero's attitude towards the woman of *Le Masque*
and he may pity J.G.F. in *L'Héautontimorouménos*.

The last four stanzas of the poem invite the reader to see
in this seemingly crude and conventionally sensational little
drama, a key to the tragedy of the poet-hero's life. But he is
also invited to see it as a parable of the tragedy of human life
in general for there are several levels on which one can interpret the 'vorace Ironie' of the situation which the poet sums
up in these lines:

> Je suis la plaie et le couteau!
> Je suis le soufflet et la joue!
> Je suis les membres et la roue,
> Et la victime et le bourreau.

On the most general level of meaning, it is true of all sinners
provided that there is a reckoning in an after-life. For many
there will be a reckoning in this life if vice should lead to
material ruin, physical disease or delayed remorse. For the

---

[1] JOP, II, p. 94.

[2] *Op. cit.*, pp. 36–37. ('On a fort valablement soutenu que le célèbre marquis
était avant tout un masochiste, et la plupart des psychologues ont montré
que le sadique ne peut jouir de la souffrance de sa victime qu'en s'identifiant
d'une façon idéale avec elle.') Such identification takes place in pity also, and
pity, too, may yield a 'volupté' of varying degrees of purity.

poet-hero there is an immediate reckoning, since his pleasure itself is mixed with a pain that he will feel as genuine pain as soon as the pleasure wears off. Just as his sordid little drama is a parable of the wilful perversity of sin, so is he as much the archetype of the sinner as is 'ce pâle et ennuyé Melmoth',[1] from whom he derives his 'rire terrible'.[2] The importance that Baudelaire himself attached to the poem is proved by the letter of April 7, 1855, which summarized the original plan. There it is indicated that Baudelaire hoped to use it as an epilogue to the selection of poems soon to be published in the *Revue des Deux Mondes* with *Au Lecteur* as the prologue. His seemingly light-hearted description of it as a 'joli feu d'artifice de monstruosités' is balanced and contradicted by his insistence that it would be *'un véritable Épilogue* digne du *prologue* au lecteur, une réelle Conclusion'.

It is, however, in *L'Irrémédiable* that the full irony of the poet-hero's situation is brought out. The poem with its nightmare cosmic setting is the most powerful of the group. It shows the destiny of the poet as irremediably determined and corrupted by the same feature of the poet's temperament that has been analysed in previous poems, first calmly, then with a note of tragic irony and despair which reaches a climax in this poem.

The first seven stanzas illustrate, in a kaleidoscopic series of images, the fact that the poet is somehow, for some reason,

[1] CE, p. 378. Robert Vivier (*op. cit.*, p. 266) is surely correct in relating this laughter to Melmoth.

[2] CE, p. 383. (Cf. p. 380: '. . . les nations se mettent à rire diaboliquement du rire de Melmoth . . .') As regards the final line of *l'Héautontimorouménos* ('Et qui ne peuvent plus sourire!'), a smile for Baudelaire may have an innocence which laughter has not. Cf. p. 383: 'Le rire des enfants est comme un épanouissement de fleur . . . Aussi, généralement, est-ce plutôt le sourire.'

trapped in an unbearable situation. Stanza eight attributes this to the agency of Satan. Stanzas nine and ten present the extremely complex image by means of which the poet sums up the moral and psychological cause of his downfall:

> Tête à tête sombre et limpide
> Qu'un coeur devenu son miroir!
> Puits de Vérité, clair et noir,
> Où tremble une étoile livide,
>
> Un phare ironique, infernal,
> Flambeau des grâces sataniques,
> Soulagement et gloire uniques,
> —La conscience dans le Mal!

The poet is depicted as looking into his own heart and seeing there the reflection of an 'étoile livide' which is finally identified as 'la conscience dans le Mal'. The first function of 'la conscience dans le Mal' is therefore to enable the poet to see its own reflection within him—that is, to see his own evil, his own vice. In so far as it does so, it promotes the qualities of lucidity and mental honesty and far from being evil in itself it is a positive aid to virtue. As Baudelaire remarked in his notes on *Les Liaisons dangereuses*: 'Le mal se connaissant était moins affreux et plus près de la guérison que le mal s'ignorant. G. Sand inférieure à de Sade'.[1] It is in this sense that the 'conscience dans le Mal' can be 'soulagement et gloire uniques'.

But this is not by any means the only function of 'la conscience dans le Mal'. The poet does not merely see the evil that is within him *by the light of* the star which is 'la conscience

[1] JOP, I, p. 330.

dans le Mal'. The evil that he sees is itself the reflection of that star. In some sense 'la conscience dans le Mal' must be a synonym for his vice and itself a form of vice. This is its second and evil function, explained by the lines:

> Un phare ironique, infernal,
> *Flambeau des grâces sataniques,*

If 'la conscience dans le Mal' can act as a 'phare' or 'flambeau' which reveals the evil within the poet himself, it can likewise reveal evil in any other place where evil may be. What is more, it causes this evil to be seen as 'grâces', that is, as attractive. And this attraction is dependent on the fact that the things in question are evil ('sataniques') and recognized as such. Were they innocent or were their evil quality not recognized, they would be too insipid to excite. The reader is faced here with more than the simple idea of a sinner who sins with full know-ledge of what he is doing. Nothing could be more common and there is no valid reason why such a sinner should be 'englué dans son propre péché par la "conscience du mal" qui exclut toute excuse, et par conséquent tout remède'—to quote Marcel Ruff.[1] The remedy for sin is surely quite indep-endent of excuses for sin. Even the tendency to detect evil in remorse and repentance, the only means whereby the sinner can reform, cannot explain why the poet-hero should remain 'bloqué dans la conscience du Mal' as Jacques Crépet put it.[2]

---

[1] *Op. cit.*, p. 113.

[2] FM (Crépet), p. 437. ('De même que l'Idée, l'Ange ou le Damné qui sont descendus dans le gouffre ne peuvent plus remonter, de même l'homme qui est descendu assez profondément en lui-même pour y installer un dialogue ironique, ne peut plus s'évader. De même que le navire cerné par les glaces se trouve pris au piège, de même la conscience qui se livre devant le miroir à ce qu'Amiel nommait "le dévêtement de l'âme" est une "conscience bloquée", —et bloquée irrémédiablement dans la conscience du Mal.')

He can only be so 'blocked' if his attempts to reform are directed towards enjoyment of this evil instead of the good that lies beyond. And this suggests that the true reason why there can be no escape for him, is that he cannot want to escape. Sin for him is not an incidental factor in his pleasure. He sins for the sake of the thrill that comes from conscious-ness of sinning ('la conscience dans le Mal'). To his intensely moral nature, awareness of sin has come to seem the most subtly satisfying form of pain that can be incorporated into his sado-masochistic vice. To that extent, he has become a purist in sin in the same way that he is a purist in art: he believes in Sin for Sin's Sake and can find no excitement without it (for even in art it must appear in the subject-matter). But since he can find no peace of mind *with* it, and must pay the price in disgust and remorse, one can appreciate the bitter irony—as well as the truth—which enters into the words: 'Soulagement et gloire uniques'.

L'Irrémédiable is the true end of *Spleen et Idéal,* for it is doubtful whether *L'Horloge,* which is neither a poem of Spleen nor a poem of self-analysis, adds anything of value to the architecture of that book. Its real function may be to prepare the next, for it suggests a desperate awareness of the need to make some effort to escape from the vicious circle in which the poet-hero is trapped.

VIII

THE LIFE OF PARIS

THE addition of the new book of *Tableaux parisiens* to the second edition of *Les Fleurs du Mal* had a most important and beneficial effect upon the balance of the architecture as a whole. In the first edition, balance was badly lacking. *Spleen et Idéal* was a monstrous construction comprising seventy-seven out of the total of a hundred poems. The remaining four books had only twenty-three poems between them and, of these, *Fleurs du Mal* which followed *Spleen et Idéal*, accounted for twelve. Of the last three books, *Le Vin* had five poems, and the books which treated the imposing and important themes of satanic revolt and death were each allotted only three. The three concluding sonnets were amongst the most subdued of all, and the too sudden decrescendo tailed off into too marked a whisper. The book of *Tableaux parisiens* is the chief factor in the improved balance of the second edition. *Spleen et Idéal*, with eighty-five poems, has been reduced from more than three times the size of the remaining books to barely twice their size. *Le Vin* is shifted from the tail and inserted between the relatively ample books of *Tableaux parisiens* and *Fleurs du Mal* with eighteen and nine poems respectively, leaving only *Révolte* to fit between *Fleurs du Mal* and a final book of *La Mort* which was doubled in length if

one considers the number of poems and well-nigh quad-
rupled if one remembers the unusual length of *Le Voyage*.

In the first edition of *Les Fleurs du Mal*, six of the eight
poems of *Spleen et Idéal* which were later to be used as the
nucleus of the book of *Tableaux parisiens*, were placed in
sequence. They were: *A une mendiante rousse*, *Le Jeu*,
Crépuscule du Soir, *Crépuscule du Matin*, *La Servante au grand
coeur*, *Je n'ai pas oublié*. . . . It is possible that even then Baudelaire had in mind the idea of a cycle of poems dealing with
aspects of the life of Paris. It was in any case a natural development of the early socialist or humanitarian spirit that is evident
in the book of *Le Vin*, as well as of the artistic theory of 'une
beauté et un héroïsme modernes' expounded in the *Salon de
1846*, where already we may read: 'La vie parisienne est
féconde en sujets poétiques et merveilleux. Le merveilleux
nous enveloppe et nous abreuve comme l'atmosphère; mais
nous ne le voyons pas'.[1] Nor could Baudelaire have failed to
be tempted at this early date to help poetry to share the
'provinces fleuries' which had been occupied by Balzac for
the novel, and, for lithography, by Gavarni and Daumier. It
was not however until the end of 1857 that a serious attempt
was made, partly in the prose-poems, partly in the ten new
poems which were written to supplement the eight already
available for the new book to be inserted in *Les Fleurs du
Mal*.

The book is designed to fit into the architecture, no less
than to widen the scope of Baudelaire's poetry and the poetry
of the time. The first purpose that it serves is to emphasize
the universality of interest of *Les Fleurs du Mal*. Suffering

[1] CE, p. 200.

and vice are detected in human-beings other than the poet himself in seemingly impersonal poems. But the application of these poems to the personal tragedy of the poet-hero should not be neglected. Marcel Ruff has said that in this book the poet 'passe de l'introspection à une enquête extérieure, et si la première personne apparaît encore de temps en temps dans le reste de l'ouvrage, elle ne se réfère désormais qu'à un *témoin*, et non plus à un sujet',[1] It may be that Marcel Ruff, who does not make a clear distinction between Baudelaire and the hero of *Les Fleurs du Mal*, is anxious to protect Baudelaire from the unpleasant implications of the three following books, by dissociating him at this point from the 'Je' of the poems. In any case, he surely goes too far in reducing this personage, whoever he may be, to the status of a 'témoin' as opposed to a 'sujet'. Many of the poems of *Spleen et Idéal* are just as impersonal in form as those in *Tableaux parisiens* and later books. Many of the poems in the later cycles are just as personal in form as those of *Spleen et Idéal*. Even in the seemingly impersonal poems the tragedy of the poet-hero continues—in exactly the same way as it does in the cycle of the black Venus where the poet's moral and spiritual barometer can be read by the particular light in which he chooses to present particular aspects of the woman's charm. Marcel Ruff himself observes: 'Les trois seuls poèmes qui ne laissent pas une impression douloureuse, bien que d'un optimisme très relatif, sont placés en tête, comme une espérance ou une illusion bientôt dissipées'.[2] When we observe also that the book ends with the Spleen of *Crépuscule du Matin*, we may feel justified in accepting the traditional

[1] *Op. cit.*, p. 113.   [2] *Ibid.*, p. 114.

view that the book portrays the poet-hero in search of a new form of the Ideal, and in trying to reassess the degree of coherence that enters into this portrayal.

The nature of the new ideal is outlined in the first two poems, *Paysage* (published in November 1857) and *Le Soleil* (moved from its place as the second poem of *Spleen et Idéal* in the first edition). After the heights and depths of *Spleen et Idéal*, it appears as the ideal of a cautious would-be convalescent who hopes to cease from being 'le vampire' of his own heart, by turning his gaze and his imagination outwards towards his fellow-men. His aim is nothing so ambitious as spiritual salvation, although it might prove to be a first, hesitant step along that road. His aim is peace of mind, avoidance of excitement, a return to the simplest and most tranquil pleasures of contemplation and imagination. From the window of his garret, the poet will look out upon a peaceful scene:

> Je verrai l'atelier qui chante et qui bavarde;
> Les tuyaux, les clochers, ces mâts de la cité,
> Et les grands ciels qui font rêver d'éternité.

And when winter comes:

> Alors je rêverai des horizons bleuâtres,
> Des jardins, des jets d'eau pleurant dans les albâtres,
> Des baisers, des oiseaux chantant soir et matin,
> Et tout ce que l'Idylle a de plus enfantin.

The aim is a return to pleasures which, though innocent, are not connected with thoughts of God or Satan, good or evil, and calculated not to excite the malady which is the poet's

vice and the poet's Spleen. The last lines, heralding, as they
do, a return of spring and of the sun, anticipate the title of the
next poem, together with the season and atmosphere it
portrays, thus showing exceptional care for details of the
architecture. He is trying to revive in himself the pure taste
for the 'Printemps adorable', that was mourned as lost in
Poem LXXX, *Le Goût du Néant*.

Le Soleil has the same sweet gentleness of tone and mood
as *Paysage*, a quality all the more impressive in these poems
because it is rare in the volume as a whole. Here, the poet's
projected activities are extended to wandering through the
city and, by means of the poems which its life will inspire,
performing a benign and ennobling office, comparable to that
of the sun, for the 'porteurs de béquilles' and the 'choses les
plus viles'. *Le Soleil* thus serves to introduce the group of
five poems which Jean Massin has called the cycle of compassion.

In these poems, *A une mendiante rousse*, *Le Cygne*, *Les Sept
Vieillards*, *Les Petites Vieilles* and *Les Aveugles*, Baudelaire
consciously trespasses on one of Hugo's domains. Having
referred, in his article on Victor Hugo, to the great man's
love of the grandiose, he continues: 'En revanche, mais par
une tendance différente dont la source est pourtant la même,
le poète se montre toujours l'ami attendri de tout ce qui est
faible, solitaire, contristé, de tout ce qui est orphelin: attraction paternelle. Le fort qui devine un frère dans tout ce qui
est fort, voit ses enfants dans tout ce qui a besoin d'être
protégé ou consolé'.[1] In his letter to Poulet-Malassis of
October 1, 1859, accompanying *Les Sept Vieillards* and *Les*

[1] AR, p. 310.

Petites Vieilles, Baudelaire says that he has tried to imitate Hugo's manner in the second of these poems.[1] The comparison with Hugo is indeed interesting and instructive. Despite his use of some subtle effects of technique which hit off the Master's style, Baudelaire's compassion is very different from Hugo's and that difference itself has a bearing on the architecture.

From this point of view, *A une mendiante rousse* and *Le Cygne* are less interesting than the following poems and need concern us only by reason of the gradation in mood that they help to develop. In accordance with the programme set forth in *Soleil* the poet 'ennobles' the beggar-girl, and does so with considerable good humour and a not unhealthy interest in her physical charms. Even in this poem his attitude is noticeably more 'fraternelle' than 'paternelle'. He cannot condescend because he himself is on a level with those he pities. This is still more evident in *Le Cygne*, where the mood changes to a resigned melancholy. Despite some deeper undertones (as when the swan seems to address 'des reproches à Dieu' on behalf of all earthly exiles) the poem is one of sympathy rather than intense compassion. But what the feeling lacks in strength, it makes up for in purity, and it combines with the mastery that Baudelaire displays in handling his contrasting themes (Andromaque and *la voirie*!) to make this a fascinating poem.

Les Sept Vieillards is not a poem of compassion but an essay in the fantastic which recalls Gautier's *Vieux de la Vieille*. The mood, as grim and unpleasant as the apparitions themselves, provides the first hint that the programme of

[1] CORR, II, p. 351.

Paysage and *Soleil* may not be carried out as planned. In itself the poem is chiefly remarkable for the brilliance of the verbal caricature of the first of the seven identical old men:

> Il n'était pas voûté, mais cassé, son échine
> Faisant avec sa jambe un parfait angle droit,
> Si bien que son bâton, parachevant sa mine,
> Lui donnait la tournure et le pas maladroit
>
> D'un quadrupède infirme ou d'un juif à trois pattes.

This is a talent that Mathurin Régnier would have envied. The exaggeration of the characteristic features and the reduction of the figure to three lines forming two right angles, are carried out with the same bold strokes and the same cruel irony that one associates with the pictorial art of caricature. In its mixture of harsh realism and horrifying phantasy, the poem as a whole is indeed reminiscent of some of the drawings of Goya or the elder Breughel.

Les Petites Vieilles shows the same gift for caricature, but instead of being grotesque and horrifying, the subjects here are grotesque and pathetic. The first stanza is a confession more appropriate to the poet of *Spleen et Idéal*, than to the poet of *Paysage* and *Soleil*:

> Dans les plis sinueux des vieilles capitales,
> Où tout, même l'horreur, tourne aux enchantements,
> Je guette, obéissant à mes humeurs fatales,
> Des êtres singuliers, décrépits et charmants.

It is this increasing obedience to the 'humeurs fatales' which determines the plan of the book, the corruption of the new ideal and the final return to Spleen.

Stanzas three and four present a portrait of the subjects which brings out very clearly the principal difference between Baudelaire's pity and that of Hugo. Whereas Hugo tends to idealize the weak and defenceless on whom he looks paternally, and so to raise them up towards him, Baudelaire's eye is on a level with their misery, nothing of their 'grotesque triste' escapes him, and he cannot help caricaturing it with a fascinated, cruel compassion:

> Ils trottent, tout pareils à des marionnettes;
> Se traînent, comme font les animaux blessés,
> Ou dansent, sans vouloir danser, pauvre sonnettes
> Où se pend un Démon sans pitié! . . .

The following stanza converts the grotesque into pathos and reminds us that Baudelaire admitted to having imitated Hugo in this poem:

> . . . ils ont des yeux perçants comme une vrille,
> Luisants comme ces trous où l'eau dort dans la nuit;
> Ils ont les yeux divins de la petite fille
> Qui s'étonne et qui rit à tout ce qui reluit.
>
> —Avez-vous observé que maints cercueils de vieilles
> Sont presque aussi petits que celui d'un enfant?

One wonders if Hugo was altogether pleased at the perfection of this *pastiche* which excels the models. Hugo had written of a little girl: 'Une petite fille avec des yeux divins'. In applying almost the same words to his grotesque old women, Baudelaire obtains a far more powerful effect than that achieved by the original. The marked assonance of the 'i' in the final line of the stanza is a favourite trick of Hugo's (cf. in *Dans le*

cimetière de . . ., 'La foule des vivants rit et suit sa folie').
A much more subtle form of imitation is provided by the
beginning of the following stanza. There is a sudden break in
the continuity of the description; an appeal is made to the
reader's observation in a calm, familiar, conversational tone
which is designed to reinforce, through contrast, the emotional effect of the content of the question. It is the same device
that Hugo had used in his *Souvenir de la Nuit du Quatre*:

> . . . Sa bouche,
> Pâle, s'ouvrait; la mort noyait son oeil farouche;
> Ses bras pendants semblaient demander des appuis.
> Il avait dans sa poche une toupie en buis.
> On pouvait mettre un doigt dans les trous de ses plaies.
> Avez-vous vu saigner la mûre dans les haies?

Hugo's pity is like the effect of this rustic image—too senti-
mental because too obviously designed to appeal to the reader.
Baudelaire's is characteristically more cruel, much less 'pleasant', but perhaps better poetry.

The poet clearly derives some satisfaction from watching
over his strange family of 'Eves octogénaires', but *Les Petites
Vieilles* ends as grimly as it began, and so leads on to *Les
Aveugles* which ends the entire group on a note of unrelieved
horror and Spleen. The last lines of the sonnet contain the
third reference to God—or, in this case, to Heaven—which
has been made in this cycle. The first depicted the swan
reproaching God for his sufferings and exile; the second
concerned the 'griffe effroyable de Dieu' which weighed
down upon the 'petites Vieilles'; the last puts the highly
suggestive question: 'Que cherchent-ils au Ciel, tous ces
aveugles?', and answers it by implying that the poet, at least,

expects no help from that quarter. It is perhaps more than a coincidence that these poems should, albeit in passing, serve to suggest the severance of the poet from the ideal of God and even the remote possibility of *Révolte*.

A une Passante continues the street-scenes and provides an echo of the love-poems of *Spleen et Idéal*. Then, in a book-stall on the quays, the poet comes across a copy of the engraving of Breughel described in *Le Squelette laboureur*, and again the mood darkens with a vision, not only of death in the midst of Parisian life, but also, thanks to the suggestions of the engraving itself, of a possible life in death that is not at all to the taste of the poet-hero. For to judge from the words: '. . . envers nous le Néant est traître', the poet-hero's attitude has changed little since the writing of *Obsession* and *Le Goût du Néant*. This suggestion strengthens the anti-religious implications of the previous poems.

From this point onwards, the plan of the book is governed by considerations of time inasmuch as *Le Crépuscule du Soir* and *Le Crépuscule du Matin* form a frame into which the remaining seven poems fit very neatly indeed. The gradation in mood continues also, and *Le Crépuscule du Soir* marks the first entry into this book of the theme of vice, in the shape of the prostitution and crime which evening brings. But the poet reacts in the manner most appropriate to the architecture at this point:

> Recueille-toi, mon âme, en ce grave moment,
> Et ferme ton oreille à ce rugissement.

He turns his thoughts to the misery of the sick in a brief continuation of the cycle of compassion—but the following poem, *Le Jeu*, finds him preoccupied with a nightmare vision of a gambling-hell. And the poet-hero is surely as much a *sujet* as a *témoin* when, in the concluding stanzas, he reaffirms the attraction, as well as the horror, which vice still holds for him:

> Voilà le noir tableau qu'en un rêve nocturne
> Je vis se dérouler sous mon oeil clairvoyant.
> Moi-même, dans un coin de l'antre taciturne,
> Je me vis accoudé, froid, muet, enviant,
>
> Enviant de ces gens la passion tenace,
> De ces vieilles putains la funèbre gaieté,
> Et tous gaillardement trafiquant à ma face,
> L'un de son vieil honneur, l'autre de sa beauté!
>
> Et mon coeur s'effraya d'envier maint pauvre homme
> Courant avec ferveur à l'abîme béant,
> Et qui, soûl de son sang, préférerait en somme
> La douleur à la mort et l'enfer au néant!

In these stanzas we find the poet-hero so far 'recovering' from his moral convalescence that he can feel the urge to join these people in their search for an infinite, albeit one of vice. The ideal of peaceful pleasure and the final peace of 'le néant', which characterizes *Tableaux parisiens*, is already threatened by a resurgence of energy which will carry the poet-hero further into 'la douleur' and closer to 'l'enfer'. It is already difficult to say whether the excitement expressed by this poem is of the pleasurable kind connected with the ideal of vice, or of the purely painful kind connected with Spleen.

The same is true of *Danse macabre* where the scene shifts from the gambling-hell to the ball attended by Christophe's statue of a skeleton dressed for the occasion. The source of the excitement here is the horror of death and the horror of seeing all life as inseparable from death:

> Pourtant, qui n'a serré dans ses bras un squelette,
> Et qui ne s'est nourri des choses du tombeau?

But the concluding stanzas with their description of 'Le branle universel de la danse macabre', capture something of the moralistic tone of *Le Voyage* and the dance becomes suggestive of 'Le spectacle ennuyeux de l'immortel péché'. For in this poem, the sky is not altogether empty, and the poet, at least, is aware of the gaping mouth of 'la trompette de l'Ange' which pokes through it. It is not certain whether this Angel is a figurative way of referring to death, or whether he implies belief in God and the other occupants of Heaven by representing either Azrael or Gabriel (who would suggest the terrors of judgement and retribution). In the latter case, we might justifiably point to some inconsistency in the poet's expressed beliefs, for near the end of the following poem, *L'Amour du Mensonge*, there comes the line: 'plus vides, plus profonds que vous-mêmes, ô Cieux', recalling 'Que cherchent-ils au Ciel, tous ces aveugles?' But such uncertainty is not out of keeping with the poet-hero's present state, and is paralleled by his uncertainty regarding a future life. Throughout this book, as at the end of *Spleen et Idéal*, he appears to hope for the peace of absolute death. Yet he may still fear and secretly believe in immortality and retribution. Similarly, hopeful, bitter or defiant references to the emptiness of the heavens, may be punctuated by expressions of a belief in God which is never really shaken.

The fifth stanza of *Danse macabre* adds an appendix to the poet's analysis of his ideal of relative beauty:

> Aucuns t'appelleront une caricature,
> Qui ne comprennent pas, amants ivres de chair,
> L'élégance sans nom de l'humaine armature.
> Tu réponds, grand squelette, à mon goût le plus cher!

Unlike Gautier, who deserted this macabre beauty for the Venus of Milo, Baudelaire continued to defend the skeleton of Christian art. In his *Salon de 1859* he wrote:

> Le sculpteur comprit bien vite tout ce qu'il y a de beauté mystérieuse et abstraite dans cette maigre carcasse, à qui la chair sert d'habit, et qui est comme le plan du poëme humain. Et cette grâce caressante, mordante, presque scientifique, se dressa à son tour, claire et purifiée des souillures de l'humus, parmi les grâces innombrables que l'Art avait déjà extraites de l'ignorante Nature.[1]

The ideal of the skeleton provides a middle term between the fleshly beauty of living human-beings and the mineral beauty of a precious stone. It is in the skeleton that the beauty of animate things passes into what Baudelaire calls the abstract beauty of inanimate things, and for that very reason its attraction is ambiguous. When the skeleton is regarded as the end of the process of growth and decay which is human life, it can arouse the horrified excitement that dominates *Danse macabre* and the other skeleton poems. Nevertheless, as Baudelaire claims in the *Salon de 1859*, the skeleton's freedom from the sinful associations of the flesh and the decay of 'humus', may be appreciated as a kind of purity. It may then be looked at in the same way as things of the mineral world

---

[1] CE, p. 359.

or such products of man's art as the ship which is admired in *Fusées* for its complex yet coherent structure.[1]

L'Amour du Mensonge puts a woman of flesh and blood in place of the skeleton dancer and expresses the poet-hero's reawakened desire for a 'savant amour'. This will have an unusual touch of perversity, for the poet welcomes the possibility that the woman, whose ageing, painted beauty suggests fascinating moral depths, may be stupid or indifferent. The thought that his love will be based on a lie, rejoices 'un coeur qui fuit la vérité'.

The mood softens momentarily in *Je n'ai pas oublié . . .*, and both pity and remorse are present in *La servante au grand coeur . . . . Brumes et Pluies* is a poem of Spleen and helps to prepare the ending of the book. But to complete this long Parisian night, there is the strange *Rêve parisien* of Poem CII.

The dream brings out to the full the poet's love for a purely mineral beauty. It brings out also his love of the artificial as opposed to the natural, for the beauty of this metal, marble and water has the added purity of owing more to art than to Nature and accords with Baudelaire's condemnation of the natural in his long essay on Constantin Guys to whom the poem is addressed.[2] Like the human skeleton, the Paris of his dream owes as much of its effect to a sense of what is absent as to awareness of what is present. Three absent features are commented on in the poem itself: 'le végétal irrégulier' has

[1] JOP, II, p. 71. It is true that Baudelaire's taste carries him through the abstract to rejoin the human on the imaginative level. His analysis of the beauty of the ship concludes with the words: 'L'idée poétique qui se dégage de cette opération du mouvement dans les lignes est l'hypothèse d'un être vaste, immense, compliquée, mais eurythmique, d'un animal plein de génie, souffrant et soupirant tous les soupirs et toutes les ambitions humaines.'

[2] AR, p. 96.

been expressly banned, the sun and other heavenly bodies have gone, and (despite the passion expressed in *Les Bijoux* for combinations of light and sound) there is no noise. The last impression left by the account of the dream is that of 'un silence d'éternité'. And so the reader is made aware of what is possibly the most important absence of all—that of human life in any shape or form. Along with the 'irregular' vegetable, the poet has banished the no less 'irregular' animal. The city of his heart's desire which the poet constructs in his dreams is free from the horror, the evil and the Spleen of Paris that has marked the previous poems. But that has been accomplished only by suppressing life itself. This poem could well be classed with others in the book and volume in which the poet, consciously or unconsciously, seems to renounce existence as an evil and aspire to some form of 'le néant'. For this 'terrible paysage', where an eternity of mineral light and movement creates a cold, unfeeling illusion of life, is a 'néant' in its own right. The suggestion that the dream springs from Spleen is strengthened by the return, at the awakening, to the horror of the 'taudis', the 'soucis maudits', the 'triste monde engourdi'.

Le Crépuscule du Matin makes a perfect conclusion for the book and a perfect reply to *Paysage* which begins it. Here, 'l'homme est las d'écrire', and his last impression of the city is not only one of unrelieved evil and suffering, but of evil and suffering which bring him personally, not pleasurable excitement, but only the unrelieved pain of Spleen. The pursuit of the new ideal has gone astray, has led to a temporary revival of the old ideal of vice, and this, as always, has been followed by the return to Spleen.

IX

THE JOURNEY THROUGH EVIL

I. THE ARTIFICIAL PARADISE (POEMS CIV–CVIII)

OF all the books of *Les Fleurs du Mal*, *Le Vin* presents the most baffling problem. That is as true of the first edition, where it followed *Révolte* and preceded *La Mort*, as it is of the second, where it followed *Tableaux parisiens* and preceded *Fleurs du Mal*. In neither edition does the attitude of mind expressed or implied by the poems correspond to their place in the volume and the apparent requirements of the architecture.

Commenting on the function of *Le Vin* in the first edition, Marcel Ruff remarks: '*Le Vin* proposé comme un moyen efficace d'évasion après les terribles séquences de *Fleurs du Mal* et de *Révolte*, en atténuait singulièrement la portée.'[1] It is true that the poems do, for the most part, present wine as a not unhealthy and efficacious remedy for human woes. It is also true that this weakening of the moral tension weakens the effect of the preceding books,—and, we might add, of *La Mort* which follows. We must therefore conclude either that Baudelaire was sadly in error in placing *Le Vin* where he did, or else that since writing the poems he had altered the overall plan of his volume in a manner which led him to alter his view of the poems and the subject they treated.

[1] *Op. cit.*, p. 94.

The passage is interesting as an indication that Baudelaire's attitude towards wine could change in exactly the same way as his attitude towards man. The manner in which it could change is foreshadowed in the same articles when he speaks of wine and hashish as 'ces deux moyens artificiels, par lesquels l'homme, exaspérant sa personnalité, crée, pour ainsi dire, en lui une sorte de divinité'.[1] In 1851, the would-be 'homme-dieu' is not condemned. But by early 1858, Baudelaire's attitude had changed to that which is expressed in the article he was completing for the *Revue Contemporaine*, *De l'Idéal artificiel—Le Haschish*, better known as *Le Poëme du Haschish* of 1860. There Baudelaire wrote: 'En effet, tout homme qui n'accepte pas les conditions de la vie, vend son âme. Il est facile de saisir le rapport qui existe entre les créations sataniques des poëtes (Baudelaire has referred to Melmoth) et les créatures vivantes qui se sont vouées aux excitants. L'homme a voulu être Dieu, et bientôt le voilà, en vertu d'une loi morale incontrôlable, tombé plus bas que sa nature réelle. C'est une âme qui se vend en détail.'[2]

This change of attitude, or perhaps only of emphasis, on the part of Baudelaire is at least as likely to have occurred before the publication of *Les Fleurs du Mal* as in the ten or so months which separated that literary occasion from the date of the publication of *Le Haschish*. And it could well have altered Baudelaire's conception of the poems of *Le Vin* without his being able, or feeling any urgent need, to clarify the new conception by means of new poems. The cycle, as it is, could be considered in the ironical light which it derives from the very context of the volume, and special importance

[1] PA, p. 215.   [2] PA, pp. 64–65

attached to the third and fourth poems, *Le Vin de l'Assassin*
and *Le Vin du Solitaire*. In *Le Vin de l'Assassin*, wine per-
suades the assassin that his crime itself raises him above other
men (by proving that he alone has known 'l'amour véritable
—Avec ses noirs enchantements'), and makes him as con-
temptuous of death, as of God, the Devil and the 'Sainte
Table'. The ending of *Le Vin du Solitaire* is also relevant:

> Tout cela ne vaut pas, ô bouteille profonde,
> Les baumes pénétrants que ta panse féconde
> Garde au coeur altéré du poëte pieux;
>
> Tu lui verses l'espoir, la jeunesse et la vie,
> —Et l'orgueil, ce trésor de toute gueuserie,
> Qui nous rend triomphants et semblables aux Dieux!

The preceding quatrains are themselves an invitation to
interpret this piety, hope and youth in an ironical way, since
the 'baumes' to which wine is preferred are such mockingly
perverse ones as 'le regard singulier d'une femme galante',
'le dernier sac d'écus dans les doigts d'un joueur', 'un baiser
libertin de la maigre Adeline', and 'les sons d'une musique
énervante et câline,—Semblable au cri lointain de l'humaine
douleur'. When it is remembered also that one of Baudelaire's
principal arguments in defence of wine is that it promotes
sociability as opposed to solitary vice,[1] it may seem possible
that Baudelaire intended both *Le Vin du Solitaire* and *Le
Vin de l'Assassin* to balance the effect of the two opening
poems by stressing the dangerous duality that wine shares
with its human creator. The position of the final poem, *Le
Vin des Amants*, is obviously due to its connection with the

[1] PA, p. 231.

first poem of the book of *La Mort*, *La Mort des Amants* (and, in the second edition, to its connection with the sexual vice of *Fleurs du Mal*). In itself, the poem is a curious and ironically effective echo both of *Élévation* and of *L'Invitation au Voyage*. The comparison, which surely fits in with Baudelaire's intentions, serves to emphasize, not without a touch of pathos, the relatively degraded nature of this ideal.

Thus understood, the book of *Le Vin* would appear less incongruous as an intermediate stage between *Révolte* and *La Mort*. After turning his back on Satan as well as on God, it would be logical for the poet to aim at independence of the supernatural and to avail himself, as a last resort before death, of what Baudelaire described in 1851 as 'la faculté d'augmenter outre mesure la personnalité de l'être pensant, et de créer, pour ainsi dire, une troisième personne, opération mystique, où l'homme et le vin, le dieu animal et le dieu végétal, jouent le rôle du Père et du Fils dans la Trinité; ils engendrent un Saint-Esprit, qui est l'homme supérieur, lequel procède également des deux'.[1]

Of the new place assigned to *Le Vin* in the second edition, Marcel Ruff writes: '*Le Vin*, faisant suite aux *Tableaux parisiens* dont il forme comme un prolongement naturel, prend un sens nouveau qui en retire l'idée d'efficacité que sa place primitive conférait à l'ivresse comme moyen d'évasion. Cette efficacité reste exprimée dans les poèmes, mais le lecteur qui les rencontre entre *Tableaux parisiens* et *Fleurs du Mal* ne peut la considérer que comme un effet passager impuissant à sauver l'homme de sa misère'.[2] Even though the remedy of *Le Vin* may seem particularly efficacious in the first edition

[1] PA, p. 214.   [2] *Op. cit.*, p. 114.

in so far as it brings apparent forgetfulness of Satanism, the greatest of sins, its effect is no less transitory there, where it is followed by *La Mort*, than in the second edition where it is followed by *Fleurs du Mal*. What is diminished by the transfer of *Le Vin* to an earlier position in the volume, is rather the impression one receives of the gravity or extremity of the measure which it represents. The transfer is therefore more in accord, not less, with what is anodyne in the poems themselves. They might in fact pass, as Marcel Ruff suggests, as little more than an appendix to what is equally anodyne in the *Tableaux parisiens*. On the other hand, it is hard to believe that Baudelaire failed to see, or did not want, the great advantage to be gained from incorporating into the architecture of *Les Fleurs du Mal* the 'Idéal artificiel' that he had defined in 1858—and defined in terms that have an unmistakable relation to the architecture of *Les Fleurs du Mal*. Drugs of all kinds, including alcohol, are regarded as an artificial means of attaining to the natural Ideal of blissful enthusiasm which itself 'corresponds' to heavenly bliss. But they provide a degraded sinful form of the 'goût de l'infini', and one which leads to the transmutation of a passion for good into a passion for evil through the dissolution of the will for good, exactly as represented in *Au Lecteur*:

(L'homme) oublie, dans son infatuation, qu'il se joue à un plus fin et plus fort que lui, et que l'Esprit du Mal, même quand on ne lui livre qu'un cheveu, ne tarde pas à emporter la tête. Ce seigneur visible de la nature visible (je parle de l'homme) a donc voulu créer le paradis par la pharmacie, par les boissons fermentées, semblable à un maniaque qui remplacerait des meubles solides et des jardins véritables par des décors peints sur toile et montés sur châssis. C'est dans cette dépravation du sens de l'infini que gît, selon moi, la raison de tous les excès coupables, depuis l'ivresse solitaire et concentrée du littérateur (*Le Vin du Solitaire* could represent such a case), qui, obligé de chercher dans l'opium un soulagement à une douleur physique, et ayant ainsi découvert une source de jouissances morbides, en a fait peu à peu son unique hygiène et comme le soleil de sa vie spirituelle, jusqu'à l'ivrognerie la plus répugnante des faubourgs, qui, le cerveau plein de flamme et de gloire, se roule ridiculement dans les ordures de la route (cf. *Le Vin de l'Assassin*).[1]

This is the true significance of the cycle of *Le Vin* in the second edition of *Les Fleurs du Mal*. Though the poems tend to be impersonal in form, they must none the less be applied to the tragedy of the poet-hero just as that tragedy, as revealed in the more obviously personal poems, must be applied to sinners and mankind in general. The poet-hero's intention in seeking this new ideal is not necessarily more consciously evil than that which is envisaged at the outset of *Tableaux parisiens*. It is, in the first place, a consequence of the failure of that ideal, an attempt by the poet to create what is substantially a new environment by altering his mental attitude towards the familiar one. The aim as Baudelaire describes it in *Le Poëme du Haschish* is—'de déranger les conditions primordiales de l'existence et de rompre l'équilibre de ses facultés avec les milieux où elles sont destinées à se mouvoir, en un mot, de déranger son destin pour y substituer une fatalité d'un nouveau genre'.[2] This revolt against the 'condition humaine' satisfies his pride as well, in seeming to confer upon him a kind of divinity. But although the revolt may be aimed no less at Satan than at God, it is Satan who profits

[1] PA, p. 6.   [2] PA, p. 64.

by garnering in the human soul which has been robbed by drugs of its taste for purer pleasures, along with its will. Even if the poet-hero is not attracted to the artificial paradise *because* he recognizes it as evil from the start, even if pursuit of the ideal is not itself an expression of his sado-masochist vice, it has the effect of enabling that vice to express itself in exacerbated form in the following book of *Fleurs du Mal.*

2. SEXUAL VICE (POEMS CIX–CXVII)

After the relative calm of *Tableaux parisiens* and *Le Vin*, the fourth book appears as a return to the state of crisis depicted in the cycle of the black Venus, and a marked acceleration in the downward trend of the poet's spiritual life. The opening poem, *La Destruction*, indicates very clearly that a personal significance should be attached even to the most impersonal poems of the cycle, and also indicates precisely what that significance is. Nor does this exhaust the interest of the poem. It points to the most essential feature of the poet's past, present and future. It reminds the reader of *Au Lecteur* and summarizes the architectural pattern of the tragedy.

It is indeed fitting that Satan should reappear at this point in the volume and in closer contact with the poet-hero than at any previous time. It is also fitting that the hero's passion for the Ideal should now be described as 'un désir éternel et coupable' and attributed to the agency of the Devil whose influence is drunk in (cf. 'Je l'avale') like the Wine of the previous book. The second quatrain illustrates the form taken by the desire which has thus been identified with the Tempter himself:

> Parfois il prend, sachant mon grand amour de l'Art,
> La forme de la plus séduisante des femmes,
> Et, sous de spécieux prétextes de cafard,
> Accoutume ma lèvre à des philtres infâmes.

These lines summarize the drama of the first half of *Spleen et Idéal* as far as the end of the cycle of the black Venus. In all good faith the poet was led from the ideal of pure artistic Beauty ('l'amour de l'Art') to the ideal of Woman and so to that of sexual vice. The black Venus, by her very nature, brought out his taste for the 'philtres infâmes', that is, for a type of excitement in which pleasure and the pain of 'la conscience dans le Mal' are inextricably mixed.

The first tercet deals with the consequences of habitual sin and refers to the journey through Spleen:

> Il me conduit ainsi, loin du regard de Dieu,
> Haletant et brisé de fatigue, au milieu
> Des plaines de l'Ennui, profondes et désertes, ...

The final stanza explains the contents of the book of *Fleurs du Mal*:

> Et jette dans mes yeux pleins de confusion
> Des vêtements souillés, des blessures ouvertes,
> Et l'appareil sanglant de la Destruction.

The Destruction referred to here is not only the sadistic murder of *Une Martyre* but also (as the original title of *Volupté* proves) sexual passion itself, which may destroy body and soul together. And the poet's only escape from Spleen must now be the horrified excitement of contemplating this evil in its most violent and repulsive forms. His position is analogous to that the monster *Ennui* in the final stanzas of

Au Lecteur, who dreams of scaffolds. Here the scaffolds are replaced by studies of sadism, Lesbianism, and *l'amour maudit*, until the excitement turns into the unbearable self-torment of introspection and Spleen.

Une Martyre corresponds exactly to the programme outlined in *La Destruction* and may, from the point of view of the architecture, be considered to represent indulgence in mental vice on the part of the poet-hero. Nevertheless it is clear that in writing the poem Baudelaire tried to achieve a similar effect to that which he felt David had achieved in his painting of the death of Marat. Baudelaire wrote of this work: 'le drame est là, vivant dans toute sa lamentable horreur, et par un tour de force étrange qui fait de cette peinture le chef-d'oeuvre de David et une des grandes curiosités de l'art moderne, elle n'a rien de trivial ni d'ignoble . . . Ceci est le pain des forts et le triomphe du spiritualisme; cruel comme la nature, ce tableau a tout le parfum de l'idéal'.[1] In his poem, Baudelaire has sought this 'parfum' in the contrast between the violence and horror to which the beheaded corpse testifies, and the calm of its repose, of the still and silent room, of the suave voice of the poet who, like Flaubert in the death-scene of *Madame Bovary*, sees all, understands all and gives absolution in the form of the serenity of art.

But for the banning of the first two poems of the series, *Une Martyre* would be followed in the second edition as well as the first by the *Lesbiennes*, *Lesbos*, *Delphine et Hippolyte*, and *Femmes damnées* (Poem CXI in the second edition).

The sixth stanza of *Lesbos* explains the importance of this brief cycle:

[1] CE, p. 208.

Tu tires ton pardon de l'éternel martyre,
Infligé sans relâche aux coeurs ambitieux,
Qu'attire loin de nous le radieux sourire
Entrevu vaguement au bord des autres cieux!
Tu tires ton pardon de l'éternel martyre!

A link is thus established with the preceding poem, *Une Martyre*, and it, together with *Les Lesbiennes*, is revealed as a continuation of the cycle of compassion. What is more, the reasons for this compassion are indicated and it is seen to be a compassion of complicity. The poet-hero is conscious of an analogy between his own state and that of the Lesbians, as well as of the analogy which links his vice to their vice and to vice in general. Hence the extreme complexity of the feelings that are expressed in these poems, and implied by *La Destruction* and the architecture. The poet's pity, and even the cruelty which may enter into it, do not emphasize the difference between writer and subject: the pity and cruelty reflect back upon the writer himself who is impersonally personal, committed yet detached. It is his own martyrdom, his own destruction and his own evil that he contemplates in those whom he pities. And in so far as his contemplation itself is an acceptance of evil and a source of immediate *volupté*, it is further evidence of the personal martyrdom confessed to in *La Destruction* and a furtherance of the same process of destruction.

In the stanza of *Lesbos* quoted above, there is already a hint of the spirit of *Révolte*. The eternal martyrdom of which the poet speaks, is actually that of the wicked, who are euphemistically referred to as 'coeurs ambitieux'. And although Baudelaire may have been tempted by the view that suffering alone, and even the suffering inherent in sin, is a 'divin remède' and a payment in full, the pardon that is in question here is granted, not by any god, but by the religion of love or sexual passion itself. For the eighth stanza runs:

> Que nous veulent les lois du juste et de l'injuste?
> Vierges au coeur sublime, honneur de l'archipel,
> Votre religion comme une autre est auguste,
> Et l'amour se rira de l'Enfer et du Ciel!
> Que nous veulent les lois du juste et de l'injuste?

As in the cycle of the black Venus, we find—to quote Baudelaire's essay on *Tannhäuser*—'l'amour effréné, immense, chaotique, élevé jusqu'à la hauteur d'une contre-religion, d'une religion satanique'.[1] In speaking for the Lesbians, the poet-hero allows himself to repeat the error which has been his in earlier books, and which consists in believing that one can adopt a neutral position and mock both 'le ciel' and 'l'enfer' at one and the same time. The same mistake is made by Delphine in the following poem *Delphine et Hippolyte* when she counters the moral scruples of her companion with the savage reply:

> —Qui donc devant l'amour ose parler de l'enfer?

> Maudit soit à jamais le rêveur inutile,
> Qui voulut le premier, dans sa stupidité,
> S'éprenant d'un problème insoluble et stérile,
> Aux choses de l'amour mêler l'honnêteté!

> Celui qui veut unir dans un accord mystique
> L'ombre avec la chaleur, la nuit avec le jour,
> Ne chauffera jamais son corps paralytique
> A ce rouge soleil que l'on nomme l'amour!

[1] AR, p. 223.

But in this poem (as in the second *Femmes damnées*) the poet-hero corrects the error in the final address, which recalls *Duellum*:

> —Descendez, descendez, lamentables victimes,
> Descendez le chemin de l'enfer éternel!

The evil may be recognized as evil, but this does not suffice to make the poet-hero's attitude a moral one. The acceptance of evil, the 'aspiration à la douleur' which he makes on behalf of his tragic heroines, is an attitude which enters into the aesthetic of tragedy. In its most serene form it is the height of that aesthetic. But this is by no means its most serene form, nor does it need to be, since we are dealing here with feelings that enter into *subject-matter* as opposed to appreciation. The intensely fascinated and consenting horror which is all that is *expressed* in these lines, and all that need be expressed, is itself an expression of the poet-hero's vice.

For the rest, the poet-hero's sympathy for the Lesbians is to be explained by the same theory of the 'dépravation du sens de l'infini' that determines the meaning of the preceding book of *Le Vin*. What must however be recognized, what constitutes a new and important feature in the development of the tragedy and the architecture, is that the ideal of the Lesbians is envisaged in a far more heroic light than that of the alcoholic or drug-addict could ever be. However often Baudelaire may insist in *Du Vin et du Haschish* and in *Le Poëme du Haschish* that the taste for the infinite and the very vices to which it leads, are a sign of man's grandeur, the escapist character of the drug-habit deprives it of any vestige of heroism. In other vices, including sexual vice, the escapist character is less obvious. It can then be argued that only those who have the force of character and passion to aspire to the heights can be so dissatisfied with the mediocre level of ordinary life as to take the plunge into the depths. The more flagrant and horrible the vice, the more strongly can it be argued that 'Les charmes de l'horreur n'enivrent que les forts' (Poem XCVII). This reasoning is applied to the unnatural vice of the Lesbians, these 'coeurs ambiteux', these 'Chercheuses d'infini, —De la réalité grands esprits contempteurs'. The very degree of suffering which enters into vice can be regarded as an element in its grandeur, and it is here that the poet finds the closest analogy between the vice of the Lesbians and his own:

> Jamais vous ne pourrez assouvir votre rage,
> Et votre châtiment naîtra de vos plaisirs.

Contemplation of the vice of the Lesbians therefore leads the poet-hero to see in evil a combination of energy, suffering and horror which together constitute a kind of tragic heroism. Such tragic heroism, as we know from the cycle of poems on Beauty, is synonymous for the poet with relative beauty itself—the beauty of Milton's Satan. But heroism in general is synonymous with pride and revolt. In this case, the revolt, like that of Delphine, is against those forces which would suppress her vice in the name of good. Though Delphine refuses to recognize it, the revolt is satanic. The poet-hero is conscious of kinship with her, and all the more attracted to her 'grâce satanique' because he shares Hippolyte's consciousness of sin. Behind Delphine, as behind the black Venus, he can see the figure of Satan himself. And at this stage in the volume, his position relative to Satan is analogous to that of

Hippolyte relative to Delphine. Like Hippolyte he is a novice trembling on the verge of initiation into a new and terrible religion. It is not in his case the 'contre-religion' or 'religion satanique' of sexual vice, for into that he has already been initiated by the black Venus. Nor indeed is it the sexual element as such which fascinates him now in his contemplation of Lesbianism: without exception, the remaining six poems of the book are poems of Spleen in which he turns his back on sex. What fascinates him now is the quintessential evil which lies in and beyond sexual vice, the tragic heroism and awful beauty of Satan himself. What fascinates him is the possibility of the tremendous emotional surge and release which is expressed in Hippolyte's cry:

> Mais l'enfant épanchant une immense douleur,
> Cria soudain:—'Je sens s'élargir dans mon être
> Un abîme béant; cet abîme est mon coeur!

> Brûlant comme un volcan, profond comme le vide,
> Rien ne rassasiera ce monstre gémissant
> Et ne rafraîchira la soif de l'Euménide
> Qui, la torche à la main, le brûle jusqu'au sang.'

Here again is 'abîme béant' of *Le Jeu* in *Tableaux parisiens*, albeit sited within the human heart:

> Et mon coeur s'effraya d'envier maint pauvre homme
> Courant avec ferveur à l'abîme béant . . .

Moreover the image used by Hippolyte is remarkably similar to that used by the poet-hero in *Destruction*:

> Sans cesse à mes côtés s'agite le Démon;
> Il nage autour de moi comme un air impalpable;
> Je l'avale et le sens qui brûle mon poumon
> Et l'emplit d'un désir éternel et coupable.

The new form of this desire, which is the poet-hero's vice, is the temptation to widen and deepen the 'abyss' of his heart to accommodate Satan himself, not in the idolatrous form of the religion of sexual vice, but in the pure form of orthodox Satanism. Satan has not ceased to disguise himself as 'la plus séduisante des femmes' (cf. *La Destruction*) in order to achieve his ends, and here he has used his 'Femmes damnées' to show the poet-hero something of his own satanic grandeur and something of the grandeur that might be the poet-hero's own in the final revolt. All that remains in order to make the poet-hero drink the last of the 'philtres infâmes', is to provide him with the incentive of escape from the Spleen that is represented by the six other poems of this book.

These, to which may be added the banned *Métamorphoses du Vampire*, correspond perfectly to the needs of the architecture. *Les Deux Bonnes Soeurs* and *La Fontaine de Sang* are presented as personal confessions of the destructive power of sex in which women appear only as unidentified prostitutes. The next two poems, *Allégorie* and *La Béatrix*, shift attention to two individual women who represent particularly dangerous agents of destruction, firstly the woman who is devoid of any moral sense and is simply amoral, secondly the coquette who is immoral and unfaithful. Marcel Ruff has made a curious comparison between *Allégorie* and the sonnet of *La Beauté*. Having insisted that the beauty of the latter poem contradicts Baudelaire's aesthetic, he continues: '*Allégorie*, poème de la même époque, ressortit à la même esthétique; mais aussi Baudelaire le placera dans le chapitre *Fleurs du Mal*, c'est-à-dire celui des erreurs criminelles'.[1] The parallel does little to

[1] *Op. cit.*, p. 27.

support the sentence pronounced upon *La Beauté*. Prarond dates *Allégorie* before 1843, but has not mentioned *La Beauté*, of which nothing is known until its publication in April 1857. And even though *Allégorie* might conceivably serve to represent several aspects of artistic beauty, it is manifestly not as an allegory of artistic beauty that Baudelaire has used the poem and condemned this strange creature who is as human as *La Beauté* is superhuman—even to the extent of letting her hair trail in her wine!

Les Métamorphoses du Vampire, *Un Voyage à Cythère* and *L'Amour et le Crâne*, end the book with three nightmare visions of physical destruction that constitute the poet's farewell to the ideal of love and sexual vice.

3. SATAN (POEMS CXVIII–CXX)

The three poems of this short but important cycle present the three clearly defined stages in which the poet-hero's revolt or conversion to Satanism is accomplished. There is no introduction save that which is provided by implication in the preceding cycle and particularly in the Lesbian poems.

In *Le Reniement de Saint Pierre* we have the first expression of a revolt which has already begun—a blasphemous denial of God's interest in man, coupled with a denial of the value of the sacrifice of Christ. The motive for the poet's revolt has no obvious connection at all with his vice. It is based, it would seem, on the values of a disappointed idealist, values which attach to an ideal of good, and it is for having fallen short of this ideal that first God and then Christ are judged and rejected.

In the first two stanzas, which may recall the end of *Les Phares*, God's omnipotence is opposed to his seeming inaction and the conclusion drawn that he is a sadistic tyrant. Christ is then portrayed and pitied as one of God's victims before being condemned for his own inaction. The poet opposes the doctrine of passive resistance and hope in an after-life, in which he sees the basis of Christianity, to the doctrine of social, political and metaphysical revolt, but although he gives his preference to the latter, it does not imply disbelief either in Christianity or in God. On the contrary his blasphemy is accompanied or followed by the conviction that his act will recoil upon himself in the form of a malediction pronounced by God. So it is that in the following poem, which presents the second stage of the revolt, he is identified with Cain.

In *Abel et Caïn* the reply to the supposed malediction is hate, directed in the first place at the servile race of Abel. The sinner who pretends to have revolted in the name of good, turns on the innocents who have not renounced God, and hate is strengthened by envy of those amongst them whose material circumstances suggest that they enjoy the favour of Providence. The metaphysical revolt is strengthened by the social revolt, and the threat of political socialism and communism lends substance to the poet's vision of the triumph of the race of Cain, the despised and rejected of God and of bourgeois society alike.

The third and last stage in the revolt consists quite logically in an alliance with the being who is presented by Christian theology itself as the first and most powerful of all rebels against God. In *Les Litanies de Satan*, the true sense and purpose of the poet-hero's revolt is revealed as he becomes a Satanist in the full sense of the term by worshipping the spirit of Evil in person in the orthodox form of the litany. The Satan depicted here has, as we might expect, all the tragic beauty and heroism of Milton's fallen angel, and his wisdom as well. He is the culmination of the poet-hero's search for his ideal of relative beauty, which is the same as his ideal of vice.

The logic underlying the process of conversion is perfect, even to the ambiguity and irony which enter into it. Like all other ideals, the ideal of Revolt or Satan is ambiguous in the sense that it has a negative aspect and a positive aspect: it is at once an escape *from* Spleen and an aspiration *towards* pleasurable excitement. In so far as it is an attempt to escape from Spleen, it is an attempt to escape from the pain that comes from the poet-hero's consciousness of his own sinfulness—at least in moods of Spleen. The way to counteract that pain is to persuade himself that what is evil, and what is to blame, is not himself but the laws of God that make him sinful. This entails a reversal of values which identifies God with evil, and himself and Satan with good. The three poems show the stages in which this reversal of values is *ostensibly* brought about.

The ideal, however, is positive as well as negative. The principal aim is pleasurable excitement, which is also the surest way of drowning Spleen. The reversal of values itself can help, by providing fuel for resentment and defiance directed at God and sympathy and admiration directed towards the tragic ideal of Satan. But if this were all, the tragedy of the poet-hero would *end* in Satanism — and a Satanism of a relatively anodyne kind. For this Satanist would be no 'esprit salamandrin'[1] attempting to assuage his insatiable thirst by swallowing the very source of the flame which torments him. In embracing Satanism, the poet-hero would have been miraculously converted from a wilfully perverse sinner, into a self-righteous and consciously virtuous idealist, defending the right against the tyrant God. In Baudelaire's eyes, he would surely lose, not gain in tragic stature. And although no poems have been included in *Révolte* itself to prove it, the following book of *La Mort* is surely a clear indication that the ideal of Satanism collapses like all the others. The reason is rooted in the nature of the poet-hero and the poet-hero's vice.

It would indeed be surprising if the poet of *L'Irrémédiable* ('la conscience dans le Mal') and *La Destruction*, were duped, or duped for long, by the sophisms and semi-righteous wrath which he expresses in the first two poems of *Révolte*. They may, for all we know, have been written in all sincerity. This does not alter the fact that the tenor of Baudelaire's foreword to *Révolte* in the first edition, agrees with the implications of the architecture by warning the reader of ironical intentions.[2] Not only is the author Baudelaire not deceived by the 'sophismes', but even in the case of the poet-hero they must be understood as 'spécieux prétextes' which, like Spleen itself, encourage further expression of what is

---

[1] JOP, I, p. 232.

[2] FM, p. 473. The essential portion of the introductory note ran as follows: 'Parmi les morceaux suivants, le plus caractérisé a déjà paru dans un des principaux recueils littéraires de Paris où il n'a été considéré, du moins par les gens d'esprit, que pour ce qu'il est véritablement: le pastiche des raisonne-ments de l'ignorance et de la fureur. Fidèle à son douloureux programme, l'auteur des *Fleurs du Mal* a dû, en parfait comédien, façonner son esprit à tous les sophismes comme à toutes les corruptions.'

called, in *La Destruction*, the 'désir éternel et coupable', that is, the poet-hero's vice. The absence of any indication of horror or repulsion in *Les Litanies de Satan* should not blind the reader to the fact that the real motive underlying the poet-hero's revolt must be understood as the desire to enjoy the painful excitement of conscious indulgence in the greatest of all sins—what Baudelaire calls in the essay on *Tannhäuser*: 'le sentiment presque ineffable, tant il est terrible, de la joie dans la damnation'.[1] This implies, not a reversal of the values of good and evil as applied to God and Satan, but awareness of the sinfulness of the latter ideal and a continued though tacit adherence to the law of God.

The negative and positive aspects of the satanic ideal therefore lead to an apparent moral contradiction, and only the negative aspect—the reversal of values—is expressed in these three poems. It is not surprising that the cycle should have given rise to widely different interpretations and judgements.

Amongst critics who have brought out the positive aspect of the satanic ideal are Aldous Huxley and T. S. Eliot. In his essay on Baudelaire, Huxley remarks: 'Only a believer in absolute goodness can consciously pursue the absolute of evil; you cannot be a Satanist without being at the same time, potentially or actually, a Godist'.[2] Huxley, who was attempting at the time to become a thoroughly healthy 'life-worshipper' in the image of D. H. Lawrence, roundly condemns this perversity. T. S. Eliot also fails to envisage the possibility

[1] AR, p. 226.
[2] *Do what you will*, New York, Doubleday, Doran, 1929, pp. 196–197. Quoted by Arnolds Grava: *L'Aspect métaphysique du Mal dans l'oeuvre de Charles Baudelaire et d'Edgar Allan Poe*, University of Nebraska Studies, June 1956, p. 130.

that Baudelaire is portraying a Satanist in an ironical manner. But, like Huxley, he is not deceived by the apparent reversal of values.[1]

More recent criticism has preferred a simpler view of the matter. The reversal of values in the poems is taken seriously and the poet is regarded as a Romantic Satanist who prefers the unjustly persecuted Lucifer to the tyrant God. This interpretation goes hand in hand with the presentation of a 'humanist' Baudelaire. Thus, Jean Prévost sees in the poems of *Révolte*: 'tout autre chose que les lieux communs d'impiété; une revendication humaine, la charité contre la religion'.[2] Although their subject becomes neither less nor more 'commonplace' as a result, this may be true, for all we know, of the spirit in which the poems were originally written. But it is much less likely to be true of the spirit in which the poems were presented in *Les Fleurs du Mal*. Pascal Pia has underlined the contrast between the Baudelaire of 1846 who admired Pierre Dupont, and the Baudelaire of 1865 who wrote to Édouard Manet: 'Mais je me fous du genre humain'.[3]

More recently still, L. J. Austin has found support in Prévost and in Thibaudet for his own theory, which ascribes to Baudelaire an ambivalent attitude towards Satan. He suggests that '(Baudelaire) a voulu faire de Satan un symbole riche et complexe, présidant non seulement aux vices de l'homme, mais à ses plus nobles activités spirituelles', and there follows the quotation from the *Poëme du Haschisch*: 'Hélas! les vices de l'homme, si pleins d'horreur qu'on les

---

[1] *Baudelaire* in *Selected Essays*, 1917–1932, London, Faber and Faber, 1932.
[2] *Op. cit.*, p. 122.
[3] *Baudelaire par lui-même*, Éditions du Seuil, 1956, pp. 74–75.

suppose, contiennent la preuve ... de son goût de l'infini'.[1]
But why the 'Hélas!' if Baudelaire wished to present Satan
as presiding over man's noblest activities? Baudelaire's point
is surely that man's noblest instincts can be corrupted by
Satan's temptations ('Il (l'homme) oublie, dans son infatuation
qu'il se joue à un plus fin et plus fort que lui'[2]), and in so
far as they are corrupted, they surely lose their moral nobility,
they become vice, and it is over vice that Satan presides, not
over vice *and* noble activities.

Nor can support for the theory be found in Baudelaire's
statements that 'l'art moderne a une tendance essentiellement
démoniaque', or that poets need 'une diabolique personnalité'.[3] Granted that art and poetry are noble activities, this is
slender evidence on which to base the view that Baudelaire
wished to present Satan as presiding over them. The value of
the demoniac tendency and the diabolic personality is largely
relative to Baudelaire's own particular age, in which 'les
nations se mettent à rire diaboliquement du rire de Melmoth'.[4]
The value proper to art and poetry is, like the absolute
beauty with which it is synonymous, clearly and invariably
identified by Baudelaire with a celestial world and hence with
God. All that is identified with Satan is a conception of
relative beauty which seems to Baudelaire to determine the
subject-matter of much modern art (he surprisingly fails to
emphasize its relevance to the tragic art of all ages). And
considered in itself, as a representation of human thoughts,
feelings and actions, this subject-matter need be none the
less vicious and ignoble, for all that it is *associated* with

---

[1] *Op. cit.*, p. 56. Cf. *ibid.*, p. 279.   [2] PA, p. 6.
[3] Quoted by L. J. Austin, *op. cit.*, p. 279.   [4] CE, p. 380.

the genuinely noble activity of art. As has been shown in earlier chapters of this study, the entire tragedy presented by *Les Fleurs du Mal* turns upon this very fact, for the same experiences which serve the poet-hero so well in the noble activity of writing poetry, nevertheless spell his moral and spiritual ruin. It is over them that Satan presides, and they can scarcely be termed noble. As for Satan himself, the only 'good' or 'nobility' that Baudelaire finds in the figure (outside *Les Litanies de Satan*) is the ambiguous fascination which he shares with the character of Melmoth, Lady Macbeth and Baudelaire's own poet-hero—the double fascination of energy which is directed towards evil that is recognized as such and not in any way confused with ethical good. Of Melmoth, it is said:

Quoi de plus grand, quoi de plus puissant relativement à la pauvre humanité que ce pâle et ennuyé Melmoth? Et pourtant, il y a en lui un côté faible, abject, antidivin et antilumineux . . . Il est, qu'on me comprenne bien, la résultante nécessaire de sa double nature contradictoire, qui est infiniment grande relativement à l'homme, infiniment vile et basse relativement au Vrai et au Juste absolus.[1]

The ethical judgement contained in the last words is unequivocal. And despite appearances, it is always implicit in Baudelaire's attitude towards the great criminals, of whom Satan is the prototype. It is true that from an amoral point of view, he could admire them as a Corneille, a Stendhal or a Flaubert might do, for their sheer energy and vitality—the most primitive of all human values. But it is doubtful whether Baudelaire could ever adopt an attitude that was completely

[1] CE, p. 378.

amoral. The vice or human weakness that he evidently shared with his poet-hero, caused him to be attracted towards the great criminals all the more strongly because he was instinctively horrified and repelled by clear recognition of their ethical evil, what was ethically 'vile' and 'basse' in their natures. His ethical condemnation of them was therefore an actual condition of their attraction, their relative and satanic beauty. Apart from the poems of *Révolte* themselves, there is not the slightest evidence to suggest that Baudelaire was ever inclined to reverse ethical and theological values as Nerval was inclined to do, at least before writing *Aurélia*. And as Georges Blin has shown, Baudelaire differed also from Sade, who '... donnait des recettes pour éteindre les brûlures de la conscience',[1] by proving to his own satisfaction that in doing evil he was merely obeying the dictates of the universal principle which was evil itself. As far as we can tell, Baudelaire never ceased to reckon with two opposed principles, between which man must choose—in the knowledge that he would suffer a just and merited punishment if he chose Satan and evil. And whatever Baudelaire's feelings may have been when he wrote the poems of *Révolte*, there seems every reason to suppose that when he published them in *Les Fleurs du Mal*, he intended them to represent the 'spécieux prétextes' by means of which the 'héautontimorouménos' might be encouraged to let his sado-masochistic vice express itself in the form of the supreme sin.

The poems, then, do not explicitly testify to indulgence in the vice, inasmuch as the poet merely mistakes, or pretends to mistake, evil for good and *vice versa*. Nor do the poems

[1] *Op. cit.*, pp. 70–71.

reflect any Spleen or remorse which would herald and explain
the eventual abandonment of this ideal. The law which governs
the transition to the next and last ideal, is nevertheless identical
with that which operates in previous cycles. The poet-hero
cannot reverse his ingrained moral values, and to do so would
be to destroy the essential excitement provided by his sin.
Not to do so, is to leave himself open, when the excitement
wears off, to the worst remorse and Spleen he has ever
known. Because of this Spleen he cannot find a lasting ideal
in Satanism any more than he could in previous forms of the
Ideal. But now he can go no deeper into sin—unless one can
so regard the change to a state of would-be indifference to
both the supernatural forces which still hold him in their
grip. This may well be the implication of the final book of
La Mort, as it appears in the second edition.

4. DEATH (POEMS CXXI–CXXVI)

The three poems which made up the book of *La Mort* in
the first edition are related by their titles and general intention, and perhaps even by the dates of their composition,
to the poems of the book which immediately preceded them:
Le Vin. They seem to belong to a fairly early, humanitarian,
and relatively less sombre conception of the architecture,
one which required the poet to speak with a degree of
impersonality for classes of people other than his own. These
are, in fact, the poems which most obviously fit the plan of
Les Limbes, announced in 1850 and 1851 as a work 'destiné à
retracer l'histoire des agitations spirituelles de la jeunesse
moderne'. And we have certain evidence to show that six of
the eight poems in question had been written by 1852, the

exceptions being *Le Vin du Solitaire* (Poem CVII) and *Le Vin des Amants* (Poem CVIII).

Albert Feuillerat has said that in this conclusion to the first edition, Baudelaire 'avait affirmé sa croyance qu'il rentrerait triomphalement dans le paradis perdu où Dieu et les anges accueilleraient la malheureuse créature dès lors purgée de ses péchés'.[1] And comparing *La Mort* with *Le Vin*, he remarks: 'La seconde solution, la mort, est définitive et satisfaisante, car elle nous remet entre les mains des anges compatissants. C'est le triomphe promis au poète au début du livre, l'admission dans les "rangs bienheureux des Saintes Légions", "l'éternelle fête des Trônes, des Vertus, des Dominations". Au Paradis perdu succède le Paradis re-trouvé'.[2] It is certainly possible to find in these poems two references to an angel (in *La Mort des Pauvres*, the angel is Death itself), a reference to Gods in the plural (Death is said to be 'la gloire des Dieux' in *La Mort des Pauvres*), a pre-diction of a joyous resumption of love for 'les Amants', and a reference to a 'patrie antique' and a 'portique ouvert sur les Cieux inconnus' in the case of 'les Pauvres'. But even when these elements are taken out of their context in the individual poems, and put together, they still fall considerably short of the picture which is painted by Feuillerat. The mood of the poems is as far removed from triumph as it is from a spirit of dogmatic affirmation about the world that lies beyond the grave. The mood is one of fascinated contemplation or reverie in which the macabre horror of death is 'subdued and chastened' (as Poe would put it), much as in *Une Martyre*, by being made to 'correspond' with the gently pathetic dreams

[1] *Op. cit.*, p. 318.   [2] *Op. cit.*, p. 289.

and *hopes* of the 'Amants' and 'Pauvres' themselves. The poet
may be merely the sympathetic interpreter of these hopes
which relate to 'Cieux' that are indeed 'inconnus' (cf. the last
line of *La Mort des Pauvres*), and owe their fascination to this
very uncertainty. Moreover, of the three poems, none is
less in accord with Feuillerat's interpretation than *La Mort
des Artistes*, the poem which is presumably most appropriate
to the hopes and beliefs of the poet-hero himself. Unless
one 'borrows' the references to angels and Gods and 'Cieux'
from the two preceding poems, this one is as indefinite in its
way as the ending of *Le Voyage*. We are not told what may
be the attitude towards death adopted by the fortunate artists
who have looked on 'leur Idole'.[1] But the others—

> N'ont qu'un espoir, étrange et sombre Capitole!
> C'est que la Mort, planant comme un Soleil nouveau,
> Fera s'épanouir les fleurs de leur cerveau!

Why should this hope, or the 'Capitole' to which it is likened,
be described as 'étrange et sombre', if it is associated with a
triumphant entry of the redeemed sinner into Paradise (as
Feuillerat suggests)? The epithets are perhaps to be explained
by the macabre ambiguity of the concluding 'vegetative'
image, and may therefore serve to emphasize the fact that the

---

[1] Feuillerat apparently identifies with God Himself the 'Idole' and the
'Grande Créature', whilst admitting that in the first version of the poem
'il n'était nullement question de retrouver Dieu' (*op. cit.*, p. 286 note). He
also assumes that 'la grande Créature' will be contemplated in the 'patrie
antique' referred to *in the preceding poem*. In *La Mort des Artistes* it is surely
made clear that 'la grande Créature' may be contemplated in this life, as a
result of artistic activity. If the words are to be interpreted in terms of supernatural beings, which hardly seems necessary, Satan is more likely to be in
question than God, since he is at least a creature, not a creator, and provides a
better object for an '*infernal* désir'.

reader is left in doubt as to whether there *is* any real 'Capitole' for the artists beyond their tomb itself. If there is, no hint has been given as to its geographical location, once again we are concerned with 'un espoir', and neither this poem nor the two preceding ones need be taken to commit the poet-hero to any definite—let alone optimistic—view of his own future.

One of Feuillerat's main arguments in support of his interpretation, appears to be that the optimism of the conclusion would confirm that of *Bénédiction* and bring the wheel full circle. It would do so, however, only by contradicting the unrelieved pessimism of *Au Lecteur*, *L'Irréparable* (Poem LIV), *L'Irrémédiable* (Poem LXXXIV), *La Destruction* (Poem CIX) and all the other poems in the first edition which link its plan to the plan of the second edition far more closely than Feuillerat is prepared to admit. The passage to Paradise of the ex-devotee of Bacchus and of Satan would be too smooth and too swift to be other than a *dénouement postiche*—one which would justify us in condemning the first edition for its lack of unity in much the same way as Feuillerat condemns the edition of 1861.

If it is true that the poems under consideration do not express at all clearly the ideas which Feuillerat finds in them, Baudelaire's own satisfaction with the 'conclusion excellente' of the first edition[1] may be regarded as further evidence against Feuillerat's interpretation. It must however be conceded that the alternative view of the matter which has been advanced in this study does little to explain or justify Baudelaire's self-congratulation. Like the poems of *Le Vin* and *Révolte*, the poems of *La Mort*, in the first edition, scarcely

[1] See FM, p. 310.

seem equal to the grandeur of the conceptions outlined in *Spleen et Idéal* and *Fleurs du Mal*. Nevertheless the weakness can be attributed to the imperfect adaptation to the architecture of the 1857 edition, of poems written to conform with an earlier plan. Feuillerat's theory obliges him to impute to Baudelaire a far greater error of judgement, inasmuch as the poet is thought to have failed to see that his additions to the first edition detracted from the virtual perfection of some of its parts, including *La Mort*. And Feuillerat is faced with the need to explain why Baudelaire should so far have altered his 'conclusion excellente' as to give it, in 1861, a meaning directly opposed to that which Feuillerat believes it to have in 1857.

The poems added to the book in the second edition tend to confirm the view that the three original ones present contrasted attitudes towards the exciting subject of death, in the course of meditations which do not commit the poet-hero to any definite view of his own future.

La Fin de la Journée, the first of the added poems, attributes to 'le Poëte' a longing for repose and sleep that anticipates Baudelaire's words in his *Projets de Préface*: 'Ne rien savoir, ne rien enseigner, ne rien vouloir, ne rien sentir, dormir et encore dormir, tel est aujourd'hui mon unique voeu'.[1] *Le Rêve d'un Curieux*, on the other hand, anticipates a death that brings no observable change to satisfy the deceased's curiosity as to what death is. It is also the first poem of the series to contain a reference to the poet-hero's vice, which appears here as 'le goût de l'horreur', and to suggest that this contemplation of death is itself a way—the last way—of indulging it:

[1] FM, p. 375.

> Connais-tu, comme moi, la douleur savoureuse,
> Et de toi fais-tu dire: 'Oh! l'homme singulier!'
> —J'allais mourir. C'était dans mon âme amoureuse,
> Désir mêlé d'horreur, un mal particulier; . . .

But these poems count for little in comparison with *Le Voyage* which makes an admirable conclusion to the volume.

The voyage in question relates both to the past and to the future. It is the voyage of life as well as that of death, and in describing the former the poet-hero is able to recall the themes and even the outline of the architecture of *Les Fleurs du Mal.* The first section connects departure with the thirst for the Ideal—

> De vastes voluptés, changeantes, inconnues,
> Et dont l'esprit humain n'a jamais su le nom.

The second converts the voyage into a vicious circle of aspiration and disappointment, a search for the Ideal followed by Spleen:

> Chaque îlot signalé par l'homme de vigie
> Est un Eldorado promis par le Destin;
> L'Imagination qui dresse son orgie
> Ne trouve qu'un récif aux clartés du matin.

Sections three and four describe the fabulous voyage in more picturesque detail, whilst insisting that the limited satisfactions achieved serve only to make satisfaction more difficult and to exasperate desire for the absolute:

> —La jouissance ajoute au désir de la force.
> Désir, vieil arbre à qui le plaisir sert d'engrais,
> Cependant que grossit et durcit ton écorce,
> Tes branches veulent voir le soleil de plus près!

In sections five and six, the itinerary is shown to pass from
start to finish through ubiquitous sin. Well-nigh all the deadly
sins are attributed to men and women in their personal relations but the *péché mignon* of the poet-hero is implicit in his
striking description of man as 'Esclave de l'esclave'. It is
referred to more explicitly in the passages dealing with justice,
politics and religion:

> Le bourreau qui jouit, le martyr qui sanglote;
> La fête qu'assaisonne et parfume le sang;
> Le poison du pouvoir énervant le despote,
> Et le peuple amoureux du fouet abrutissant;
>
> Plusieurs religions semblables à la nôtre,
> Toutes escaladant le ciel; la Sainteté,
> Comme en un lit de plume un délicat se vautre,
> Dans les clous et le crin cherchant la volupté;

The irreligious section of humanity is in frantic revolt:

> Criant à Dieu, dans sa furibonde agonie:
> 'O mon semblable, ô mon maître, je te maudis!'

and the 'moins sots' seek an escape in 'L'opium immense'.

The first function served by this part of *Le Voyage* considered in relation to the architecture is to sum up in terms of
universal experience the principal stages in the poet-hero's
own career. The second function is to confirm the findings of
Au Lecteur by envisaging life from a different and complementary point of view. In *Au Lecteur*, the poet, so to speak,
insinuated himself into the heart and mind of the individual
and described this subjective universe. In *Le Voyage*, the
relative objectivity which attaches to the poet-hero's account
of his own adventure, is developed into a God's-eye view of
the external manifestations of sin throughout the world in

such spheres of activity as personal relations, justice, politics and religion, which are shown to be governed by the same forces that cause the poet-hero's private tragedy. In this way *Le Voyage* complements *Au Lecteur*. *Au Lecteur* however is outside the framework of the narrative or drama. *Le Voyage* is within it and completes it. We therefore find a subtle difference in the moral and indeed the religious attitude of the writer, which is to be explained by the dramatic situation of the poet-hero at this the last stage in his adventure. In *Au Lecteur* the outspoken condemnation of all signs of the *postulation vers Satan* implies in the writer an equally strong *postulation vers Dieu*. In *Le Voyage*, sin is still recognized and condemned as sin, but if there is no sign in the writer of any conscious *postulation vers Satan*, there is considerable doubt right up to the concluding sections as to the presence of a *postulation vers Dieu*. The poet is so completely disillusioned as to be detached from saint and sinner alike, from God and Satan. And in the concluding sections the doubt is converted into certainty that this is indeed the case.

Section seven of the poem begins the moral preparation for the second voyage, or continuation of the voyage, which is the journey into death. This death is not 'la Mort des Amants' nor 'la Mort des Pauvres' nor 'la Mort des Artistes'. It is the death of the poet-hero of *Les Fleurs du Mal* and in the stanzas which picture it, Baudelaire does full justice to his talent and to the theme:

> Nous nous embarquerons sur la mer des Ténèbres
> Avec le coeur joyeux d'un jeune passager.
> Entendez-vous ces voix, charmantes et funèbres,
> Qui chantent; 'Par ici! vous qui voulez manger

Le Lotus parfumé! c'est ici qu'on vendange
Les fruits miraculeux dont votre coeur a faim;
Venez vous enivrer de la douceur étrange
De cette après-midi qui n'a jamais de fin!'

The full tragic splendour of the final appeal to Death emerges
when one sees behind it all the similar aspirations that have
been made towards all the other forms of the Ideal, and
especially the ideal of Beauty. The prayer to Beauty was:

Que tu viennes du ciel ou de l'enfer, qu'importe,
O Beauté! monstre énorme, effrayant, ingénu!
Si ton oeil, ton souris, ton pied, m'ouvrent la porte
D'un Infini que j'aime et n'ai jamais connu?

De Satan ou de Dieu, qu'importe? Ange ou Sirène,
Qu'importe, si tu rends,—fée aux yeux de velours,
Rhythme, parfum, lueur, ô mon unique reine!—
L'univers moins hideux et les instants moins lourds?

The prayer to Death is:

O mort, vieux capitaine, il est temps! levons l'ancre!
Ce pays nous ennuie, ô Mort! Appareillons!
Si le ciel et la mer sont noirs comme de l'encre,
Nos coeurs que tu connais sont remplis de rayons!

Verse-nous ton poison pour qu'il nous réconforte!
Nous voulons, tant ce feu nous brûle le cerveau,
Plonger au fond du gouffre, Enfer ou Ciel, qu'importe?
Au fond de l'Inconnu pour trouver du *nouveau*!

It is understandable that commentators should have been
impressed with the negative aspect of this conclusion to *Les
Fleurs du Mal*. Marcel Ruff speaks of 'la lassitude et l'accable-

ment' that it expresses.[1] Albert Feuillerat makes this 'lassitude'
and 'découragement' the basis of his distinction between the
second edition and the first, which gives 'une image plus
virile' of Baudelaire.[2] But there is less excuse in this cycle than
in the preceding cycle of *Révolte*, for overlooking the positive
aspect of the ideal, since that is so clearly brought out in the
last six stanzas of *Le Voyage*. And it is most important that it
should not be overlooked, because it determines the final
impression that is left by the tragedy.

The end of *Le Voyage* certainly implies that the poet-hero
has lost all hope of satisfying his restless aspirations in this
life. But despite all the past disillusionment and suffering, his
mood is not in fact weary or depressed: his heart is 'le coeur
joyeux d'un jeune passager'; it is '(rempli) de rayons'. When
faith is lost in all else, in life on earth, in God, in Satan, one
thing still remains—the affirmation of the immensity of
human desire, the 'abîme du coeur' (cf. *Delphine et Hippolyte*)
which has swallowed up the ideals of God and Satan with all
the rest, and is now taking in the 'gouffre' of death and all
that may lie beyond. For Baudelaire, this indifference to
salvation may indeed be sinful folly and presented to the
reader as such, in Baudelaire's ironic way. Yet he cannot have
been blind to the fact that his poet-hero attains in this to a
far greater tragic stature than he enjoyed before, even as a
Satanist. For here at last he finds himself, not as a willing
dependent of either of his supernatural masters, but as a man
who is free at least to *will* his freedom from them both. And
even if this freedom be impossible, he will not will to die, in
the absolute sense of the word, but to go on living, come what

---

[1] *Op. cit.*, p. 118.   [2] *Op. cit.*, p. 319.

may. The poet-hero may look forward to death as the only possible solution to his problem, but suicide is not in question. It is only when Death itself 'mettra le pied sur (leur) échine', that the poet-hero and his companions will embark. And their prayer is not in fact a prayer to Death but to Life-in-death.

It is in this final poem that the ultimate significance of the 'goût de l'infini' and even of the perverted form of it which is the poet-hero's vice, emerges most clearly. Vice or not, it represents 'Désir, vieil arbre à qui le plaisir sert d'engrais'. As such, it is the moral principle of life itself, the basis of the all-important will to live—to live in this life or any life hereafter. Whoever or whatever may be defeated in *Les Fleurs du Mal*, it is not the will to live, in the broad sense of the expression which has just been defined. In that sense, it is exalted not merely indirectly through poetic emotion, the pleasure peculiar to art, but directly also, through the passions expressed in the fiction itself. In this, Baudelaire shows his complete fidelity to the aesthetic of tragedy. To exalt the will to live by the equivocal passions attendant on the spectacle of its denial, may well be a primitive use of tragedy. Nor perhaps has the development of a highly civilized artistic appreciation rendered it wholly out-of-date.

CONCLUSION

Les Fleurs du Mal is not a 'pur album': it is a very rich dramatic poem. In the first chapter of this study, emphasis was placed on the remarkable degree of coherence which governs the complexity of structure and action in the second edition. In this conclusion, the claims made in the first chapter will be qualified with reference to the weaknesses in the architecture and suggestions concerning its likely historical development. Thereafter, the central figure of the poet-hero will be examined with a view to assessing the psychological and dramatic value of his tragedy, together with its universal, philosophic interest. Included under the latter heading is the special interest that it may have held for Baudelaire as a reflection of his own character and beliefs.

The books of *Les Fleurs du Mal* which appear least well adapted to their role in the architecture are *Le Vin*, *Révolte* and, in the first edition, *La Mort*. They are also the shortest books and the ones which contain the highest proportion of poems known to have been written in or before 1852. Together with the Lesbian poems of the book of *Fleurs du Mal*, they form a nucleus of relatively impersonal poems which could combine with the more personal poems of Spleen and the early love-poems, to fulfil the promise made in 1850 and 1851 of a volume 'destiné à retracer l'histoire des agitations spirituelles de la jeunesse moderne'. This was the period—or perhaps the end of the period—when Baudelaire could think and write in the optimistic, humanitarian manner of his essay on Pierre Dupont: 'En effet, la nature est si belle, et l'homme est si grand, qu'il est difficile, en se mettant à un point de vue supérieur, de concevoir le sens du mot: irréparable . . . Disparaissez donc, ombres fallacieuses de René, d'Obermann et de Werther . . . Le génie de l'action ne vous laisse plus de place parmi nous'.[1] This spirit was almost certainly reflected in Baudelaire's conception of the architecture of *Les Limbes*, and in some of the poems that were composed to fit it. It is the 'ton d'agressive vitalité' which seems to Albert Feuillerat to characterize the 1857 edition and to distinguish it from the sombre pessimism of the 1861 edition.[2] Feuillerat concludes that a radical change took place in Baudelaire's outlook on life, and hence in his architectural plan, after 1857. It is possible, however, that we should reckon in the first place with a change that took place between 1852 and 1857. Amongst the poems published in the *Revue des Deux Mondes* of June 1, 1855, two years before the appearance of the first edition of *Les Fleurs du Mal*, was *Au Lecteur*—already perfectly in keeping with the spirit of the second edition. It was accompanied by such other key-poems as *Le Vampire*, *L'Irréparable*, *La Destruction*, and followed in May 1857 by *L'Héautontimorouménos* and *L'Irrémédiable*, published in *L'Artiste*. Indeed, of the poems added to the volume in 1861, only *Obsession*, *Le Goût du Néant*, *L'Horloge*, *La Fin de la Journée* and *Le Voyage* can compare in respect of 'lassitude' and 'découragement'

---

[1] AR, p. 195. Cf. *L'Irréparable* (Poem LIV), and Baudelaire's praise of 'la grande école de la mélancolie, créée par Chateaubriand', in the essay on Théophile Gautier published in *L'Artiste* in March 1859, and in the *Projets de lettre à Jules Janin* of 1865.

[2] *Op. cit.*, p. 330.

with the most dispirited poems of the first edition. Feuillerat is certainly correct in maintaining that the altered arrangement of poems at the end of *Spleen et Idéal*, the new position allotted to *Le Vin* and the additions to *La Mort* deepen the impression of pessimism. But this may not be entirely due to an increase of pessimism in Baudelaire himself between 1857 and 1861. It may result from a more systematic and artistic presentation of the elements that the poet had designedly introduced into the first edition, from a deliberate effort to make the spirit of the work as a whole conform more nearly with that which, even in the first edition, is proper to the tragedy of the central figure, as distinct from the other classes of humanity to whom reference is made. Certainly, resigned pessimism is to be found side by side with 'agressive vitalité' in 1857, and if they clash in 1861 they should do so in 1857 also. The difference can be no more than a matter of degree. Unless one's taste in relative beauty leads one to prefer aggressive vitality to resigned pessimism as a matter of course, there seems to be no good reason why one should not regard the second edition as a definite artistic improvement on the first.

If we feel obliged to explain the change in Baudelaire's plan with reference to a change that took place in his outlook on life between 1852 and 1857, we need not suppose that either was a particularly sudden or radical one. Baudelaire's optimistic and humanitarian phase seems to reach an extreme between 1848 and 1852, followed by a gradual recession. Nor is it only a question of emotional outlook, since this phase is closely linked with the literary attitude that sprang from Baudelaire's conception of 'l'héroïsme de la vie moderne' and gives him undoubted affinities with the Realists. In any case, the stated intention underlying *Les Limbes* allowed the sombre side of the poet's nature sufficient scope for the transition to the plan of the first edition of *Les Fleurs du Mal* to have been a smooth and gradual one. That would help to explain why he failed to see any urgent need to alter the books of *Le Vin*, *Révolte* and (before the preparation of the second edition) *La Mort*. He nevertheless seems to have ceased to write the type of relatively impersonal poem that refers to 'Chiffonniers', 'Pauvres', etc., and—at least until the composition of *Tableaux parisiens* led him to revive the practice, in a different vein—he elaborated more and more on the adventure of the central figure whose task it was to represent humanity in general. Unfortunately, though the poems of *Le Vin* and *Révolte* were adequate as expressions of the 'agitations spirituelles de la jeunesse moderne', they fell short of the demands placed on them by the tragedy of the highly particularized poet-hero in the more ambitious architecture of the editions of 1857 and 1861.

Despite these imperfections, the architecture of *Les Fleurs du Mal* provides an impressive poetic drama built around a worthy successor to the Fausts, Renés and Lorenzaccios of Romanticism. As is clearly shown by comparison of the endings of the *Hymne à la Beauté* and *Le Voyage*, to which may be added *Bénédiction*, the source of this tragic hero's energy lies in his instinctive need to make a movement of aspiration toward an ideal. In his constant repetition of this movement lies the *raideur* of his character, a quality which, *pace* Bergson, belongs to tragic characters no less than to comic ones, and serves to give this tragedy and the character of its hero their unusual degree of coherence or unity. To judge by Baudelaire's article on Flaubert's novel, he was not blind to the relation between his own hero's nature and what Jules de Gaultier was later to call 'le Bovarysme'. As this writer's philosophical use of the idea suggests, what is in question is a fundamental 'rhythm' of all energy endowed with life. What is more, this characteristic of living energy needs only to be 'exaggerated', or given unusually strong emphasis, to take on potential artistic value as the basic *formal* rhythm that appears in the subject-matter of dramatic literature. Envisaged in imaginary space as a visual pattern, it may be detected both in the overall 'rise and fall' of tragic and comic characters and in the minor rises and falls, the minor set-backs and renewed efforts, which punctuate the overall movement and give rise to the impression of a character's *raideur*, be it the positive *raideur* which comes with an ideal of action or the negative *raideur* of inaction or weakness. In so far as the expression of the energy of desire is considered merely as coherent pattern or form, it gives rise to the specifically artistic satisfaction which such patterns produce when they build or represent corresponding patterns of emotion within the sensibility. In so far as it is considered or felt as the corresponding pattern of emotion, it appears in the reader as the fluctuation of feeling due to an instinctive vicarious sympathy (which implies corresponding antipathies) with the principle of desire itself.

The extreme coherence which the repeated assertion of desire gives to the character of Baudelaire's poet-hero (and, as we have seen, to the related formal and emotional patterns) is not sufficient in itself to constitute genuine artistic merit. It must be measured against the complexity of what is made coherent. In the poet-hero of *Les Fleurs du Mal*, complexity goes hand in hand with coherence inasmuch as the very abundance of the energy of desire leads it to seek many different ideals: complexity is present both in the variety of forms taken by the movement of aspiration or escape and in the temperament which admits of such variety. The quest for pleasure can extend to any activity whatever, but in few individuals does it range between such paradoxical extremes as in Baudelaire's poet-hero. In turn, he seeks his ideal in God, art, beauty, woman, Paris, drugs, evil, the author of evil, before turning to death and the beyond. Nothing in life can provide a lasting form of the excitement craved by his insatiable soul—insatiable because too easily satiated, too easily satiated because more energetic and harder to satisfy than the mediocre soul of the 'hypocrite lecteur'.

This complexity in the hero gives complexity to the related formal and emotional patterns. It enables the basic formal rhythm or pattern—which is simply that of successive aspirations towards a constant ideal—to exploit a new 'dimension'. Instead of plotting the hero's movements merely in terms of proximity or distance from his ideal whatever it may be, the reader is invited to plot his movements also in terms of a scale of *values* which are more than the values of success and failure and can only be termed 'moral' in an extremely broad sense of the word. This is the new 'dimension', one in which tragedy and art in general can adapt morality to their own basically formal purposes. For the pattern of a hero's career may reflect variations in the degree of energy or weakness, and also ethical virtue or vice, with which he pursues a single objective ideal, be it a throne, a fortune, a woman or an enemy's life. Or, as in the more exceptional case of the hero of *Les Fleurs du Mal*, he may pursue with equal fervour a set of different objective ideals which will themselves produce the moral variation on the basic pattern of success and failure. And in this case the 'moral' variation involves not only the value which attaches to energy or courage as opposed to spinelessness and cowardice, but ethical values, religious values, and even aesthetic values too, inasmuch as the poet-hero is a poet to the last.

The complexity of the formal pattern produces a corresponding complexity in the emotional pattern. The pattern of instinctive sympathy which the reader feels towards the principle of desire (and which a naive view of literature and art confuses with artistic value) is converted into an immensely complex emotional pattern—so complex that the passions appropriate to the various kinds of value have apparently clashed within readers' breasts with no less violence than they do in the breast of the poet-hero, and with widely differing fortunes of war. Baudelaire and *Les Fleurs du Mal* were to poetry much what Wagner and *Tannhäuser* were to music. It has been the aim of the present study to relate the emotional pattern of *Les Fleurs du Mal* to the formal pattern or *architecture secrète* (the words are more than a figure of speech) which resolves the conflicts of life in the harmony or unity of art.

Both the coherence of the character of the poet-hero and his complexity can be used to prove that he is a most exceptional and even a freakish individual. His *raideur* may be deemed as unnatural as the wide range of his tastes in pleasure. This appearance of being an exception is none the less a distinction that he would welcome. Not only does it separate him from the common herd of humanity, but it also puts him in the distinguished company of many of the greatest characters in literature. And the paradox of art which ensures that these other great individualists lose nothing in respect of universality, operates in his favour too.

On the plane of appetency, nothing could be more universal than the search for pleasure which he so fully exemplifies. Even the corruption of his taste in pleasure is merely an extreme illustration of the fact that pleasure and pain, like heat and cold, merge into one another to an indefinite extent in a manner familiar to all. In one sense it may make the poet-hero appear exceptional. It is none the less an important factor in his universality inasmuch as his experience covers a wider range than it could otherwise do—'tantôt très-haut et puis très-bas', as Baudelaire wrote to Calonne in 1858.[1]

On the plane of morality, the corruption of his taste appears as a vice which, even though it lacks a name outside the field of individual psychology, is no less universal than the avarice of Harpagon or the hypocrisy of Tartuffe and may be thought to enter into all other vices. It is the tendency to derive pleasurable excitement from what pains and repels, whether through plain brutality or—and here lies the tragic irony of the poet-hero's fate—through the very intensity of one's revulsion from brutality, ugliness and immorality in all its forms, for the higher one climbs the greater may be the fascination of the depths beneath ('Un Ange, imprudent voyageur—Qu'a tenté l'amour du difforme . . .'[2]).

[1] CORR, VI, p. 233.
[2] *L'Irrémédiable* (Poem LXXXIV). Cf. the identification of *le difforme* with Baudelaire's ideal of relative beauty in JOP, II, p. 62.

On the plane of theology, this same vice, understood as the essence of all sin, the conscious *postulation vers Satan*, has a still more obvious universal significance. The idea is not advanced as a definite belief of Baudelaire, and certainly not as a belief of the writer of this study, but the *postulation vers Satan* as it appears in Baudelaire's poet-hero could reasonably be supposed to underlie the desire for knowledge of good and evil which is used in Genesis to explain whatever is narrated or allegorized in the account of the Fall. The attraction of the desire for something unknown and *forbidden* is itself 'la conscience *dans* le mal', and 'la conscience *du* mal' necessarily dates from the prohibition. The serpent is the natural form for the 'mauvaises pensées' of which Baudelaire speaks in the letter to Toussenel of 1856.[1] However that may be, the sin of Ennui referred to in *Au Lecteur* is clearly not the greatest: it is a sin only in so far as it is specially conducive to this essential one which is 'la conscience dans le Mal' and may consist of dreaming of 'échafauds' or discovering, desiring and plucking other species of forbidden fruit and 'Fleurs du Mal'. The unjustly criticized title of the work is a perfect expression of the Romantic and Decadent artistic convention or *poncif* which Baudelaire, although he certainly did not invent it,[2] elevated to the status of a universal psychological, moral and theological problem—and an aesthetic one also.

On the plane of aesthetics, one must certainly accord universality to the attraction of tragic emotion, especially if one extends the meaning of the term to cover the feelings produced by reading the sensational popular press—which

[1] CORR, I, p. 370.
[2] Cf. 'Créer un poncif, c'est le génie'. (JOP, II, p. 70.)

has changed little since the days when Baudelaire wrote: 'Guerres, crimes, vols, impudicités, tortures ... Je ne comprends pas qu'une main pure puisse toucher un journal sans une convulsion de dégoût'.[1] But whether it be found in a newspaper, in *Phèdre* or in *Les Fleurs du Mal*, the attraction of tragic subject-matter may well be similar to the attraction which his ideal of relative beauty holds for Baudelaire's poethero, and it points to tastes in the public which are akin to the poet-hero's vice. Far from being peculiar to him and his creator, the ideal expressed in the poems on Beauty is that which is implied in mankind at large by the existence of the tragic genre itself. It is even more universal than the ideal of absolute beauty which complements it, in theory and practice alike, in the extraordinary work which uses aesthetic theory as a basis for one of the great tragedies of French literature.

That the aesthetic theory of the poet-hero is indeed identical with that to which Baudelaire himself subscribed, at least from 1852 onwards, appears to be beyond dispute. It is not beyond dispute that Baudelaire was a more consistent thinker in matters of aesthetics than has generally been assumed, but this is nevertheless one of the most important conclusions to which the preceding chapters have led.

Baudelaire's theological beliefs were evidently much less settled, and all that can be said of the theological implications of the architecture of *Les Fleurs du Mal* is that they reflect an attitude towards these matters which is probably more characteristic of Baudelaire than any other. That is to say, the poet-hero's despairing dualism and defiant affirmation of his will to live his own life, must be understood as the

[1] JOP, II, pp. 119-20.

'religion travestie' of which Baudelaire speaks in the letter to
Ancelle:[1] the author of the work must be understood to look
upon his hero with condemnation as well as sympathy, as if
his own attitude were one of complete acceptance of the law
of God. It was not perhaps easy for Baudelaire to know, at any
given period of his life, to what extent he actually *believed* in
God (how much more difficult for critics and biographers!),
and his very hesitations may be taken as evidence of disbelief.
Nevertheless, the conclusion to which this study of the architecture points, is that Paul Bourget was largely right when he
affirmed, as early as 1883, that although religious faith might
weaken, 'le mysticisme, même expulsé de l'intelligence,
demeurera dans la sensation'.[2] L. J. Austin has disputed this
view.[3] Baudelaire himself, he reminds us, affirmed that his
work 'partait d'une pensée catholique'. True,—but, strictly
speaking, this proves nothing as to his *personal* beliefs.
Secondly, L. J. Austin argues that the religious experience
of a thinker like Baudelaire cannot be reduced to mere
'sensations invétérées'. But this may be thought to evade the
question in so far as 'sensations invétérées' may be the constant accompaniment to any amount of more or less vacillating
'pensée'. Siding therefore with the psychologists, one might
say that Bourget is explained by Georges Blin, who believes
that Baudelaire's sado-masochistic tendencies expressed
themselves on the moral and metaphysical planes as much as on
any others.[4] To put the matter as simply as possible, whatever
else Baudelaire did or did not believe in, he believed in *sin*—

---

[1] CORR, V, p. 279.
[2] *Essais de psychologie contemporaine*, Paris, Plon, 1901, t.l, pp. 7–8.
[3] *Op. cit.*, pp. 110–11.   [4] *Op. cit.*, p. 47.

which implies a corresponding belief in purity. This could well be the principal meaning of the opening remarks of *Fusées*: 'Quand même Dieu n'existerait pas, la religion serait encore Sainte et *divine*—Dieu est le seul être qui, pour régner, n'ait même pas besoin d'exister'.[1] God and religion must reign as symbols of the purity that is the opposite of impurity or sin. There is no lack of documentary evidence to prove that Baudelaire, thanks perhaps to his upbringing, thanks to Joseph de Maistre, and thanks above all to his temperament, believed in sin quite unthinkingly with a fervour that was never seriously weakened and led him to detect sin in the most unlikely places. But even if, at times, he was prepared to see evil in God himself (if God existed), he was too conscious of the existence of pure joy and of his own impurity, to do so for long: both demanded that he be in the wrong—as did his vice itself, by demanding the excitement of 'la conscience dans le Mal'. His temperament could let his thought embrace dualism, but not, apparently, the doctrine of redemption, monism, or a Satanism which implied a reversal of the values of good and evil. He could not help making such a fiercely puritanical distinction between purity and impurity, that the sphere of sin was enlarged to include the whole of creation, and the sphere allotted to purity was identified with a lost paradise and a remote heaven. In this life, purity was to be found less in good works than in the form of the pure joy vouchsafed to man in the perception of absolute beauty, and in other fleeting moments of spiritual elevation. Here lies the connection between Baudelaire's aesthetic theory and his theology and ethics. Absolute beauty

[1] JOP, II, p. 53.

and aesthetic emotion correspond to the soul of man, to ethical goodness, to Paradise and to God (if he exists). Relative beauty in art and the excitement of 'passion' correspond to the body of man, and in a world corrupted by original sin, it is likely to partake of ethical evil: it may therefore be related to Hell and Satan (if Satan exists). In this system of *correspondances* lies the unity of Baudelaire's thought. The unity is based on a strong conviction of the duality of things. The only uncertainty is a consequence of the strength of that conviction, for it is uncertainty as to how the duality can ever be resolved. And the answer that seemed to him to be the least unsatisfactory, evidently lay, as Georges Blin saw clearly,[1] in the hope that suffering itself might be a 'divin remède de nos impuretés'. For it appealed both to his longing for purity, and to the vice that was the perversion of that longing.

Analysis of Baudelaire's theology and ethics, like analysis of his aesthetic, brings us back in the end to the temperament which he undoubtedly shared with his poet-hero, one in which the very intensity of the revulsion from impurity combines with the frustration of the longing for a well-nigh impossible purity, to lead to the deliberate exploitation of impurity as a source of excitement. As Alison Fairlie has remarked, no one can judge this temperament as harshly as Baudelaire appears to have done himself.[2] And remembering the implications of its impurity and the likely degree of incidence of 'sins' of the imagination which are never allowed to reach the light of day, much less find expression in great poetry and tragic art, many will prefer not to judge it at all.

[1] *Op. cit.*, p. 72. Cf. A. R. Chisholm, *op. cit.*, p. 85.   [2] *Op. cit.*, p. 315.

If we do, let it be in the light of the ending of *Mademoiselle Bistouri*, one of the strangest and perhaps one of the most personal of his poems in prose: it expresses not only a Christian point of view but the point of view of art itself in so far as art is faced with such problems:

Quelles bizarreries ne trouve-t-on pas dans une grande ville, quand on sait se promener et regarder? La vie fourmille de monstres innocents.—Seigneur, mon Dieu! vous, le Créateur, vous, le Maître; vous qui avez fait la Loi et la Liberté; vous, le souverain qui laissez faire, vous le juge qui pardonnez; vous qui êtes plein de motifs et de causes, *et qui avez peut-être mis dans mon esprit le goût de l'horreur pour convertir mon coeur, comme la guérison au bout d'une lame;* Seigneur, ayez pitié, ayez pitié des fous et des folles! O Créateur! peut-il exister des monstres aux yeux de Celui-là seul qui sait pourquoi ils existent, comment ils *se sont faits* et comment ils auraient pu *ne pas se faire?*[1]

Baudelaire's 'message' is no more a didactic solution of the problems of life than is that of any other writer. He might none the less be credited with his refusal—or inability—to simplify the complexity of human-nature and human problems, a complexity which gives rise to clashes within the nature of civilized man between sets of values so fundamentally different as to make it impossible to order them into a permanent and universally valid harmony or hierarchy. The probability that Baudelaire failed more signally than most to order them in his own life, in no way detracts from the value of his achievement as an artist, in giving to this complexity the coherence and harmony proper to poetry and tragic art.

[1] PPP, pp. 163-4. (Only in the last sentence quoted, are the italics Baudelaire's own.)

APPENDIX

THE ORDER OF THE POEMS IN THE 1861 EDITION[1]	THE ORDER OF THE POEMS IN THE 1857 EDITION[2]
Au Lecteur	*Au Lecteur*
(Spleen et Idéal)	*(Spleen et Idéal)*
I *Bénédiction* (I)	*Bénédiction* (I)
II *L'Albatros* (—)	*Le Soleil* (LXXXVII)
III *Élévation* (III)	*Élévation* (III)
IV *Correspondances* (IV)	*Correspondances* (IV)
V *J'aime le souvenir* (V)	*J'aime le souvenir* (V)
VI *Les Phares* (VI)	*Les Phares* (VI)
VII *La Muse malade* (VII)	*La Muse malade* (VII)
VIII *La Muse vénale* (VIII)	*La Muse vénale* (VIII)
IX *Le Mauvais Moine* (IX)	*Le Mauvais Moine* (IX)
X *L'Ennemi* (X)	*L'Ennemi* (X)
XI *Le Guignon* (XI)	*Le Guignon* (XI)
XII *La Vie antérieure* (XII)	*La Vie antérieure* (XII)
XIII *Bohémiens en Voyage* (XIII)	*Bohémiens en Voyage* (XIII)
XIV *L'Homme et la Mer* (XIV)	*L'Homme et la Mer* (XIV)
XV *Don Juan* (XV)	*Don Juan* (XV)
XVI *Châtiment de l'Orgueil* (XVI)	*Châtiment de l'Orgueil* (XVI)
XVII *La Beauté* (XVII)	*La Beauté* (XVII)
XVIII *L'Idéal* (XVIII)	*L'Idéal* (XVIII)

[1] The numbers in brackets which follow the titles are the numbers which were given to poems in the 1857 edition.
[2] The numbers in brackets which follow the titles are the numbers which were given to poems in the 1861 edition.

APPENDIX—continued

THE ORDER OF THE POEMS IN THE 1861 EDITION[1]	THE ORDER OF THE POEMS IN THE 1857 EDITION[2]
XLV Confession (XLI)	Le Poison (XLIX)
XLVI L'Aube spirituelle (XLII)	Ciel brouillé (L)
XLVII Harmonie du Soir (XLIII)	Le Chat (LI)
XLVIII Le Flacon (XLIV)	Le Beau Navire (LII)
XLIX Le Poison (XLV)	L'Invitation au Voyage (LIII)
L Ciel brouillé (XLVI)	L'Irréparable (LIV)
LI Le Chat (XLVII)	Causerie (LV)
LII Le Beau Navire (XLVIII)	L'Héautontimorouménos (LXXXIII)
LIII L'Invitation au Voyage (XLIX)	Franciscae meae laudes (LX)
LIV L'Irréparable (L)	A une Dame créole (LXI)
LV Causerie (LI)	Moesta et Errabunda (LXII)
LVI Chant d'Automne (—)	Les Chats (LXVI)
LVII A une Madone (—)	Les Hiboux (LXVII)
LVIII Chanson d'Après-Midi (—)	La Cloche fêlée (LXXIV)
LIX Sisina (—)	Spleen (LXXV)
LX Franciscae meae laudes (LIII)	Spleen (LXXVI)
LXI A une Dame créole (LIV)	Spleen (LXXVII)
LXII Moesta et Errabunda (LV)	Spleen (LXXVIII)
LXIII Le Revenant (LXXII)	Brumes et Pluies (CI)
LXIV Sonnet d'Automne (—)	L'Irrémédiable (LXXXIV)

¹ The numbers in brackets which follow the titles are the numbers which were given to poems in the 1857 edition.
² The numbers in brackets which follow the titles are the numbers which were given to poems in the 1861 edition.

APPENDIX—continued

THE ORDER OF THE POEMS IN THE 1861 EDITION [1]	THE ORDER OF THE POEMS IN THE 1857 EDITION [2]
	L'Amour et le Crâne (CXVII)
	(Révolte)
	Le Reniement de Saint Pierre (CXVIII)
	Abel et Caïn (CXIX)
	Les Litanies de Satan (CXX)
	(Le Vin)
LXXXIX Le Cygne (—)	L'Âme du Vin (CIV)
	Le Vin des Chiffonniers (CV)
XC Les Sept Vieillards (—)	Le Vin de l'Assassin (CVI)
XCI Les Petites Vieilles (—)	Le Vin du Solitaire (CVII)
XCII Les Aveugles (—)	Le Vin des Amants (CVIII)
	(La Mort)
XCIII A une Passante (—)	La Mort des Amants (CXXI)
XCIV Le Squelette laboureur (—)	La Mort des Pauvres (CXXII)
XCV Le Crépuscule du Soir (LXXVII)	La Mort des Artistes (CXXIII)
XCVI Le Jeu (LXVI)	
XCVII Danse macabre (—)	
XCVIII L'Amour du Mensonge (—)	
XCIX Je n'ai pas oublié (LXX)	
C La Servante au grand coeur (LXIX)	
CI Brumes et Pluies (LXIII)	
CII Rêve parisien (—)	
CIII Le Crépuscule du Matin (LXVIII)	
	(Le Vin)
CIV L'Âme du Vin (XCIII)	

248

[1] The numbers in brackets which follow the titles are the numbers which were given to poems in the 1857 edition.
[2] The numbers in brackets which follow the titles are the numbers which were given to poems in the 1861 edition.

BIBLIOGRAPHY

The following list of authors is limited to those whose works have been mentioned in the foregoing chapters. For the works of Baudelaire, see the List of Abbreviations.

AUSTIN, L. J.: *L'Univers poétique de Baudelaire*, Paris, Mercure de France, 1956.

BENEDETTO, L. F.: *L'Architecture des "Fleurs du Mal"* in *Zeitschrift für franzÖsische Sprache und Literatur*, vol. 39, 1912.

BLIN, G.: *Le Sadisme de Baudelaire*, Paris, José Corti, 1947. See also: *Baudelaire*, Paris, Gallimard, 1939.

BOURGET, P.: *Essais de psychologie contemporaine*, Paris, Plon, t. l, 1901.

CASTEX P.-G.: *La Beauté—Fleur du Mal* in *Revue des Sciences humaines*, Juillet-Septembre, 1959.

CHISHOLM, A. R.: *Towards Hérodiade. A literary Genealogy*, Melbourne University Press, 1934.

DECAUNES, L.: *Charles Baudelaire*, Paris, Seghers, 1952.

ELIOT, T. S.: *Selected Essays*, 1917–1932, London, Faber and Faber, 1932.

FAIRLIE, A.: *Some remarks on Baudelaire's "Poëme du Haschish"* in *The French Mind, Studies in Honour of Gustave Rudler*, Oxford, Clarendon Press, 1952.

FEUILLERAT, A.: *L'Architecture des "Fleurs du Mal"* in *Studies by members of the French Department of Yale University*, New Haven, Yale University Press, 1941.
See also: *Baudelaire et la Belle aux cheveux d'or*, Yale University Press, 1941, and *Baudelaire et sa mere*, Montreal, Variétés, 1947.

FRANÇOIS, A.: *Le Sonnet sur "la Beauté"* in *Le Mercure de France*, 1ᵉʳ Juin, 1954.

GRAVA, A.: *L'Aspect métaphysique du Mal dans l'oeuvre de Charles Baudelaire et d'Edgar Poe*, University of Nebraska Studies, June 1956.

HUXLEY, A.: *Do what you will*, New York, Doubleday, Doran, 1929.

JOHANSEN, S.: *Le Symbolisme*, Copenhagen, Einar Munksgaard, 1945.

LÉVY O.: *Baudelaire, son esthétique et sa technique littéraire*, Brno, 1947.

MALLARMÉ, S.: *Oeuvres complètes*, Paris, Bibliothèque de la Pléiade, 1951.

MANSELL-JONES, P.: *Baudelaire*, Cambridge, Bowes and Bowes, 1952.

MASSIN, J.: *Baudelaire entre Dieu et Satan*, Paris, R. Juillard, 1945.

MICHAUD, G.: *Message poétique du Symbolisme*, Première partie, Paris, Nizet, 1947.

OUROUSOFF, Prince A.: See *Le Tombeau de Charles Baudelaire*, Paris, Bibliothèque artistique et littéraire, 1896.

PIA, Pascal: *Baudelaire par lui-même*, Paris, Editions du Seuil, 1956.

POE, E. A.: *The Works of Poe*, edited by John H. Ingram, London, A. and C. Black, 1901.

POMMIER, J.: *La Mystique de Baudelaire*, Paris, Les Belles-Lettres, 1932.

See also: *Dans les chemins de Baudelaire*, Paris, José Corti, 1945.

PORCHÉ, F.: *Baudelaire et la Présidente*, Geneva, Ed. du Milieu du Monde, 1941, and Paris, Gallimard, 1959.

See also: *La Vie douloureuse de Charles Baudelaire*, Paris, Plon-Nourrit, 1924, and *Baudelaire, histoire d'une âme*, Paris, Flammarion, 1945.

PRÉVOST, J.: *Baudelaire*, Paris, Mercure de France, 1953.

PROUST, M.: *Du côté de chez Swann*, t.l, Paris, Gallimard, 1929.

REYNOLD, Gonzague de: *Charles Baudelaire*, G.Crès, 1920.

RUFF, M.: *Baudelaire, l'homme et l'oeuvre*, Paris, Hatier-Boivin, 1955.

See also: *L'Esprit du mal et l'esthétique baudelairienne*, Paris, Armand Colin, 1955.

STARKIE, E.: Introduction to *Les Fleurs du Mal*, Oxford, Basil Blackwell, 1947.
See also: *Baudelaire*, London, Gollancz, 1933; revised edition, 1957.

SWEDENBORG, E.: *Angelic Wisdom*, London, Swedenborg Society, 1931.
Heaven and Hell, London, Swedenborg Society, 1931.
Compendium of Swedenborg's Theological Writings, London, Swedenborg Society, 1939.

TOKSVIG, S.: *Emmanuel Swedenborg*, London, Faber and Faber, 1949.

VALÉRY, P.: *Oeuvres complètes*, Paris, Bibliothèque de la Pléiade, t.l, 1957.

VIVIER, R.: *L'Originalité de Baudelaire*, Bruxelles, Palais des Académies, 1952.

INDEX OF PERSONS

(The numbers refer to pages)